Workshop on Natural Language Processing and Computational Social Science (NLP + CSS 2016)

Held at the Conference on Empirical Methods in Natural Language Processing (EMNLP 2016)

Austin, Texas, USA
5 November 2016

ISBN: 978-1-5108-3148-3

Introduction

Language is a profoundly social phenomenon, both shaped by the social context in which it is embedded (such as demographic influences on lexical choice) and in turn helping construct that context itself (such as media framing). Although this interdependence is at the core of models in both natural language processing (NLP) and (computational) social sciences (CSS), these two fields still exist largely in parallel, holding back research insight and potential applications in both fields.

This workshop aims to advance the joint computational analysis of social sciences and language by explicitly connecting social scientists, network scientists, NLP researchers, and industry partners. Our focus is squarely on integrating CSS with current trends and techniques in NLP and to continue the progress of CSS through socially-informed NLP for the social sciences. This workshop offers a first step towards identifying ways to improve CSS practice with insight from NLP, and to improve NLP with insight from the social sciences.

Areas of interest include all levels of linguistic analysis, network science, and the social sciences, including (but not limited to): political science, geography, public health, economics, psychology, sociology, sociolinguistics, phonology, syntax, pragmatics, and stylistics.

The program this year includes 41 papers presented as posters. We received 47 submissions, and due to a rigorous review process, we rejected 6. There are also 5 invited speakers, Jason Baldridge (co-founder People Pattern / Linguistics, University of Texas Austin), Cristian Danescu-Niculescu-Mizil (Information Science, Cornell University), James Pennebaker (Psychology, University of Texas, Austin), Molly Roberts (Political Science, University of California, San Diego), and Hanna Wallach (Microsoft Research / University of Massachusetts Amherst).

The Doctoral Consortium event is part of a workshop at EMNLP, one of the top conferences in natural language processing. Doctoral consortium aims to bring together students and faculty mentors across NLP and the social sciences, to encourage interdisciplinary collaboration and cross-pollination. The consortium event is part of a workshop at EMNLP, one of the top conferences in natural language processing. Student participants will have the opportunity to present their dissertation work, and will be paired with a senior researcher as a mentor. Applications are welcome from doctoral students in both the social sciences and in computer science. Members of groups that are underrepresented in computer science are especially encouraged to apply.

We would like to thank the Program Committee members who reviewed the papers this year. We would also like to thank the workshop participants. Last, a word of thanks also goes to the National Science Foundation for providing travel grant funding for travel grants for doctoral students at US universities.

David Bamman, A. Seza Doğruöz, Jacob Eisenstein, Dirk Hovy,
David Jurgens, Brendan O'Connor, Alice Oh, Oren Tsur, Svitlana Volkova
Co-Organizers

Organizers:

David Bamman, University of California Berkeley
A. Seza Doğruöz, Independent Researcher and Strategy Advisor
Jacob Eisenstein, Georgia Tech
Dirk Hovy, University of Copenhagen
David Jurgens, Stanford University
Brendan O'Connor, University of Massachusetts Amherst
Alice Oh, KAIST
Oren Tsur, Harvard University and Northeastern University
Svitlana Volkova, Pacific Northwest National Laboratory

Program Committee:

Nikolaos Aletras (Amazon)
Yoram Bachrach (Microsoft Research)
Tim Baldwin (Computing and Information Systems, The University of Melbourne)
David Bamman (Information School, University of California Berkeley)
Nick Beauchamp (Political Science, Northeastern)
Eric Bell (Pacific Northwest National Laboratory)
Yejin Choi (Computer Science, University of Washington)
Court Corley (Pacific Northwest National Laboratory)
Andy Cowell (Pacific Northwest National Laboratory)
Munmun De Choudhury (Computer Science, Georgia Tech)
Aron Culotta (Computer Science, Illinois Institute of Technology)
A. Seza Doğruöz (Tilburg University, Netherlands)
Bill Dolan (Microsoft Research)
Jacob Eisenstein (Computer Science, Georgia Tech)
Eric Gilbert (Computer Science, Georgia Tech)
Oul Han (Political Science, Freie Universität Berlin)
Marti Hearst (Information School, University of California Berkeley)
Brent Hecht (Computer Science, University of Minnesota)
Graeme Hirst (University of Toronto)
Nathan Hodas (Computer Science, Pacific Northwest National Laboratory)
Dirk Hovy (Center for Language Technology; University of Copenhagen)
Ed Hovy (Computer Science, Carnegie Mellon University)
Anders Johannsen (Center for Language Technology; University of Copenhagen)
David Jurgens (Computer Science, Stanford University)
Brian Keegan (Harvard Business School)
Vasileios Lampos (Computer Science, University College London)
Yuru Lin (University of Pittsburgh)
Drew Margolin (Department of Communication, Cornell)

Winter Mason (Facebook)
Kathy McKeown (Columbia University)
David Mimno (Information Science, Cornell)
Dong Nguyen (Tilburg University)
Brendan O'Connor (Computer Science, University of Massachusetts, Amherst)
Alice Oh (Computer Science, KAIST)
Katya Ognyanova (School of Communication and Information, Rutgers)
Jahna Otterbacher (Social Information Systems, Open University Cyprus)
Michael Paul (Computer Science, University of Colorado, Boulder)
Thierry Poibeau (CNRS)
Chris Potts (Linguistics, Stanford University)
Vinod Prabhakaran (Computer Science, Stanford)
Daniel Preotiuc (Computer Science, University of Pennsylvania)
Daniele Quercia (University of Cambridge)
Tina Eliassi-Rad (Computer Science, Rutgers University)
Alan Ritter (Computer Science, The Ohio State University)
Molly Roberts (Political Science, University of California San Diego)
Carolyn Penstein Rose (Carnegie Mellon University)
Derek Ruths (Computer Science, McGill University)
Andy Schwartz (Computer Science, Stony Brook)
Dan Simonson (Linguistics, Gerorgetown University)
Anders Søgaard (Center for Language Technology, University of Copenhagen)
Brandon Stewart (Sociology, Princeton University)
Oren Tsur (IQSS, Harvard; Network Science, Northeastern)
Rob Voigt (Linguistics, Stanford University)
Svitlana Volkova (Computer Science, Pacific Northwest National Laboratory)
Hanna Wallach (Computer Science, Microsoft Research)
Wei Xu (Computer Science, University of Pennsylvania)

Invited Speaker:

Jason Baldridge, co-founder People Pattern / Linguistics, University of Texas, Austin
Cristian Danescu-Niculescu-Mizil, Information Science, Cornell University
James Pennebaker, Psychology, University of Texas, Austin
Molly Roberts, Political Science, University of California, San Diego
Hanna Wallach, Microsoft Research / University of Massachusetts Amherst

Table of Contents

Workshop Program

Saturday, November 5, 2016

9:00–10:30 **Session 1**

09:00–09:15 *Welcome*
Workshop organizers

09:15–10:00 *Invited talk*
James Pennebaker

10:00–10:30 ***Doctoral consortium presentations***

10:30–11:00 ***coffee break***

11:00–12:30 **Session 2**

11:00–11:45 *Invited talk*
Hanna Wallach

11:45–12:30 *Invited talk*
Cristian Danescu-Niculescu-Mizil

12:30–14:00 ***Lunch break***

14:00–15:30   Session 3

14:00–14:45   *Invited talk*
Jason Baldridge

14:45–15:30   *1-minute poster madness*

Relating semantic similarity and semantic association to how humans label other people
Kenneth Joseph and Kathleen M. Carley

Identifying News from Tweets
Jesse Freitas and Heng Ji

Obfuscating Gender in Social Media Writing
Sravana Reddy and Kevin Knight

Social Proof: The Impact of Author Traits on Influence Detection
Sara Rosenthal and Kathy McKeown

Generating Politically-Relevant Event Data
John Beieler

User profiling with geo-located posts and demographic data
Adam Poulston, Mark Stevenson and Kalina Bontcheva

Gov2Vec: Learning Distributed Representations of Institutions and Their Legal Text
John J. Nay

#WhoAmI in 160 Characters? Classifying Social Identities Based on Twitter Profile Descriptions
Anna Priante, Djoerd Hiemstra, Tijs van den Broek, Aaqib Saeed, Michel Ehrenhard and Ariana Need

Identifying Stance by Analyzing Political Discourse on Twitter
Kristen Johnson and Dan Goldwasser

Learning Linguistic Descriptors of User Roles in Online Communities
Alex Wang, William L. Hamilton and Jure Leskovec

The Effects of Data Collection Methods in Twitter
Sunghwan Mac Kim, Stephen Wan, Cecile Paris, Jin Brian and Bella Robinson

Expressions of Anxiety in Political Texts
Ludovic Rheault

Constructing an Annotated Corpus for Protest Event Mining
Peter Makarov, Jasmine Lorenzini and Hanspeter Kriesi

Demographer: Extremely Simple Name Demographics
Rebecca Knowles, Josh Carroll and Mark Dredze

Bag of What? Simple Noun Phrase Extraction for Text Analysis
Abram Handler, Matthew Denny, Hanna Wallach and Brendan O'Connor

News Sentiment and Cross-Country Fluctuations
Samuel Fraiberger

The Clinical Panel: *Leveraging Psychological Expertise During NLP Research*
Glen Coppersmith, Kristy Hollingshead, H. Andrew Schwartz, Molly Ireland, Rebecca Resnik, Kate Loveys, April Foreman and Loring Ingraham

Are You a Racist or Am I Seeing Things? Annotator Influence on Hate Speech Detection on Twitter
Zeerak Waseem

Disentangling Topic Models: A Cross-cultural Analysis of Personal Values through Words
Steven Wilson, Rada Mihalcea, Ryan Boyd and James Pennebaker

15:30–16:00   *coffee break*

Relating semantic similarity and semantic association to how humans label other people

Kenneth Joseph
Northeastern University
k.joseph@northeastern.edu

Kathleen M. Carley
Carnegie Mellon University
kathleen.carley@cs.cmu.edu

Abstract

Computational linguists have long relied on a distinction between semantic similarity and semantic association to explain and evaluate what is being learned by NLP models. In the present work, we take these same concepts and explore how they apply to an entirely different question - how individuals label other people. Leveraging survey data made public by NLP researchers, we develop our own survey to connect semantic similarity and semantic association to the process by which humans label other people. The result is a set of insights applicable to how we think of semantic similarity as NLP researchers and a new way of leveraging NLP models of semantic similarity and association as researchers of social science.

1 Introduction

Computational linguists often find it useful to distinguish between the *semantic similarity* and *semantic association* of two concepts (Resnik, 1999; Agirre et al., 2009; Hill et al., 2016). Two concepts are highly semantically *associated* if when we think of one, we almost always think of the other. In contrast, two concepts are semantically *similar* if they share some salient property. Resnik (1999) differentiates between similarity and association via the following example: "cars and gasoline [are] more closely [associated] than, say, cars and bicycles, but the latter pair are certainly more similar".

This distinction between semantic similarity and semantic association is important to computational linguists for two reasons. First, different types of models are engineered to infer one versus the other (Sahlgren, 2006). For example, topic models (Blei et al., 2003) are geared towards inferring sets of semantically associated concepts, while neural embedding models (Mikolov et al., 2013; Levy and Goldberg, 2014; Zhang et al., 2013) aim to place concepts into a latent space where proximity indicates semantic similarity. Second, distinguishing between semantic similarity and semantic association can help us understand how well these models are optimizing for their intended purpose. For example, Hill et al. (2016) develop a dataset of semantic associations and similarities measured via survey which is used to show that many neural embedding models are actually much better at capturing association than they are at capturing similarity.

The present work uses these survey-based measurements from Hill et al. (2016) to better understand an entirely different question - what is the process by which individuals label other people? Specifically, we focus on understanding how semantic associations and similarities between *identities*, defined as the labels that we apply to people (e.g. man, woman, etc.) (Smith-Lovin, 2007), impact this labeling process. We focus here on the following two hypotheses:

- *H1:* The higher the semantic similarity between two identities, the more likely two identities are to be applied to the same person (e.g. this person is both a woman and a scholar)

- *H2:* The higher the semantic association between two identities, the more likely two identities are to be applied to two people in the same

1

Proceedings of 2016 EMNLP Workshop on Natural Language Processing and Computational Social Science, pages 1–10,
Austin, TX, November 5, 2016. ©2016 Association for Computational Linguistics

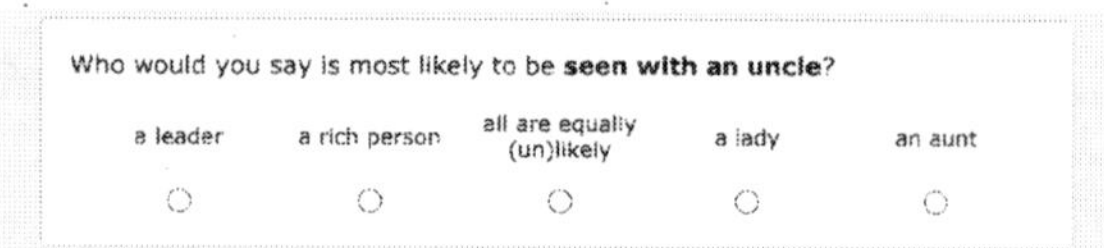

Figure 1: An example of a "SeenWith" question as seen by participants

context (e.g. a doctor is often seen with her patient)

As a canonical question in the social sciences, a significant amount of work has studied the way people label others. Social psychologists have studied both how we label ourselves (Stryker and Burke, 2000; Owens et al., 2010) and how we label others (Heise, 2007; Penner and Saperstein, 2013), as have cognitive psychologists (Kunda and Thagard, 1996; Freeman and Ambady, 2011), neuroscientists (Cikara and Van Bavel, 2014) and linguists (Recasens et al., 2011; Bucholtz and Hall, 2005). Despite the depth and breadth of this work, however, few quantitative models exist that can actually *predict* how an individual will be labeled in a particular situation. Where such models do exist, they tend to either focus explicitly on similarity *or* association (Joseph et al., 2017), to conflate the two and treat them both as semantic "links" in cognitive networks (Freeman and Ambady, 2011), or to ignore relationships between identities all together in favor of feature-based models of individual identities (Heise, 2007).

By testing the two hypotheses above, the present work hopes to achieve three related goals that further our understanding of the identity labeling process. First, we would like to provide additional evidence that rather than focusing simply properties of identities in isolation, we must incorporate identity relationships into our models of how people label other people (Kang and Bodenhausen, 2015; Joseph et al., 2017). Second, we hope to provide evidence that it is not merely enough to consider relationships between identities - if our hypotheses are correct, they would indicate that different types of relationships impact how we label others in distinct ways. Finally we hope to show that differentiating similarity from association is a useful and parsimonious way to characterize these different types of relationships.

In the following sections, we describe the data

from Hill et al. (2016) that we use as measurements of semantic associations and semantic similarities. We then detail the development of a survey, intended to test the two hypotheses above, that asks respondents to label people in hypothetical social situations. The survey asks respondents to perform identity labeling by providing answers to multiple choice questions, an example of which is given in Figure 1 for one of the many identities (uncle) we consider here.

In addition to asking questions of the form "who would you say is most likely to be *seen with* an uncle?", as shown in Figure 1, we also ask questions of the form "given that someone is an uncle, what other identity is *that same person* most likely to also be?" These two different types of questions get at H1 (above) and H2 (Figure 1). Even intuitively, we can see that they should have different mechanisms by which individuals determine the appropriate label. In the first question above, for example, people would be likely to respond with "aunt". However, this is among the least likely answers to be given in the second question, as "uncle" and "aunt" are mutually exclusive role identities. While these questions shrink the complex process by which identity labeling occurs down to a simple survey, they therefore are useful as a starting point for exploring the importance of semantic similarity and semantic association in the identity labeling process.

2 Data

For this study, we use a set of 88 pairs of identity words for which data on semantic similarity and semantic association scores already exists. These scores are drawn from the SimLex-999 dataset of Hill et al. (2016), which includes survey measurements of both semantic association and semantic similarity for 999 pairs of concepts. For the purposes of the present work, we were only interested in concept pairs from the SimLex-999 dataset in which both concepts were unambiguously identities, thus the reduction to only 88 pairs of words.[1]

To measure semantic association, Hill et al.

---

[1] We did not consider the pair heroine-hero, as it appeared that the former term was interpreted as the drug rather than the female hero. We also ignored the terms god, devil and demon, judging them to be more representative of the religious concepts than their alternative identity meanings

(2016) used the USF free association dataset compiled by Nelson et al. (2004). This dataset contains five thousand "cue" words that were given to at least ninety-four survey respondents (mean = 148). For each cue, respondents were asked to write the first word that came to mind that they thought of when shown the cue. As a result, for each cue word one can construct a distribution of its association to other words based on the percentage of survey respondents that gave that word as an answer.

For a survey-based measure of semantic similarity, Hill et al. (2016) pulled 900 of the 72,000 possible pairs of cue-association words from the USF Free Association dataset. To this dataset, they add 99 pairs of words found in the USF Free Association dataset where each was either a cue word or a response word but that were not themselves associated. For each of these 999 pairs of concepts, the authors then asked approximately 50 respondents on Amazon's Mechanical Turk to rate the similarity of each pair of concepts. They used a scale defined via examples similar to the one from Resnik (1999) presented above and allowed respondents to compare the similarity of concept pairs. Additionally, it should be noted that Hill et al. (2016) assume semantic similarity is symmetric, but do not directly test this point.

Table 1 presents some examples of the 88 identity pairs we extracted from the SimLex-999 data based on whether they were higher or lower than average on one or both dimensions. Broadly, we see that identities which are highly similar seem to be those one might be willing to apply to the same individual, and identities that are highly associated are those one might tend to see together in similar social contexts. These obvious examples suggest support for our hypotheses - we now detail the survey we develop in order to more formally test these intuitions.

3   Identity Labeling Survey Description

Let us assume two identities A and B make up one of the 88 pairs of identities we draw from the SimLex-999 dataset. To construct our surveys, we first generated eighty randomized questions with this pair, twenty each from four types:

- **"IsA" A questions:** "Given that someone is a[n] **A**, what is **that same person** most likely to also be?"

- **"IsA" B questions:** "Given that someone is a[n] **B**, what is **that same person** most likely to also be?"

- **"SeenWith" A questions**: "Who would you say is most likely to be **seen with** a[n] **A**?

- **"SeenWith" B questions**: "Who would you say is most likely to be **seen with** a[n] **B**?

Each of these questions had five multiple choice answers. Within the answer set, the identity not in the question itself (i.e. B if A was in the question, or vice versa) was given as one of the answers. As shown in Figure 1, we then included three random identities from a set of 234 commonly occurring identities[2] as alternative choices, along with the option "all answers are equally (un)likely" in order to allow respondents to opt out of answering questions they were uncomfortable with.

These questions were then distributed as surveys where each respondent saw 40 random questions. With 80*88=7,040 questions to ask, we therefore required 176 respondents. Surveys were deployed on Amazon's Mechanical Turk to only "Masters"[3] and only those with IP addresses within the United States. To assess accuracy for respondents, we randomly sampled 5 questions from each respondent and ensured that answers appeared reasonable. No personally-identifiable information was collected, and all (anonymized) survey questions, responses and analyses presented here are available at `https://github.com/kennyjoseph/nlp_css_workshop`.

4   Results

As we will show in this section, our results show support for both hypotheses. High similarity between identities led to more 'IsA' attributions (H1),

---

[2]Due to space constraints, how these identities were chosen is not described here - for more details, we refer the reader to Section 5.4.2 of (Joseph, 2016)

[3]`https://www.mturk.com/mturk/help?helpPage=worker#what_is_master_worker`

Similarity, Association	Examples
High Similarity, High Association	physician & doctor, friend & buddy; student & pupil; teacher & instructor
High Similarity, Low Association	buddy & companion; adversary & opponent; author & creator; champion & winner; leader & manager; politician & president
Low Similarity, High Association	wife & husband; woman & man; child & adult
Low Similarity, Low Association	adult & baby; author & reader; boy & partner; chief & mayor; dad & mother; daughter & kid; friend & guy; girl & maid; guy; & partner; king & princess; lawyer & banker

Table 1: Examples of identities that are higher or lower than average for each combination of high/low of semantic similarity and semantic association.

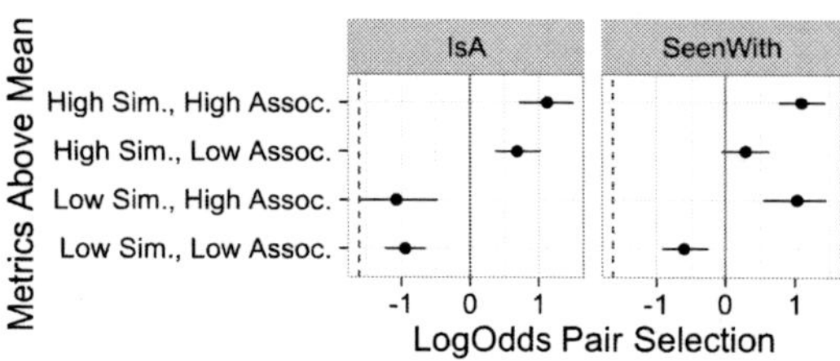

Figure 2: On the x-axis, the log odds of selection. On the y-axis, identity pairs are split into the same categories as in Table 1; see text for details. For each category, 95% bootstrapped Confidence Intervals are presented for mean log odds of selection of all identity pairs within the category. Vertical lines are drawn at a log-odds of selection of 0 (red solid line; 50-50 chance of selection) and at $log(\frac{1}{5})$ (blue dashed line; random chance of selection)

while high association led to more 'SeenWith' attributions (H2).

Figure 2 presents a high-level overview of the results in terms of the classification of high/low similarity/association presented in Table 1. Similarly to Table 1, the y-axis of Figure 2 presents four "categories" of identity pairs based on whether they were above ("high") or below ("low") average on the two different semantic metrics.[4] The x-axis of Figure 2 shows a 95% confidence interval for the *log-odds of selection* of all identity pairs in the given category. The *log-odds of selection* for an identity pair is the (log) proportion of times an identity pair element in the answer set was selected out of the 20 randomized questions generated for that question type and that arrangement of identities. So, for exam-

ple, if "woman" were selected 19 out of 20 times when given as a possible answer for the question "Who would you say is most likely to be seen with a man?", then the log-odds of selection for the "man-woman" pair for "SeenWith" questions would be $\frac{19+1}{1+1}$, where a $+1$ is added to avoid zero-valued denominators. Finally, Figure 2 also displays two baselines to consider- a red, solid line is drawn at a log-odds of 0, representing the odds of the identity being selected as the answer more than 50% of the time. The blue, dashed line is drawn at a log-odds of 20%, that is, the odds of the identity being selected more often than random.

Figure 2 provides evidence that high semantic similarity breeds high log-odds of selection for "IsA" questions (H1), and high association breeds high log-odds of selection for "SeenWith" questions (H2). However, two anomalies not suggested by our hypotheses are worth considering as well. First, note that when both similarity and association are low, the log-odds of selection are still noticeably greater than chance. This is likely due to the way that word pairings were selected in the SimLex-999 dataset- Hill et al. (2016) sampled largely from existing cue/response pairs in the USF free association data. Consequently, we work here with identity pairings that already have some form of association in at least one direction; their relationship is therefore stronger than a random baseline in almost all cases. Second, we see that semantic similarity appears to have a strong impact on "SeenWith" questions - that is, identities which are above average in semantic similarity but *not* on semantic association still are perceived to frequently exist together in the same context.

---

[4]Note that Table 1 shows only some examples of each category, whereas Figure 2 uses the entire dataset

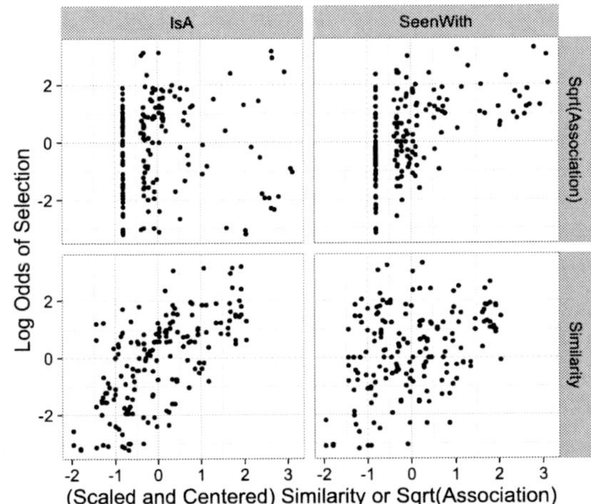

Figure 3: A scatterplot of bivariate relationships between the two dependent variables and the independent variable. Each point represents one identity pair. Results for association for IsA questions (top left), association for SeenWith questions (top right), similarity for SeenWith questions (bottom right) and similarity for IsA questions (bottom left) are presented

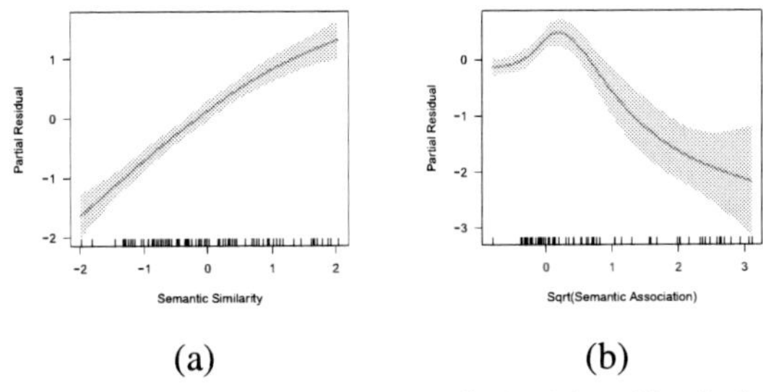

Figure 4: Results from a GAM fit to logit of the odds of selection for "IsA" questions. Figures a) and b) show fit lines (blue bar) and 95% confidence intervals of the fit (grey shadows) for semantic similarity and semantic association, respectively.

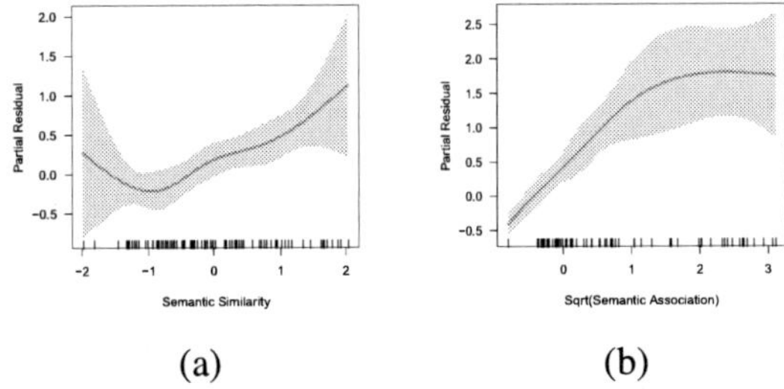

Figure 5: The same GAM model as in Figure 4, except here we fit to data from only "SeenWith" questions

These observations are also supported by Figure 3, which portrays four scatterplots of the bivariate relationships between similarity and the square root of association[5] for both IsA and SeenWith questions. However, because similarity and association are themselves related, it is important to leverage a more rigorous statistical approach that allows us to see the relationship between one of our factors (similarity/association) while controlling for variance in the other. We fit a binomial generalized additive model (GAM) (Hastie and Tibshirani, 1990) using the mgcv package in R (Wood, 2006; R Core Team, 2015) to results on each type of question independently.[6] In essence, generalized additive models are generalized linear models that relax the assumption of linearity, instead fitting a (possibly multi-

dimensional) curve to each model parameter. The "wigglyness" of these curves, or functions, is controlled by some form of penalty; in the mgcv package, this penalty is determined via cross-validation.

The model we use predicts the logit of the odds of selection by fitting tensor product bases to the (scaled and centered) measures of semantic similarity and the square-root of semantic association independently as well as a multivariate tensor basis on their interaction. Figure 4a) shows the fit on semantic similarity to partial residuals of the logit odds of selection for IsA questions only. Figure 4b) shows the same for (the square root of) semantic association. Partial residuals essentially show the fit of each variable after "removing" effects of the other variable and their interaction.

Figure 4a) shows that, controlling for association and the interaction effects of the two variables, semantic similarity has a strong, positive effect on the log-odds of selection in IsA questions. This result provides further support for *H1*. Interestingly, however, we see in Figure 4b) that there exists a sort of acceptable region of association for "IsA" questions.

---

[5]We use the square root as it better represents a strong distinction between a zero-valued association and a small but non-zero association. We feel this is conceptually appropriate, as a difference between any association and no association seems more important than a difference between some association and more association. Importantly, however, results presented here are robust to this decision and also robust to removing zero-association pairs all together, see the replication material for these robustness checks.

[6]Chapter 8 and Chapter 9 of (Shalizi, 2013) provide a nice introduction to GAMs and tensor product bases.

Association increases the log odds of selection up until a point but then shows, net of similarity, a significant *negative* effect on the odds that survey respondents would label the same person with those two identities. The marginal positive relationship, which holds even when we remove zero-association identity pairs, is interesting but appears to be related to oddities with how association is measured by Hill et al. that we discuss below. On the other hand, as we will discuss in Section 5, the eventual negative effect of association on "IsA" questions seems to be largely attributable to the existence of role/counter-role pairs, such as "uncle/aunt" and "husband/wife". These relationships have been heavily theorized but have been notoriously difficult to measure (Burke, 1980), thus our finding presents a novel quantification of an important and well-known phenomena.

Figure 5 provides the same model except fit on data from SeenWith question responses. Here, we observe that semantic association has, as expected in *H2*, a strong impact on log-odds of selection. We also see that net of semantic association and the interaction term, semantic similarity still has a significant positive effect on log-odds of selection.

Figure 4 and Figure 5 thus provide confirmation of *H1* and *H2*, as well as providing two novel insights. First we see that even when identities are semantically disassociated, underlying similarity (e.g. in the case of the identity pairing adversary and opponent) can impact our perception of which identities are likely to be seen together. Second, we see that high levels of semantic association can actually decrease the odds that two labels will be applied to the same individual. This further emphasizes the need to characterize similarity and association as distinct measures in models of the identity labeling process.

Before following up on these two points, we further note that Figure 4 and Figure 5 show large standard errors for the fit lines (particularly at the ends of the distribution), suggesting the models struggled with outliers. Table 2 shows the ten cases in which the "SeenWith" model most heavily under-predicted the true log-odds of selection. The table presents some surprising scores for semantic association - for example, "king" and "princess", as well as "king" and "prince", are both less associated than the average identity pair in our dataset. Given that these

identities are drawn from a similar domain, these numbers are surprising at first sight.

The cause of this is, we believe, the use of the proportion of free association connecting two concepts by Hill et al. (2016) (and others) as a metric for semantic association. The problem with using this metric is that a single association can "eat up" a significant amount of the semantic association in a free association task, masking minor but still important associations. Specific to the case of "king", the identity "queen" takes most of the association score in a free association task, meaning other identities that are still highly associated are given lower scores than we might expect. A related example is the identity mother, which has a high free association score to "father" but no association with "dad".

Predictions for our "SeenWith" model are thus hindered by the specific way in which semantic association is measured. The same can be said for the results of the "IsA" model - more specifically, the measurement assumption of Hill et al. (2016) that semantic similarity is symmetric leads to difficulties in prediction. Table 3 presents ten identity pairs where log-odds of selection differed the most depending on which identity was presented in the question. As pairs had the same value for semantic similarity regardless of which identity was presented first, these pairs represent obvious cases where the model would be unable to capture variance in the data. They also present obvious cases where semantic similarity cannot be assumed to be symmetric. For example, a "president" tends to be a "politician", but a politician is not always a president. These asymmetries are due to the naturally occurring hierarchy of identities, and emphasize the variety of ways in which identities can be considered to be similar.

5 Discussion

Results from our survey can be summarized as follows:

1. *H1*- that higher semantic similarity would increase the likelihood two identities are to be applied to the same person, and *H2* - that higher semantic association would increase the likelihood two identities are to be applied to two people in the same context - were supported

Rank	Identity Given in Question Text	Identity Given as Possible Answer	Pred. Log-odds (from GAM)	Actual Log-odds of Selection	Scaled Semantic Association (sqrt)
1	captain	sailor	-0.40	2.35	-0.80
2	sailor	captain	0.33	3.00	-0.08
3	author	reader	-1.28	0.98	-0.80
4	worker	employer	0.23	2.40	-0.32
5	king	princess	-0.38	1.79	-0.80
6	princess	king	0.09	2.23	-0.10
7	king	prince	0.30	2.40	-0.28
8	employee	employer	1.14	3.22	1.03
9	professor	student	-0.13	1.85	-0.31
10	president	politician	0.52	2.48	-0.32

Table 2: Top ten identity pairs for the "SeenWith" model in terms of under-prediction by the model relative to the true log-odds of selection by survey respondents. "Identity Given in Question Text" is the identity presented in the survey question, i.e. the A in "Seen With" A questions above; "Identity Given as Possible Answer" would then be the B. Semantic association is mean-centered and scaled by 1SD.

	Identity 1 (ID1)	Identity 2 (ID2)	Log-odds, ID1 first	Log-odds, ID2 first
1	stud	guy	-1.61	1.73
2	president	politician	-0.17	3.14
3	princess	bride	-2.48	0.41
4	worker	employer	0.98	-1.85
5	warrior	man	-2.08	0.56
6	teacher	rabbi	0.15	-2.25
7	mayor	chief	-0.08	-2.40
8	manager	leader	-0.37	1.85
9	baby	adult	-3.09	-0.89
10	worker	mechanic	1.22	-0.76

Table 3: Top ten identity pairs in terms of difference in log-odds of selection in "IsA" questions depending on which identity was presented in the question (vs. as a possible answer)

2. High semantic similarity is indicative of high log-odds of selection for "SeenWith" questions

3. Semantic association has a curvilinear impact on "IsA" questions - after some point, high semantic association between identities translates to lower odds of selection

4. Limitations of the measurement model of Hill et al. for semantic similarity (assumption of symmetry) and semantic association (proportional measurement model) in our context breed interesting outliers

Support for *H1* and *H2* was shown in both exploratory analyses and more rigorous statistical modeling of the data. Of more interest in this section, however, are the latter three points, which we feel require some further discussion.

With respect to the fourth point above, our results suggest that evaluations using Hill et al.'s (2016) data may be better served by making two additional assumptions. First, we suggest a stricter adherence to Tversky's theory of semantic similarity (Tversky and Gati, 1978), which argues that symmetry cannot be assumed in measurements of the similarity between two concepts. Second, we suggest that alternative measurements of semantic association, such as those based on spreading activation (Collins and Loftus, 1975), may be better representations of semantic association than a simple proportion based on survey responses.

With respect to the second point above, similarity's positive impact on "SeenWith" questions, we believe this to be indicative of an important tension in the linguistic definition of semantic similarity by, e.g., Resnick (1999) and the way we apply multiple identities to the same individual. This is because two distinct forms of similarity seem to play a role in how respondents answered questions. Similarity as typically defined, and thus measured, by computational linguists tends to represent taxonomic relationships, as in, "a lawyer isA professional". However, with respect to identity, similarity also refers to labels that may apply to the same individual regardless of taxonomic relationship - in sociological terms, the extent to which two identities are cross-

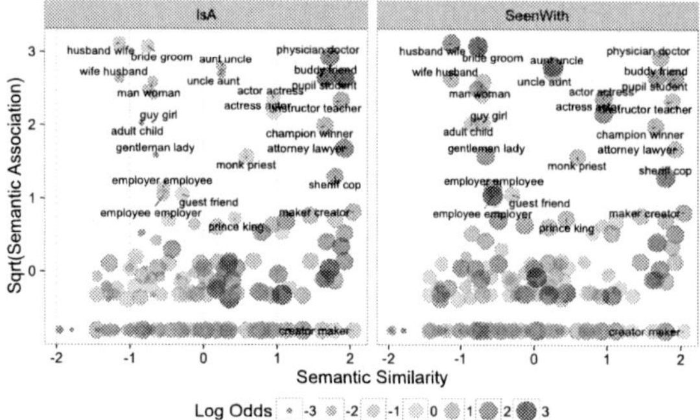

Figure 6: Results for the two different types of questions for log-odds (represented by point color and size), semantic association and semantic similarity. Within each subplot, each identity pair is shown by two points, one each depending on which identity was shown in the question and which was given as a possible answer. Outlier points are labeled based on low-probability with an overlying density estimator

cutting (Blau, 1977). Cross-cutting similarities are unlikely to be captured via denotatively organized data sets like WordNet, or even, it seems, from explicit questions about semantic similarity.

Where they do seem to be captured, however, is in the survey methods presented in this article. A good example is the identity pair "secretary-woman", which had a log-odds of selection of 1.22 (sixteen out of twenty) and a scaled semantic similarity of -1.29 (1.29 standard deviations below the mean). These two identities have little, if any, denotive similarity relationship, and it seems that when the question of similarity is posed explicitly as by Hill et al. (2016), respondents were focused on this connection.[7] In contrast, via the more subtle mechanisms utilized used in our survey, we see the well-known gender bias towards considering secretaries as being primarily women. An important question for NLP+CSS is how to understand and model these subconscious, culturally-based similarities as contrasted with the more traditional taxonomical notions of similarity, and interesting work has certainly begun along these lines (van Miltenburg, 2016; Beukeboom and others, 2014; Bolukbasi et al., 2016).

Finally, Figure 6 provides some insight into the third point above, the negative relationship between semantic association and "IsA" questions. In the figure, we show two subplots, one each for the two different types of questions. Within each subplot, each of the 88 identity pairs studied is given by two points, one each depending on which identity was shown in the question and which was given as a possible answer. The x-axis displays the (scaled) semantic similarity of the identity pair, the y-axis displays the (scaled) square root of semantic association.[8] Finally, each point is colored and sized in Figure 6 by the log-odds of selection - the darker the blue and larger the point, the higher the log-odds, the darker the red and smaller the point, the lower the log-odds.

Figure 6 shows that identities high in association but low in similarity do indeed have very low log odds of selection in "Is-A" questions. Looking at the labels of these identity pairs, we see that they tend to be, intuitively at least, in direct opposition to each other - e.g. husband and wife, man and woman, etc. A more restricted class of such opposing identity pairs, those that fill opposing *roles*, are referenced in classic quantitative models of identity as *role/counter-role* pairs (Burke, 1980). We observe a broader class of *identity/counter-identity* pairs in Figure 6 which are easily discerned by contrasting their semantic association with their semantic similarity.

While many identity/counter-identity pairings are intuitive and have long been studied by social scientists, to the best of our knowledge no methods currently exist to automatically enumerate such pairs. Antonym definitions in lexical databases like WordNet would seem to be one useful resource for this task, but are missing several of what we consider to be basic identity/counter-identity pairings (e.g. groom/bride). Our work also certainly does not fit this bill of automated methods, as we use data curated by survey. Thus, as NLP tools develop to better infer semantic similarity, uncovering identity/counter-identity pairings is one useful

---

[7]This extends to lexical databases like WordNet as well, where there is no obvious taxonomical connection between these concepts

[8]Note that several zero-associations in Figure 6 are the result of our use of both "directions" of each identity pair. Thus, while we are guaranteed some non-zero association in most of the pairs collected by Hill et al. (2016) in one "direction", in the other there is no such guarantee.

application. While observing intuitive pairings, e.g. man-woman, may not be particularly interesting, extracting less intuitive identity/counter-identity relationships from text, for example, those marking opposing ethnic factions, is a very important avenue of application for these models.

6 Conclusion

In the present work, we leverage measurements and conceptualizations of semantic similarity and semantic association by NLP researchers to study how individuals label other people, a canonical problem in sociology and social psychology. We find strong support for our hypotheses that semantic similarity is related to which identities we choose to apply to the same individual and that semantic association is related to which identities we choose to apply to different individuals in the same context.

Beyond confirmation of these hypotheses, our work presents several other useful contributions of use to the fields of NLP and Computational Social Science (CSS). With respect to NLP, an analysis of outliers in our results suggests that Hill et al.'s (2016) measurements, commonly used to evaluate neural embedding models, may have important restrictions not previously noted by the community. Thus our results suggest that the way people label others provides unique insights into measurements of similarity and association beyond those currently explored by common NLP evaluation datasets.

With respect to CSS, we have given evidence that identity relationships are important in understanding the identity labeling process, that there are unique types of these relationships with disparate impacts on this process, and that similarity and association are a powerful yet parsimonious means of characterizing these types of relationships. In addition, we find that differentiating identities by their semantic associations and semantic similarities provides an interesting socio-theoretic definition of identity/counter-identity pairs, a classic relational model of identity measurement (Burke, 1980). Our work therefore suggests new directions for theoretical development in CSS beyond just the way we label others. As we move towards better understandings of and better models of extracting semantic similarity from text, we see this as an exciting avenue of future work at the intersection of NLP and CSS.

Future work should also serve to address the limitations of the efforts presented here. In particular, the bias in using these particular 88 identity pairs from the SimLex-999 dataset is unclear. Further, social scientists also often assume that both affective meaning of identities and the actions taken by individuals with particular identities both play strong roles in how we label other people (Heise, 1987). How semantic similarity and semantic association play into these more theoretically driven and advanced theories of identity labeling remains to be seen.

Acknowledgments

We would like to thank the MTurk workers for their efforts on this project, in particular Heather Wilcox, who gave some really insightful post-survey thoughts that improved the analysis of this data and helped to hone inquiries into future work. We also thank the reviewers for this paper, who offered several helpful critiques that greatly improved the article. We would also like to thank Lynn Smith-Lovin for her assistance in developing the surveys presented. Support was provided, in part, by the Office of Naval Research (ONR) through a MURI N00014081186 on adversarial reasoning and the ONR through a MINERVA N000141310835 on State Stability.

References

Eneko Agirre, Enrique Alfonseca, Keith Hall, Jana Kravalova, Marius Paca, and Aitor Soroa. 2009. A study on similarity and relatedness using distributional and WordNet-based approaches. In *Proceedings of Human Language Technologies: The 2009 Annual Conference of the North American Chapter of the Association for Computational Linguistics*, pages 19–27. Association for Computational Linguistics.

Camiel J. Beukeboom and others. 2014. Mechanisms of linguistic bias: How words reflect and maintain stereotypic expectancies. *Social cognition and communication*, 31:313–330.

Peter M. Blau. 1977. A macrosociological theory of social structure. *American journal of sociology*, pages 26–54.

David M. Blei, Andrew Y. Ng, and Michael I. Jordan. 2003. Latent dirichlet allocation. *J. Mach. Learn. Res.*, 3:993–1022, March.

Tolga Bolukbasi, Kai-Wei Chang, James Zou, Venkatesh Saligrama, and Adam Kalai. 2016. Man is to computer programmer as woman is to homemaker? debiasing word embeddings. *arXiv preprint arXiv:1607.06520*.

Mary Bucholtz and Kira Hall. 2005. Identity and interaction: A sociocultural linguistic approach. *Discourse studies*, 7(4-5):585–614.

Peter J. Burke. 1980. The self: Measurement requirements from an interactionist perspective. *Social psychology quarterly*, pages 18–29.

Mina Cikara and Jay J. Van Bavel. 2014. The Neuroscience of Intergroup Relations An Integrative Review. *Perspectives on Psychological Science*, 9(3):245–274.

Allan M. Collins and Elizabeth F. Loftus. 1975. A spreading-activation theory of semantic processing. *Psychological review*, 82(6):407.

Jonathan B. Freeman and Nalini Ambady. 2011. A dynamic interactive theory of person construal. *Psychological review*, 118(2):247.

Trevor J. Hastie and Robert J. Tibshirani. 1990. *Generalized additive models*, volume 43. CRC Press.

David R. Heise. 1987. Affect control theory: Concepts and model. *The Journal of Mathematical Sociology*, 13(1-2):1–33, December.

David R. Heise. 2007. *Expressive Order*. Springer.

Felix Hill, Roi Reichart, and Anna Korhonen. 2016. Simlex-999: Evaluating semantic models with (genuine) similarity estimation. *Computational Linguistics*.

Kenneth Joseph, Wei Wei, and Kathleen M. Carley. 2017. Girls rule, boys drool: Extracting semantic and affective stereotypes from Twitter. In *2017 ACM Conference on Computer Supported Cooperative Work.(CSCW)*.

Kenneth Joseph. 2016. *New methods for large-scale analyses of social identities and stereotypes*. Ph.D. thesis, Carnegie Mellon University.

Sonia K. Kang and Galen V. Bodenhausen. 2015. Multiple Identities in Social Perception and Interaction: Challenges and Opportunities. *Annual Review of Psychology*, 66(1):547–574.

Ziva Kunda and Paul Thagard. 1996. Forming impressions from stereotypes, traits, and behaviors: A parallel-constraint-satisfaction theory. *Psychological Review*, 103(2):284–308.

Omer Levy and Yoav Goldberg. 2014. Dependency-based word embeddings. In *Proceedings of the 52nd Annual Meeting of the Association for Computational Linguistics*, volume 2, pages 302–308.

Tomas Mikolov, Kai Chen, Greg Corrado, and Jeffrey Dean. 2013. Efficient estimation of word representations in vector space. *arXiv preprint arXiv:1301.3781*.

Douglas L. Nelson, Cathy L. McEvoy, and Thomas A. Schreiber. 2004. The University of South Florida free association, rhyme, and word fragment norms. *Behavior Research Methods, Instruments, & Computers*, 36(3):402–407.

Timothy J. Owens, Dawn T. Robinson, and Lynn Smith-Lovin. 2010. Three faces of identity. *Sociology*, 36(1):477.

Andrew M. Penner and Aliya Saperstein. 2013. Engendering Racial Perceptions An Intersectional Analysis of How Social Status Shapes Race. *Gender & Society*, 27(3):319–344, June.

R Core Team, 2015. *R: A Language and Environment for Statistical Computing*. R Foundation for Statistical Computing, Vienna, Austria.

Marta Recasens, Eduard Hovy, and M. Antnia Mart. 2011. Identity, non-identity, and near-identity: Addressing the complexity of coreference. *Lingua*, 121(6):1138–1152, May.

Philip Resnik. 1999. Semantic similarity in a taxonomy: An information-based measure and its application to problems of ambiguity in natural language. *J. Artif. Intell. Res.(JAIR)*, 11:95–130.

Magnus Sahlgren. 2006. The Word-Space Model: Using distributional analysis to represent syntagmatic and paradigmatic relations between words in high-dimensional vector spaces.

Cosma Rohilla Shalizi. 2013. Advanced data analysis from an elementary point of view. *URL: http://www. stat. cmu. edu/cshalizi/ADAfaEPoV/13*, 24.

Lynn Smith-Lovin. 2007. The Strength of Weak Identities: Social Structural Sources of Self, Situation and Emotional Experience. *Social Psychology Quarterly*, 70(2):106–124, June.

Sheldon Stryker and Peter J. Burke. 2000. The past, present, and future of an identity theory. *Social psychology quarterly*, pages 284–297.

Amos Tversky and Itamar Gati. 1978. Studies of similarity. *Cognition and categorization*, 1(1978):79–98.

Emiel van Miltenburg. 2016. Stereotyping and Bias in the Flickr30k Dataset. In *Workshop on Computer Vision and Language Processing*.

Simon Wood. 2006. *Generalized additive models: an introduction with R*. CRC press.

Ziqi Zhang, Anna Lisa Gentile, and Fabio Ciravenga. 2013. Recent advances in methods of lexical semantic relatedness - a survey. *Natural Language Engineering*, 19(4):411–479, October.

Identifying News from Tweets

Jesse Freitas and Heng Ji
Computer Science Department
Rensselaer Polytechnic Institute
Troy, NY, USA
{freitj,jih}@rpi.edu

Abstract

Informal genres such as tweets provide large quantities of data in real time, which can be exploited to obtain, through ranking and classification, a succinct summary of the events that occurred. Previous work on tweet ranking and classification mainly focused on salience and social network features or rely on web documents such as online news articles. In this paper, we exploit language independent journalism and content based features to identify news from tweets. We propose a novel newsworthiness classifier trained through active learning and investigate human assessment and automatic methods to encode it on both the tweet and trending topic levels. Our findings show that content and journalism based features proved to be effective for ranking and classifying content on Twitter.

1 Introduction

Due to the massive amount of tweets posted on a daily basis, automatic tweet ranking has become an important task to assist fast information distillation. Previous work (Inouye and Kalita, 2011; Yang et al., 2011; Liu et al., 2012; Ren et al., 2013; Shou et al., 2013; Chua and Asur, 2013; Chang et al., 2013) focused on selecting informative tweets based on a variety of criteria such as readability, author's influence and users' interest. In addition, (Štajner et al., 2013) studied selection of user's responses to news by optimizing an objective function which jointly models the messages' utility scores and their entropy. (Wei and Gao, 2014) proposed using learning-to-rank techniques to help conduct single-document

summarization.

Additional work has been done to improve event detection on Twitter. Previous methods relied on metadata from tweets (Cui et al., 2012) while others focus on open-domain categorization using tools trained specifically for micro-blogging services(Ritter et al., 2012a). In addition, (Cataldi et al., 2010) incorporated temporal knowledge while formalizing content to compensate for informal and short text.

Tweet ranking is also related to the previous work concerning tweet summarization which summarized important information from tweet streams. Modern summarization approaches rank sentences or phrases from informal genres such as social media, web forums, and micro-blogging sites. Some methods determine semantic relations of manually annotated hashtags and user replies using social network and web document graphs (e.g., (Huang et al., 2012)). Our goal is to accomplish ranking of micro-blogging content using natural language features to identify sentences with the most newsworthiness and relevance to the event that occurred.

We introduce a novel *newsworthiness* model to improve topic classification, and investigate both human assessment and automatic linguistic features in-depth for this new measure. Once topics are identified, we apply these methods to an ordinal ranking model to identify the tweets that make this topic newsworthy. Compared with previous work, we focus more on analysis of text than social network features for ranking and classifying tweets. In order to determine newsworthiness, we use news values based on journalism theory to encode features in-

Proceedings of 2016 EMNLP Workshop on Natural Language Processing and Computational Social Science, pages 11–16,
Austin, TX, November 5, 2016. ©2016 Association for Computational Linguistics

stead of traditional methods based on social features.

2 Approach

2.1 News Values and Definition

Newsworthiness describes the amount of new information for a general audience. (Galtung and Ruge, 1965) describe news as a spike in human communication or a signal that can be measured, and trending topics on Twitter behave this way. However, trending topics on social media can also be jokes, and ongoing and commemorative events. We hypothesize that newsworthiness would be an important factor in human distillation of media regarding events because it is a subset of salience that contains only novel information that is time relevant and new compared to an existing knowledge base. We define the following novel criteria to determine the newsworthiness of content based on news values defined by Galtung and Ruge (1965):

1. The content tends to refer to a negative event more than a positive event

2. The content must be well composed

3. The content typically refers to elite nations, people, or organizations

4. The content must have human interest

The basis behind newsworthy criteria is that (1) the content must be important to the general viewer but must provide new insight to an event that occurred; (2) because news content is salient, but salient content is not always newsworthy, understanding this subset is critical for automatic news summarization; (3) negative news is typically more viewed than positive news and usually pertains to named entities that are high profile; and (4) news must also have human interest meaning it must affect many people. Using Galtung and Ruge's metaphor of a signal for news, these principles should indicate a strong signal or spike in news.

The non-syntactic features listed in Table 1 are calculated as the number of words in the tweet and the normalized features are calculated as the ratio of the number of sentiment words to the total number of words in the tweet not including stopwords. The named entities and slangs were extracted using

Feature	News Value
Slang Usage	2
First Person Usage	4
Geo-Political Entities	3
People Recognized	3
Companies Recognized	3
Sentiment Usage	1, 4
Normalized Sentiment Usage	1, 4
Normalized Stopwords Usage	2, 4
Max Parse Tree Height	2
Max NP Parse Tree Height	2
Max VP Parse Tree Height	2

Table 1: Newsworthiness features and news values they encode.

the Twitter NLP toolkit (Ritter et al., 2011; Ritter et al., 2012b) which was designed specifically for tweet content. The syntax tree features were calculated using the Stanford parser (Manning et al., 2014) trained using the English caseless model (de Marneffe et al., 2006). The premise behind using the parse tree as a feature is that more complex speech is more likely to be newsworthy because it is well composed. Sentiment terms were determined based on lexical matching from gazetteers(Hu and Liu, 2004; Taboada and Grieve, 2004; Wiebe et al., 2004; Baccianella et al., 2010; Joshi et al., 2011) and compiled into one sentiment dictionary (Li et al., 2012). Normalized stopword usage is important for both composition and human interest particularly because of the structure of a tweet. Since tweets are short and contain few words, if a tweet uses a high proportion of stopwords, it likely doesn't have many novel terms that would contain human interest. The remaining features are encoded based on the principle that generally recognized names and events are important for detecting topically familiar and important materials.

2.2 Newsworthiness Identification

There are two tasks to complete to identify newsworthy, salient content. The first is to identify the tweets within a topic that make the trending topic newsworthy. The second task is to identify trending topics on Twitter that meet the criteria for news values. To accomplish these tasks we use two Support Vector Machine based methods to perform news classification on trending topics and ordinal regression for ranking tweets in the topic. The models are trained using an eighth order polynomial kernel with default parameters and we tune the cost parameter based on the task. In order to train these models, we use the same 11 features in both tasks based on news criteria journalists use to write articles.

For identifying trending topics, our goal was to improve the precision and recall of existing systems so the model was tuned to maximize F-score performance using three fold cross validation to maintain consistency with the validation used by Huang et al. (2012). The ordinal regression model for ranking tweets was tuned using the same cross validation method to minimize the squared error from ground truth ranking.

We also evaluate an *actively trained* model for classification similar to the committee method used by Zubiaga et al. (2015). We choose candidates using *Query-By-Committee (QBC)* (Settles, 2009) where multiple models are trained using the same data and predict the class of each Twitter trend. For our committee we use our journalism based model and Zubiaga's Twitter based model. The contradicting predictions from the two models are used to choose the new training data. We use one iteration for creating candidates and our journalism model is then retrained using the new training data subset selected by the committee.

3 Experiments

3.1 Data

Our first ground truth dataset for classifying tweets was collected using CrowdFlower[1] to annotate the newsworthiness of 3,482 topically related tweets in English about Hurricane Irene. The dataset was collected during three separate hours during three different days shown in Table 2. We hypothesize that the subevents related to the topic will affect the amount of newsworthy content we are attempting to rank and may affect the performance of the ordinal regression model.

The ordinal regression dataset is composed of the same tweets used by Huang et al. (2012). Five annotators labeled the tweets' newsworthiness from

---

[1]http://www.crowdflower.com/

Date	Event
Aug. 27th, 2011	Irene landfall in NC
Aug. 28th, 2011	Irene landfall in NYC
Sept. 1st, 2011	Irene dissipates

Table 2: Tweets were collected for one hour on each day during the storm

one to three where three is most newsworthy. Annotators were given a brief summary of the events that occurred regarding Hurricane Irene and the areas that were impacted by flooding and power outages. They were provided a guideline for newsworthiness and asked to score the tweets on whether they contained new information at the time it was tweeted and would be noteworthy content in the media. The tweets were filtered to remove annotations if the CrowdFlower site's annotator confidence score was below 50 percent.

The second dataset is comprised of 2,593 trending topics used by Zubiaga (2013). The topics were collected from February 1 to 28, 2012, and five topics were randomly sampled per hour. Each topic contains at most 1,500 tweets and the topic is labeled newsworthy or not newsworthy. The tweets are in multiple languages including English, Spanish, and Portuguese and were translated to English by both human and machine translators. This dataset was selected to evaluate the news features on a set of more diverse events than Hurricane Irene.

In order to demonstrate the effectiveness of our approaches, we evaluated the features on both the tweet ranking and trend classification tasks by comparing them to the performance of other approaches.

3.2 Evaluation

The ordinal regression and classification models were evaluated separately from each other to determine individual performance.

To compare our ranking method we used *Normalized Discounted Cumulative Gain* (nDCG) (Järvelin and Kekäläinen, 2002) and evaluated the results on the three individual hours of data.

The classification task is evaluated using precision, recall, and F-score and is compared using a baseline approach for classifying news trends (Zubiaga et al., 2015). The baseline approach classifies trending topics as news, or not news using so-

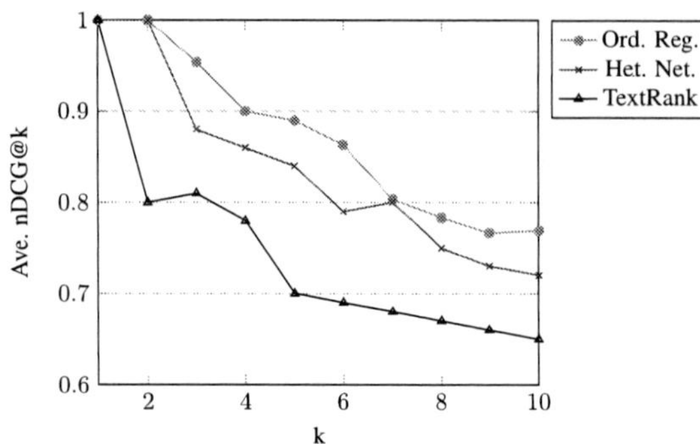

Figure 1: nDCG@k for Ordinal Regression, Heterogeneous Networks, TextRank

cial features such as user diversity, hashtag usage, and retweets about the topic, but does not consider as many language and content features.

4 Results

4.1 Ranking Individual Tweets

Figure 1 illustrates the evaluation of each method on nDCG@k from 1 to 10. The results indicate that our ordinal regression model performed better in terms of nDCG than the traditional TextRank method using the standard dampening factor with filtering and heterogeneous networks without web documents (Huang et al., 2012). The edges are calculated using cosine similarity between tweets and the filtering used removed tweets that used excessive slang or punctuation. The ordinal regression curve in Figure 1 represents the average performance of our model after evaluating the model on three different time periods of data described in Section 3.1.

4.2 Trend Classification

Method	Precision	Recall	F-Score
Baseline Features	0.582	0.670	0.623
Content Features	0.604	0.743	0.663
Active Training	**0.814**	**0.745**	**0.778**

Table 3: Trend Classification

Using journalism content features we were able to achieve better performance than our baseline(Zubiaga et al., 2015) in terms of precision and F-score while maintaining recall as shown in Table 3. Further, the model performed best when ac-

tively trained using the same journalism features and achieved a final F-score of 77.8%.

5 Discussion

We determine the statistical significance of each feature for both the trend classifier and the tweet ranker. We found features in each task were highly correlated and share overlap. For the sake of clarity, we only show significant features in Table 4.

Feature	Rank	Class
Slang Usage	***	
Geo-Political Entities	**	
Normalized Stopword Usage		***
Sentiment Terms		***
Company Entities	*	***
First Person Usage	***	***
NP Parse Tree Height	.	***

Table 4: F-statistic significant features. We show only significant features (significance codes: 0 (***) 0.001 (**) 0.01 (*) 0.05 (.) 0.1 ( )). *Rank* is the significance of the features in the tweet ranking task and *Class* is the significance of the features in the trend classification task.

Newsworthiness can affect how quickly and how much novel information can be discerned respectively. One of the goals of incorporating different criteria into ranking and classification other than traditional importance ranking was to demonstrate that salience is not the only factor that users and journalists consider when digesting material from social media. Another goal is to demonstrate that content based features can perform as well as other modern approaches that rely on web documents and social media graphs in order to bypass the challenge of understanding the short context-free nature of microblog posts.

In this paper we propose and evaluate two individual tasks used in identifying news on Twitter. We find that with the use of active learning and content based features we are able to significantly improve the precision of trend classification while maintaining recall. One challenge we faced was that Zubiaga's features for trending topics did not extend well to single tweet features for ranking. Because of this, we were unable to evaluate query-by-committee methods on ordinal regression which is something we would like to explore in the future.

While the features we used are not advanced, the application of them encode Galtung and Ruge's standards of world news for journalists and news reporting agencies. Our features attempt to capture a journalism perspective instead of previous work which focused on social media networks and social features. While this approach has limitations, the application of this approach in conjunction with web documents could improve news summarization tasks using Twitter data.

6   Acknowledgements

This work was supported by the U.S. ARL NS-CTA No. W911NF-09-2-0053, DARPA DEFT No. FA8750-13-2-0041, and NSF IIS-1523198. The views and conclusions contained in this document are those of the authors and should not be interpreted as representing the official policies, either expressed or implied, of the U.S. Government. The U.S. Government is authorized to reproduce and distribute reprints for Government purposes notwithstanding any copyright notation here on.

References

Stefano Baccianella, Andrea Esuli, and Fabrizio Sebastiani. 2010. Sentiwordnet 3.0: An enhanced lexical resource for sentiment analysis and opinion mining. In Nicoletta Calzolari (Conference Chair), Khalid Choukri, Bente Maegaard, Joseph Mariani, Jan Odijk, Stelios Piperidis, Mike Rosner, and Daniel Tapias, editors, *Proceedings of the Seventh International Conference on Language Resources and Evaluation (LREC'10)*, Valletta, Malta, may. European Language Resources Association (ELRA).

Mario Cataldi, Luigi Di Caro, and Claudio Schifanella. 2010. Emerging topic detection on twitter based on temporal and social terms evaluation. In *Proceedings of the Tenth International Workshop on Multimedia Data Mining*, MDMKDD '10, pages 4:1–4:10, New York, NY, USA. ACM.

Yi Chang, Xuanhui Wang, Qiaozhu Mei, and Yan Liu. 2013. Towards twitter context summarization with user influence models. In *Proceedings of the sixth ACM international conference on Web search and data mining*, pages 527–536. ACM.

Freddy Chong Tat Chua and Sitaram Asur. 2013. Automatic summarization of events from social media. In *ICWSM*. Citeseer.

Anqi Cui, Min Zhang, Yiqun Liu, Shaoping Ma, and Kuo Zhang. 2012. Discover breaking events with popular hashtags in twitter. In *Proceedings of the 21st ACM International Conference on Information and Knowledge Management*, CIKM '12, pages 1794–1798, New York, NY, USA. ACM.

Marie-Catherine de Marneffe, Bill MacCartney, and Christopher D. Manning. 2006. Generating typed dependency parses from phrase structure parses. In *IN PROC. INTL CONF. ON LANGUAGE RESOURCES AND EVALUATION (LREC*, pages 449–454.

Johan Galtung and Marie Holmboe Ruge. 1965. The structure of foreign news. *The Journal of Peace Research*, 2(2):64–91.

Minqing Hu and Bing Liu. 2004. Mining and summarizing customer reviews. In *KDD '04: Proceedings of the tenth ACM SIGKDD international conference on Knowledge discovery and data mining*, pages 168–177, New York, NY, USA. ACM.

Hongzhao Huang, Arkaitz Zubiaga, Heng Ji, Hongbo Deng, Dong Wang, Hieu Khac Le, Tarek F. Abdelzaher, Jiawei Han, Alice Leung, John P. Hancock, and others. 2012. Tweet Ranking Based on Heterogeneous Networks. In *COLING*, pages 1239–1256.

David Inouye and Jugal K Kalita. 2011. Comparing twitter summarization algorithms for multiple post summaries. In *Privacy, Security, Risk and Trust (PASSAT) and 2011 IEEE Third Inernational Conference on Social Computing (SocialCom), 2011 IEEE Third International Conference on*, pages 298–306. IEEE.

Kalervo Järvelin and Jaana Kekäläinen. 2002. Cumulated gain-based evaluation of ir techniques. *ACM Trans. Inf. Syst.*, 20(4):422–446, October.

Aditya Joshi, Balamurali A. R., Pushpak Bhattacharyya, and Rajat Kumar Mohanty. 2011. C-feel-it: A sentiment analyzer for micro-blogs. In *Proceedings of the 49th Annual Meeting of Association for Computational Linguistics (Demo)*. ACL.

Hao Li, Yu Chen, Heng Ji, Smaranda Muresan, and Dequan Zheng. 2012. Combining social cognitive theories with linguistic features for multi-genre sentiment analysis. In *Proceedings of the 26th Pacific Asia Conference on Language, Information, and Computation*, pages 127–136, Bali,Indonesia, November. Faculty of Computer Science, Universitas Indonesia.

Xiaohua Liu, Yitong Li, Furu Wei, and Ming Zhou. 2012. Graph-based multi-tweet summarization using social signals. In *COLING*, pages 1699–1714.

Christopher D. Manning, Mihai Surdeanu, John Bauer, Jenny Finkel, Steven J. Bethard, and David McClosky. 2014. The stanford corenlp natural language processing toolkit. In *Proc. ACL2014)*.

Zhaochun Ren, Shangsong Liang, Edgar Meij, and Maarten de Rijke. 2013. Personalized time-aware tweets summarization. In *Proceedings of the 36th international ACM SIGIR conference on research and development in information retrieval*, pages 513–522. ACM.

Alan Ritter, Sam Clark, Mausam, and Oren Etzioni. 2011. Named entity recognition in tweets: An experimental study. In *EMNLP*.

Alan Ritter, Mausam, Oren Etzioni, and Sam Clark. 2012a. Open domain event extraction from twitter. In *Proceedings of the 18th ACM SIGKDD International Conference on Knowledge Discovery and Data Mining*, KDD '12, pages 1104–1112, New York, NY, USA. ACM.

Alan Ritter, Mausam, Oren Etzioni, and Sam Clark. 2012b. Open domain event extraction from twitter. In *KDD*.

Burr Settles. 2009. Active learning literature survey.

Lidan Shou, Zhenhua Wang, Ke Chen, and Gang Chen. 2013. Sumblr: continuous summarization of evolving tweet streams. In *Proceedings of the 36th international ACM SIGIR conference on Research and development in information retrieval*, pages 533–542. ACM.

Tadej Štajner, Bart Thomee, Ana-Maria Popescu, Marco Pennacchiotti, and Alejandro Jaimes. 2013. Automatic selection of social media responses to news. In *Proceedings of the 19th ACM SIGKDD international conference on Knowledge discovery and data mining*, pages 50–58. ACM.

Maite Taboada and Jack Grieve. 2004. Analyzing appraisal automatically. In *In Proceedings of the AAAI Spring Symposium on Exploring Attitude and Affect in Text: Theories and Applications*, pages 158–161.

Zhongyu Wei and Wei Gao. 2014. Utilizing microblogs for automatic news highlights extraction. COLING.

Janyce Wiebe, Theresa Wilson, Rebecca Bruce, Matthew Bell, and Melanie Martin. 2004. Learning subjective language. *Computational Linguistics*, 30(3):277–308, January.

Zi Yang, Keke Cai, Jie Tang, Li Zhang, Zhong Su, and Juanzi Li. 2011. Social context summarization. In *Proceedings of the 34th international ACM SIGIR conference on Research and development in Information Retrieval*, pages 255–264. ACM.

Arkaitz Zubiaga, Heng Ji, and Kevin Knight. 2013. Curating and contextualizing twitter stories to assist with social newsgathering. In *Proc. International Conference on Intelligent User Interfaces (IUI2013)*.

Arkaitz Zubiaga, Damiano Spina, Raquel Martnez, and Vctor Fresno. 2015. Real-time classification of twitter trends. *Journal of the Association for Information Science and Technology*, 66(3):462–473.

Obfuscating Gender in Social Media Writing

Sravana Reddy
Wellesley College
Wellesley, MA
sravana.reddy@wellesley.edu

Kevin Knight
USC Information Sciences Institute
Marina del Rey, CA
knight@isi.edu

Abstract

The vast availability of textual data on social media has led to an interest in algorithms to predict user attributes such as gender based on the user's writing. These methods are valuable for social science research as well as targeted advertising and profiling, but also compromise the privacy of users who may not realize that their personal idiolects can give away their demographic identities. Can we automatically modify a text so that the author is classified as a certain target gender, under limited knowledge of the classifier, while preserving the text's fluency and meaning? We present a basic model to modify a text using lexical substitution, show empirical results with Twitter and Yelp data, and outline ideas for extensions.

1 Introduction

Recent work has demonstrated success in accurately detecting gender or other author attributes such as age, location, and political preferences from textual input, particularly on social media channels like Twitter (Bamman et al., 2014; Burger et al., 2011; Eisenstein et al., 2010; Li et al., 2014; Liu and Ruths, 2013; Pennacchiotti and Popescu, 2013; Rao et al., 2010; Volkova et al., 2015), weblogs (Mukherjee and Liu, 2010; Schler et al., 2006; Yan and Yan, 2006) and user-review sites (Johannsen et al., 2015).

Outside of academic research, detection of author attributes is a major component of "behavioral targeting" which has been instrumental in online advertising and marketing from the early days of the Web.

Twitter, for example, uses gender inference over textual and profile features to serve ads (Underwood, 2012) and reports over 90% accuracy. Besides advertising, companies also rely on user profiling to improve personalization, build better recommender systems, and increase consumer retention.

While automatic profiling is undoubtedly valuable, it can also be used in ethically negative ways – the problem of "dual-use" outlined by Hovy and Spruit (2016). Users may wish to mask their demographic attributes for various reasons:

1. A by-product of personalization is inadvertent discrimination: a study (Datta et al., 2015) finds that Google serves fewer ads for high-paying jobs to users profiled as female, and Sweeney (2013) shows that ads for public data about people who are profiled as black are more likely to suggest an arrest record regardless of whether the person had one.

2. Users living under authoritarian governments have the incentive to conceal their identity for personal safety (Jardine, 2016). Even outside of repressive regimes, studies have shown that users value anonymity and are more likely to share controversial content when anonymous (Zhang and Kizilcec, 2014). This is evidenced by the popularity of anonymous-posting networks like Yik Yak and Whisper. Automated demographic profiling on content in these venues compromise this assumption of anonymity.

3. Many web users are concerned about online privacy. A large number choose to opt-out of

Proceedings of 2016 EMNLP Workshop on Natural Language Processing and Computational Social Science, pages 17–26,
Austin, TX, November 5, 2016. ©2016 Association for Computational Linguistics

having their online activities tracked by blocking cookies, or installing blocking tools such as Do Not Track[1] or AdBlock Plus[2].

Turow et al. (2015) argue that the majority of users are not actually willing to compromise their privacy in order to receive benefits – rather, they are resigned to it because they believe they are powerless to limit what companies can learn about them. It is likely that a usable tool that aids in masking their demographic identity would be adopted, at least by privacy-conscious users.

4. Users may wish to conceal aspects of their identity to maintain authority or avoid harassment – some women on online forums will try to come across as male (Luu, 2015), and many female writers in literature have used male pseudonyms for this purpose.

This paper is a study addressing the following question: can we automatically modify an input text to "confound" a demographic classifier? The key challenge here is to transform the text while minimally distorting its meaning and fluency from the perspective of a human reader.

Consider this extract from a tweet:

```
OMG I'm sooooo excited!!!
```

Most classifiers would infer the author is female due to the use of multiple exclamation marks, the word *omg*, and the lengthening intensifier, features that are particularly gendered. Re-wording the tweet to

```
dude I'm so stoked.
```

conveys same message, but is more likely to be classified as male due to the words *dude* and *stoked* and the absence of lengthening and exclamation marks.

Although any distortion of text loses information (since word usage and punctuation are signals too), some of these stylistic features may be unintentional on the part of a user who isn't aware that this information can be used to profile or identify them.

---

2   Related Work

The most relevant existing work is that of Brennan et al. (2012) who explore the related problem of modifying text to defeat authorship detectors. Their program, Anonymouth (McDonald et al., 2012)[3], aids a user who intends to anonymize their writing relative to a reference corpus of writing from the user and other authors. Rather than automatically modifying the text, the program makes suggestions of words to add or remove. However, no substitutions for deleted words or placement positions for added words are suggested, so incorporating or removing specific words without being presented with alternatives requires a great deal of effort on the user's side. They also experiment with foiling the authorship detector with machine translation (by translating the text from English to German or Japanese and back to English), but report that it is not effective. Anonymouth is part of a larger field of research on "privacy enhancing technologies" which are concerned with aiding users in masking or hiding private data such as Google Search histories or network access patterns.

Another closely-related paper is that of Preotiuc-Pietro et al. (2016) who infer various stylistic features that distinguish a given gender, age, or occupational class in tweets. They learn phrases (1-3 grams) from the Paraphrase Database (Ganitkevitch et al., 2013) that are semantically equivalent but used more by one demographic than the other, and combine this with a machine translation model to "translate" tweets between demographic classes. However, since their primary objective is not obfuscation, they do not evaluate whether these generated tweets can defeat a demographic classifier.

Spammers are known to modify their e-mails to foil spam detection algorithms, usually by misspelling words that would be indicative of spam, padding the e-mail with lists of arbitrary words, or embedding text in images. It is unclear whether any of these techniques are automated, or to what extent the spammers desire that the modified e-mail appears fluent.

Biggio et al. (2013) formalize the problem of modifying data to evade classifiers by casting it as an optimization problem – minimize the accuracy of

---

the classifier while upper-bounding the deviation of the modified data from the original. They optimize this objective with gradient descent and show examples of the tradeoff between evasion and intelligibility for MNIST digit recognition. They work with models that have perfect information about the classifier, as well as when they only know the type of classifier and an approximation of the training data, which is the assumption we will be operating under as well.

Szegedy et al. (2014) and Goodfellow et al. (2015) show that minor image distortions that are imperceptible to humans can cause neural networks as well linear classifiers to predict completely incorrect labels (such as *ostrich* for an image of a truck) with high confidence, even though the classifier predicts the label of the undistorted images correctly. Nguyen et al. (2015) look at the related problem of synthesizing images that are classified as a certain label with high confidence by deep neural networks, but appear as completely different objects to humans.

A line of work called "adversarial classification" formally addresses the problem from the opposite (i.e. the classifier's) point of view: detecting whether a test sample has been mangled by an adversary. Li and Vorobeychik (2014) describe a model to defeat a limited adversary who has a budget for black box access to the classifier rather than the entire classifier. Dalvi et al. (2004) sketch out an adversary's strategy for evading a Naïve Bayes classifier, and show how to detect if a test sample has been modified according to that strategy. Within the theoretical machine learning community, there is a great deal of interest on learning classifiers that do not adversely affect or discriminate against individuals, by constraining them to satisfy some formal definition of fairness (Zemel et al., 2013).

Our problem can be considered one of paraphrase generation (Madnani and Dorr, 2010) with the objective of defeating a text classifier.

3   Problem Description

The general problem of modifying text to fool a classifier is open-ended; the specific question depends on our goals and assumptions. We consider this (simplified) scenario:

1. We do not have access to the actual classifier or even knowledge of the type of classifier or its training algorithm.

2. However, we do have a corpus of labeled data for the class labels which approximate the actual training data of the classifier, and knowledge about the type of features that it uses, as in Biggio et al. (2013). In this paper, we assume the features are bag-of-word counts.

3. The classifier assigns a categorical label to a user based on a collection of their writing. It does not use auxiliary information such as profile metadata or cues from the social network.

4. The user specifies the target label that they want the classifier to assign to their writing. Some users may want to consistently pass off as another demographic. Some may try to confuse the classifier by having half of their writing be classified as one label and the rest as another. Others may not want to fool the classifier, but rather, wish to amplify their gendered features so they are more likely to be correctly classified.[4]

5. The obfuscated text must be fluent and semantically similar to the original.

We hope to relax assumptions 2 and 3 in future work.

Our experimental setup is as follows:

1. Train a classifier from a corpus

2. Train an obfuscation model from a *separate* but similar corpus

3. Apply the obfuscation model to modify the held-out test sentences towards user-provided target labels. These target labels may be the same as the actual labels or the opposite.

4. Evaluate the accuracy of the classifier relative to the desired target labels, and compare it to the accuracy of the same classifier on the actual labels.

---

[4]Thus, while we will continue to refer to the problem as "obfuscating" the input, it is more generally interpreted as transforming the text so that it is classified as the target label.

4 Data

While our objective is to confound any user-attribute classification system, we focus on building a program to defeat a gender classifier as a testbed. This is motivated partly by of the easy availability of gender-labeled writing, and partly in light of the current social and political conversations about gender expression and fluidity.

Our data is annotated with two genders, corresponding to biological sex. Even though this binary may not be an accurate reflection of the gender performance of users on social media (Bamman et al., 2014; Nguyen et al., 2014), we operate under the presumption that most demographic classifiers also use two genders.

We use two datasets in our experiments – tweets from Twitter, and reviews from Yelp. Neither of these websites require users to specify their gender, so it's likely that at least some authors may prefer not to be profiled. While gender can be inferred from user names (a fact we exploit to label our corpus), many users do not provide real or gendered names, so a profiler would have to rely on their writing and other information.

We chose these corpora since they are representative of different styles of social media writing. Twitter has become the de facto standard for research on author-attribute classification. The writing tends to be highly colloquial and conversational. Yelp user reviews, on the other hand, are relatively more formal and domain-constrained. Both user-bases lean young and are somewhat gender-balanced.

The data is derived from a random sample from a corpus of tweets geolocated in the US that we mined in July 2013, and a corpus of reviews from the Yelp Dataset Challenge[5] released in 2016. Since gender is not known for users in either dataset, it is inferred from users' first names, an approach commonly employed in research on gender classification (Mislove et al., 2011). We use the Social Security Administration list of baby names[6] from 1990; users whose names are not in the list or are ambiguous are discarded. A name is considered unambiguous if over 80% of babies with the name are one gender rather

than the other.

We removed data that is not in English, using Twitter's language identifier for the tweet data, and the language identification algorithm of Lui and Baldwin (2011) for the Yelp reviews.

We also removed Yelp reviews for businesses where the reviewer-base was highly gendered (over 80% male or female for businesses with at least 5 reviews). These reviews tend to contain a disproportionate number of gendered topic words like *pedicure* or *barber*, and attempting to obfuscate them without distorting their message is futile. While tweets also contain gendered topic words, it is not as straightforward to detect them.

Finally, excess data is randomly removed to bring the gender balance to 50%. This results in $432,983$ users in the Yelp corpus and $945,951$ users in the Twitter data. The text is case-folded and tokenized using the Stanford CoreNLP (Manning et al., 2014) and TweetNLP (Gimpel et al., 2011; Kong et al., 2014) tools respectively.

The set of users in each corpus is divided randomly into three parts keeping the gender labels balanced: 45% training data for the classifier, 45% training data for the obfuscator, and 10% test data.

5 Obfuscation by Lexical Substitution

The algorithm takes a target label y specified by the user (i.e., the class label that the user aims to be classified as), and their original input text w. It transforms w to a new text w' that preserves its meaning, so that w' will be classified as y.

Our transformation search space is simple: each word in w can be substituted with another one.

For every token $w_i \in w$

- Compute $\mathrm{Assoc}(w_i, y)$, a measure of association between w_i and y according to the obfuscation training data.

  Positive values indicate that w_i as a unigram feature influences the classifier to label w as y and may therefore be retained (taking a conservative route), while negative values suggest that w_i should be substituted.

- If $\mathrm{Assoc}(w_i, y)$ is negative, consider the set V of all words v such that $\mathrm{SynSem}(w_i, v) >$ some threshold τ and

---

[5]https://www.yelp.com/dataset_challenge
[6]https://www.ssa.gov/oact/babynames/
limits.html

$\text{Assoc}(v, y) > \text{Assoc}(w_i, y)$, where SynSem is a measure of syntactic and semantic similarity between w_i and v. This is the set of candidat words that can be substituted for w_i while retaining semantic and syntactic *and* are more predictive of the target label y.

- Select the candidate in V that is most similar to w_i as well as to the two adjacent words to the left and right under Subst, a measure of substitutability in context. Substitute this candidate for w_i, leaving w_i unchanged if V is empty.

$$\arg\max_{v \in V} \text{Subst}(v, w_i, \{w_{i-2}, w_{i-1}, w_{i+1}, w_{i+2}\})$$

τ is a hyperparameter that controls the fidelity between w and w'. Higher values will result in w' being more similar to the original; the trade-off is that the obfuscation may not be strong enough to confound the classifier.

Descriptions of the association, similarity and substitutability functions follow.

5.1 Feature-Label Association (Assoc)

Since we don't have direct access to the classifier, an approximate measure how much a feature (word) contributes to the input being classified as a certain label is needed. For two labels y_1 and y_2, we compute the normalized pointwise mutual information between each word f and each of y_1 and y_2 from the obfuscation training set, and take the difference:

$$\text{nPMI}(f, y_1) = \log \frac{P(f, y_1)}{P(f)P(y_1)} / - \log P(f, y_1)$$

$$\text{Assoc}(f, y_1) = \text{nPMI}(f, y_1) - \text{nPMI}(f, y_2)$$

The words that have the highest associations with each gender are listed in Table 1. While these top items tend to be content/topical words that cannot be easily substituted, adjectives and punctuations that are gender-specific also rank high.

5.2 Syntactic+Semantic Similarity (SynSem)

We considered building the lexical similarity model from databases like PPDB (Ganitkevitch et al., 2013), as in Preotiuc-Pietro et al. (2016), but found that their vocabulary coverage for social media text was insufficient, particularly the words (misspellings, slang terms, etc.) that are most predictive of gender.

Distributional word representations tend to do a good job of capturing word similarity. While methods like the `word2vec` skip-gram neural network model of Mikolov et al. (2013) are effective for word similarities, we need to ensure that the substitutions are also syntactically appropriate for lexical substitution. With a skip-gram context window of 5, the most similar words to *eating* are *eat* and *stomachs*, which cannot substitute for *eating* in a sentence. On the other hand, a short content window of 1 gives high similarities to words like *staying* or *experiencing*, which are syntactically good but semantically weak substitutes.

In order to capture syntactic as well as semantic similarities, we employ dependency parses as contexts, using the `word2vec` extension of Levy and Goldberg (2014). Larger corpora of 2.2 million Yelp reviews and 280 million tweets, parsed with Stanford CoreNLP and TweetNLP, are used to train the word vectors. (According to these vectors, the most similar words to *eating* are *devouring* and *consuming*.)

The lexical similarity function $\text{SynSem}(a, b)$ is defined as the cosine similarity between the dependency-parse-based word vectors corresponding to the words a and b.

5.3 Substitutability (Subst)

This determines which of the lexically similar candidates are most appropriate in a given context. We use the measure below, adapted from Melamud et al. (2015), giving the substitutability of a for b in the context of a list of tokens C by averaging over b and the context:

$$\text{Subst}(a, b, C) = \frac{\text{SynSem}(a, b) + \sum_{c \in C} \text{Sem}(a, c)}{|C| + 1}$$

Unlike Melamud et al. (2015) who rely on the dependency-parse-based system throughout, we take $\text{Sem}(a, c)$ to be the cosine similarity between the regular window 5 skip-gram vectors Mikolov et al. (2013), and use the two adjacent words on either side of b as the context C. We found this works

Table 1: Words having the highest associations with each gender

Twitter									
Male	bro, bruh, game, man, team, steady, drinking, dude, brotha, lol								
Female	my, you, me, love, omg, boyfriend, miss, mom, hair, retail								
Yelp									
Male	wifey, wifes, bachelor, girlfriend, proposition, urinal, oem corvette, wager, fairways, urinals, firearms, diane, barbers								
Female	hubby, boyfriend, hubs, bf, husbands, dh, mani/pedi, boyfriends bachelorette, leggings, aveda, looooove, yummy, xoxo, pedi, bestie								

better, probably because social media text is syntactically noisier than their datasets.

6 Results

We train L2-regularized logistic regression classification models with bag-of-words counts for the two corpora on their classification training sets. Table 2 shows the prediction accuracies on the unmodified test data as a baseline. (Performance is lower for Twitter than Yelp, probably because of the latter's smaller vocabulary.)

The same classifiers are run on the obfuscated texts generated by the algorithm described above in §5, with target labels set to be (1) the same as the true labels, corresponding to when the test users want to amplify their actual genders, and (2) opposite to the true labels, simulating the case when all test users intend to pass off as the opposite gender. Table 2 shows the accuracy of the classifier at recovering the intended target labels, as well as the relative number of tokens changed from the original text.

The modified texts are significantly better at getting the classifier to meet the intended targets – in both directions – than the unmodified baseline. As expected, lower thresholds for semantic similarity (τ) result in better classification with respect to the target labels, since the resulting text contains more words that are correlated with the target labels.

The more important question is: do the obfuscated inputs retain the meanings of the original, and would they be considered grammatically fluent by a human reader? Future work must obtain participant judgments for a more rigorous evaluation. Examples of the modified texts are shown in Table 3, including some good outputs as well as unacceptable ones. We find that $\tau = 0.8$ is a good balance between semantic similarity of the modified texts with the original and prediction accuracy towards the target label.

Substitutions that don't change the meaning significantly tend to be adjectives and adverbs, spelling variants (like *goood* for *good*), and punctuation marks and other words – generally slang terms – that substitute well in context (like *buddy* for *friend*). Interestingly, spelling errors are sometimes introduced when the error is gendered (like *awsome* or *tommorrow*). Unfortunately, our association and similarity measures also hypothesize substitutions that significantly alter meaning, such as *Plano* for *Lafayette* or *paninis* for *burgers*. However, on the whole, topical nouns tend to be retained, and a perfunctory qualitative examination shows that most of the substitutions don't significantly alter the text's overall meaning or fluency.

7 Discussion

This paper raises the question of how to automatically modify text to defeat classifiers (with limited knowledge of the classifier) while preserving meaning. We presented a preliminary model using lexical substitution that works against classifiers with bag-of-word count features. As far as we are aware, no previous work has tackled this problem, and as such, several directions lie ahead.

Improvements A major shortcoming of our algorithm is that it does not explicitly distinguish content words that salient to the sentence meaning from stylistic features that can be substituted, as long the words are highly gendered. It may help to either restrict substitutions to adjectives, adverbs, punctuation, etc. or come up with a statistical corpus-based

Table 2: Gender identification performance of a logistic regression classifier with bag-of-words features on the original texts from the test sets and the modified texts generated by our algorithm. Performance is measured relative to the target gender label: does every user want the classifier to predict their actual gender correctly, or have it predict the *opposite* gender? Chance is 50% in all cases; higher prediction accuracies are better. Better classifier performance indicates that the texts that are successfully modified towards the users' target labels, which may be to pass off as another gender *or* to reinforce their actual gender. τ controls the trade-off between semantic similarity to the original and association to the target label.

Target		τ	Twitter		Yelp	
			Tokens Changed	Accuracy	Tokens Changed	Accuracy
	Original Text	-	0%	69.67%	0%	74.72%
Reinforce	Modified Text	0.9	2.17%	74.49%	0.38%	76.56%
Gender		0.8	4.45%	80.32%	3.42%	88.17%
		0.5	11.01%	88.73%	9.53%	96.93%
Present	Original Text	-	0%	30.33%	0%	25.28%
as Opposite	Modified Text	0.9	2.61%	37.93%	0.61%	61.19%
Gender		0.8	5.94%	51.58%	4.62%	65.27%
		0.5	15.23%	77.82%	12.74%	91.87%

Table 3: Samples where the classifier predicts the *target* gender correctly on the modified text ($\tau = 0.8$) of the user but incorrectly on the original. Predictions are shown in parentheses.

Yelp		
Original	Modified	Similar meaning/ fluency?
Took my friend here (F)	*Took my buddy here* (M)	Yes
and food still outstanding (M)	*and food still amazing* (F)	Yes
Exceptional view, excellent service,	*Impeccable view, amazing service,*	
great quality (M)	*wonderful quality* (F)	Yes
the drinks are great, too! (M)	*the drinks are wonderful, too!!* (F)	Yes
tasted as amazing as the first sip I took!	*tasted as awsome as the first sip I took;*	
Definitely would recommend (F)	*certainly would recommend* (M)	Yes
My wife and I can't wait to go back. (M)	*My husband and I can't wait to go back!* (F)	Somewhat
the creamy rice side dish - delish. (F)	*the succulent rice side dish; unreal.* (M)	Somewhat
I like burgers a lot (M)	*I like paninis a lot* (F)	No
PK was our server (F)	*PK was our salesperson* (M)	No
and I was impressed (M)	*and I is impressed* (F)	No
The girls who work there are wonderful (F)	*The dudes who work there are sublime* (M)	No
Twitter		
Original	Modified	Similar meaning/ fluency?
Yeah.. it's gonna be a good day (M)	*Yeaaah.. it's gonna be a goood day* (F)	Yes
who's up? (M)	*who's up?!* (F)	Yes
I'm so excited about tomorrow (F)	*I'm so pumped about tommorrow* (M)	Yes
I will never get tired of this #beachday (F)	*I will never get tired of this #chillin* (M)	Somewhat
all my niggas look rich as fuck (M)	*all my bitches look rich as eff* (F)	Somewhat
people from Lafayette on twitter (M)	*people from Plano on tumblr* (F)	No
#TheConjuring (F)	*#pacificrim* (M)	No

measure of whether a word carries meaning in context.

A practical program should handle more complex features that are commonly used in stylometric classification, such as bigrams, word categories, length distributions, and syntactic patterns, as well as non-linear classification models like neural networks. Such a program will necessitate more sophisticated paraphrasing methods than lexical substitution. It would also help to combine word vector based similarity measures with other existing data-driven paraphrase extraction methods (Ganitkevitch et al., 2013; Xu et al., 2014; Xu et al., 2015).

Paraphrasing algorithms benefit from parallel data: texts expressing the same message written by users from different demographic groups. While such parallel data isn't readily available for longer-form text like blogs or reviews, it may be possible to extract it from Twitter by making certain assumptions – for instance, URLs in tweets could serve as a proxy for common meaning (Danescu-Niculescu-Mizil et al., 2012). We would also like to evaluate how well the machine translation/paraphrasing approach proposed by Preotiuc-Pietro et al. (2016) performs at defeating classifiers.

We plan to extensively test our model on different corpora and demographic attributes besides gender such as location and age, as well as author identity for anonymization, and evaluate the quality of the obfuscated text according to human judgments.

Our model assumes that the attribute we're trying to conceal is independent of other personal attributes and a priori uniformly distributed, whereas in practice, attributes like gender may be skewed or correlated with age or race in social media channels. As a result, text that has been obfuscated against a gender classifier may inadvertently be obfuscated against an age predictor even if that wasn't the user's intent. Future work should model the interactions between major demographic attributes, and also account for attributes that are continuous rather than categorical variables.

Other paradigms The setup in Sec. 3 is one of many possible scenarios. What if the user wanted the classifier to be uncertain of its predictions in either direction, rather than steering it one of the labels? In such a case, rather than aiming for a high classification accuracy with respect to the target label, we would want the accuracy to approach 50%. What if our obfuscation program had no side-information about feature types, but instead had some other advantage like black-box access to the classifier? In ongoing work, we're looking at leveraging algorithms to explain classifier predictions (Ribeiro et al., 2016) for the second problem.

Security and adversarial classification Note that we have not shown any statistical guarantees about our method – a challenge from the *opposite* point of view is to detect that a text has been modified with the intent of concealing a demographic attribute, and even build a classifier that is resilient to such obfuscation.

We also hope that this work motivates research that explores provably secure ways of defeating text classifiers.

Practical implementation Eventually, we would like to implement such a program as a website or application that suggests lexical substitutions for different web domains. This would also help us evaluate the quality of our obfuscation program in terms of (1) preserving semantic similarity and (2) its effectiveness against real classifiers. The first can be measured by the number of re-wording suggestions that the user chooses to keep. The second may be evaluated by checking the site's inferred profile of the user, either directly if available, or by the types of targeted ads that are displayed. Further, while our objective in this paper is to defeat automatic classification algorithms, we would like to evaluate to what extent the obfuscated text fools human readers as well.

Acknowledgments

We thank the anonymous reviewers for their suggestions. The first author was partly supported by a Neukom Fellowship at Dartmouth College.

References

David Bamman, Jacob Eisenstein, and Tyler Schnoebelen. 2014. Gender identity and lexical variation in social media. *Journal of Sociolinguistics*, 18:135–160.

Battista Biggio, Igino Corona, Davide Maiorca, Blaine Nelson, Nedim Šrndič, Pavel Laskov, Giorgio Giacinto, and Fabio Roli. 2013. Evasion attacks against machine learning at test time. In *Proceedings of ECMLPKDD*.

Michael Brennan, Sadia Afroz, and Rachel Greenstadt. 2012. Adversarial stylometry: Circumventing authorship recognition to preserve privacy and anonymity. *ACM Transactions on Information and System Security*.

John D. Burger, John Henderson, George Kim, and Guido Zarrella. 2011. Discriminating gender on Twitter. In *Proceedings of EMNLP*.

Nilesh Dalvi, Pedro Domingos, Mausam, Sumit Sanghai, and Deepak Verma. 2004. Adversarial classification. In *Proceedings of KDD*.

Cristian Danescu-Niculescu-Mizil, Justin Cheng, Jon Kleinberg, and Lillian Lee. 2012. You had me at hello: how phrasing affects memorability. In *Proceedings of ACL*.

Amit Datta, Michael Carl Tschantz, and Anupam Datta. 2015. Automated experiments on ad privacy settings. *Proceedings on Privacy Enhancing Technologies*, 2015(1).

Jacob Eisenstein, Brendan O'Connor, Noah A. Smith, and Eric P. Xing. 2010. A latent variable model for geographic lexical variation. In *Proceedings of EMNLP*.

Juri Ganitkevitch, Benjamin Van Durme, and Chris Callison-Burch. 2013. PPDB: The paraphrase database. In *Proceedings of NAACL*.

Kevin Gimpel, Nathan Schneider, Brendan O'Connor, Dipanjan Das, Daniel Mills, Jacob Eisenstein, Michael Heilman, Dani Yogatama, Jeffrey Flanigan, and Noah A. Smith. 2011. Part-of-speech tagging for Twitter: Annotation, features, and experiments. In *Proceedings of ACL*.

Ian Goodfellow, Jonathon Shlens, and Christian Szegedy. 2015. Explaining and harnessing adversarial examples. In *Proceedings of the International Conference on Learning Representations*.

Dirk Hovy and Shannon L Spruit. 2016. The social impact of natural language processing. In *Proceedings of ACL*.

Eric Jardine. 2016. Tor, what is it good for? Political repression and the use of online anonymity-granting technologies. *New Media & Society*.

Anders Johannsen, Dirk Hovy, and Anders Søgaard. 2015. Cross-lingual syntactic variation over age and gender. In *Proceedings of CoNLL*.

Lingpeng Kong, Nathan Schneider, Swabha Swayamdipta, Archna Bhatia, Chris Dyer, and Noah A. Smith. 2014. A dependency parser for tweets. In *Proceedings of EMNLP*.

Omer Levy and Yoav Goldberg. 2014. Dependency-based word embeddings. In *Proceedings of ACL*.

Bo Li and Yevgeniy Vorobeychik. 2014. Feature cross-substitution in adversarial classification. In *Proceedings of NIPS*.

Jiwei Li, Alan Ritter, and Eduard Hovy. 2014. Weakly supervised user profile extraction from Twitter. In *Proceedings of ACL*.

Wendy Liu and Derek Ruths. 2013. What's in a name? Using first names as features for gender inference in Twitter. In *Proceedings of AAAI Spring Symposium on Analyzing Microtext*.

Marco Lui and Timothy Baldwin. 2011. Cross-domain feature selection for language identification. In *Proceedings of IJCNLP*.

Chi Luu. 2015. How to disappear completely: linguistic anonymity on the Internet. JSTOR Daily: http://daily.jstor.org/disappear-completely-linguistic-anonymity-internet/.

Nitin Madnani and Bonnie J. Dorr. 2010. Generating phrasal and sentential paraphrases: A survey of data-driven methods. *Computational Linguistics*, 36(341-387).

Christopher D. Manning, Mihai Surdeanu, John Bauer, Jenny Finkel, Steven J. Bethard, and David McClosky. 2014. The Stanford CoreNLP natural language processing toolkit. In *Proceedings of ACL (System Demonstrations)*.

Andrew W. E. McDonald, Sadia Afroz, Aylin Caliskan, Ariel Stolerman, and Rachel Greenstadt. 2012. Use fewer instances of the letter "i": Toward writing style anonymization. In *Proceedings of the Privacy Enhancing Technologies Symposium (PETS)*.

Oren Melamud, Omer Levy, and Ido Dagan. 2015. A simple word embedding model for lexical substitution. In *Proceedings of the Workshop on Vector Space Modeling for NLP (VSM)*.

Tomas Mikolov, Ilya Sutskever, Kai Chen, Greg Corrado, and Jeffrey Dean. 2013. Distributed representations of words and phrases and their compositionality. In *Proceedings of NIPS*.

Alan Mislove, Sune Lehmann, Yong-Yeol Ahn, Jukka-Pekka Onnela, and J. Niels Rosenquist. 2011. Understanding the demographics of Twitter users. In *Proceedings of the AAAI Conference on Weblogs and Social Media (ICWSM)*.

Arjun Mukherjee and Bing Liu. 2010. Improving gender classification of blog authors. In *Proceedings of EMNLP*.

Dong Nguyen, Dolf Trieschnigg, A. Seza Doğruöz, Rilana Gravel, Mariët Theune, Theo Meder, and Franciska de Jong. 2014. Why gender and age prediction from tweets is hard: Lessons from a crowdsourcing experiment. In *Proceedings of COLING*.

Anh Nguyen, Jason Yosinski, and Jeff Clune. 2015. Deep neural networks are easily fooled: High confidence predictions for unrecognizable images. In *Proceedings of CVPR*.

Marco Pennacchiotti and Ana-Maria Popescu. 2013. A machine learning approach to Twitter user classification. In *Proceedings of the AAAI Conference on Weblogs and Social Media (ICWSM)*.

Daniel Preotiuc-Pietro, Wei Xu, and Lyle Ungar. 2016. Discovering user attribute stylistic differences via paraphrasing. In *Proceedings of AAAI*.

Delip Rao, David Yarowsky, Abhishek Shreevats, and Manaswi Gupta. 2010. Classifying latent user attributes in Twitter. In *Proceedings of SMUC*.

Marco Tulio Ribeiro, Sameer Singh, and Carlos Guestrin. 2016. "Why should I trust you?" Explaining the predictions of any classifier. In *Proceedings of KDD*.

Jonathan Schler, Moshe Koppel, Shlomo Argamon, and James Pennebaker. 2006. Effects of age and gender on blogging. In *Proceedings of AAAI Spring Symposium on Analyzing Microtext*.

Latanya Sweeney. 2013. Discrimination in online ad delivery. *Communications of the ACM*, 56(5):44–54.

Christian Szegedy, Wojciech Zaremba, Ilya Sutskever, Joan Bruna, Dumitru Erhan, Ian Goodfellow, and Rob Fergus. 2014. Intriguing properties of neural networks. In *Proceedings of the International Conference on Learning Representations*.

Joseph Turow, Michael Hennessy, and Nora Draper. 2015. The tradeoff fallacy. Technical report, Annenberg School for Communication, University of Pennsylvania.

April Underwood. 2012. Gender targeting for promoted products now available. https://blog.twitter.com/2012/gender-targeting-for-promoted-products-now-available.

Svitlana Volkova, Yoram Bachrach, Michael Armstrong, and Vijay Sharma. 2015. Inferring latent user properties from texts published in social media. In *Proceedings of AAAI*.

Wei Xu, Alan Ritter, Chris Callison-Burch, William B. Dolan, and Yangfeng Ji. 2014. Extracting lexically divergent paraphrases from Twitter. *Transactions of the Association for Computational Linguistics*.

Wei Xu, Chris Callison-Burch, and Bill Dolan. 2015. Semeval-2015 task 1: Paraphrase and semantic similarity in Twitter (PIT). In *Proceedings of SemEval*.

Xiang Yan and Ling Yan. 2006. Gender classification of weblog authors. In *Proceedings of the AAAI Spring Symposium on Computational Approaches to Analyzing Weblogs*.

Rich Zemel, Yu Wu, Kevin Swersky, Toni Pitassi, and Cynthia Dwork. 2013. Learning fair representations. In *Proceedings of ICML*.

Kaiping Zhang and René F. Kizilcec. 2014. Anonymity in social media: Effects of content controversiality and social endorsement on sharing behavior. In *Proceedings of the AAAI Conference on Weblogs and Social Media (ICWSM)*.

Social Proof: The Impact of Author Traits on Influence Detection

Sara Rosenthal
IBM Research*
Yorktown Heights, NY, USA
sjrosenthal@us.ibm.com

Kathleen McKeown
Columbia University
Computer Science Department
NY, NY, USA
kathy@cs.columbia.edu

Abstract

It has been claimed that people are more likely to be influenced by those who are similar to them than those who are not. In this paper, we test this hypothesis by measuring the impact of author traits on the detection of influence. The traits we explore are age, gender, religion, and political party. We create a single classifier to detect the author traits of each individual. We then use the personal traits predicted by this classifier to predict the influence of contributors in a Wikipedia Talk Page corpus. Our research shows that the influencer tends to have the same traits as the majority of people in the conversation. Furthermore, we show that this is more pronounced when considering the personal traits most relevant to the conversation. Our research thus provides evidence for the theory of social proof.

1 Introduction

The psychological phenomenon of *social proof* suggests that people will be influenced by others in their surroundings. Furthermore, social proof is most evident when a person perceives the people in their surroundings to be similar to them (Cialdini, 2007). This tendency is known as *homophily*. One manner in which people can be similar is through shared author traits such as the demographics age (year of birth), gender (male/female), and religion (Christian/ Jewish/ Muslim/ Atheist), as well as political party (Republican/Democrat).

In this paper, we explore the impact of social proof via author traits in detecting the most influential people in Wikipedia Talk Page discussions. We present an author trait detector that can detect a suite of author traits based on prior state-of-the art methods developed for individual author traits alone, and use it to classify individuals along four author traits: age, gender, religion, and political party. We train the classifier using automatically

labeled or prior existing datasets in each trait. Our classifier achieves accuracy comparable to or better than prior work in each demographic and political affiliation. The author trait classifiers are used to automatically label the author traits of each person in the Wikipedia Talk Page discussions.

An influencer is someone within a discussion who has credibility in the group, persists in attempting to convince others, and introduces topics/ideas that others pick up on or support (Biran et al., 2012; Nguyen et al., 2013b). We use supervised learning to predict which people in the discussion are the influencers. In this paper we use the demographics and political affiliation of the authors in the Wikipedia Talk Page as features in the classifier to detect the influencers within each discussion. This is known as situational influence. In contrast, global influence refers to people who are influential over many discussions. It is important to explore situational influence because a person can be quite influential in some Wikipedia Talk Page discussions but not at all in others. We show that social proof and homophily exists among participants and that the topic of the discussion plays a role in determining which author traits are useful. For example, religion is more indicative of influence in discussions that are religious in nature such as a discussion about the Catholic Church.

In the rest of this paper we first discuss related work in influence detection. We then describe our author trait classifier, related work, and the datasets used to train the models. All of our datasets are publicly available at http://www.cs.columbia.edu/~sara/data.php. Next, we discuss the Wikipedia Talk Page (WTP) dataset and how they were labeled for influence. Afterwards we discuss our method for detecting influence, the experiments and results. Finally, we conclude with a discussion of the impact of author traits on influence detection.

---

* Work completed as graduated student at Columbia University

Proceedings of 2016 EMNLP Workshop on Natural Language Processing and Computational Social Science, pages 27–36,
Austin, TX, November 5, 2016. ©2016 Association for Computational Linguistics

2 Related Work

Influence detection has been explored in conversations and social networks. We discuss both types of influence in more detail in this section.

2.1 Influence in Conversations

Several authors have detected influencers in a single conversation using the actual discussion (Quercia et al., 2011; Nguyen et al., 2013b; Biran et al., 2012). This work has explored detecting influencers using features such as dialog structure, agreement, persuasion, sentiment, and topic control in several online corpora such as WTP, Twitter, Presidential Debates, and the ICSI meeting corpus (Janin et al., 2003). This work did not, however, explore the impact of author traits in detecting influence.

There has also been work exploring influence on the utterance level (Young et al., 2011) within hostage negotiation transcripts. The utterances were labeled for influence using Robert Cialdini's weapons of influence (Cialdini, 2007), including social proof. However, they define social proof differently as: 1) an utterance that is a reference to a social norm (e.g. referring to a way a person could be influential) and 2) an appeal to the group regarding how they should proceed. Our use of social proof is based on shared author traits. Furthermore, they do not distinguish between the weapons of influence in their results making it impossible to determine their performance on social proof alone. Other related work has looked at analyzing the interactions of persuasive arguments using dialog structure, style, and textual features in the Reddit's ChangeMyView discussions (Tan et al., 2016).

A closely related area of research has been predicting power relations in dialog (Prabhakaran and Rambow, 2014; Danescu-Niculescu-Mizil et al., 2012; Strzalkowski et al., 2013). This includes several types of power relationships, such as hierarchical and administrative power, as well as influence. Most relevant among this work, Prabhakaran et al (2012) have explored the role of gender in hierarchical power within the Enron e-mail corpus. They find that female superiors use less displays of power than male superiors, and subordinates in female environments use more conventional language than any other group. Finally, they use the actual gender of the participants to improve the accuracy of predicting who is the subordinate and who is the superior given a pair of people.

2.2 Influence in Social Networks

There has been a lot of work that has explored influence in social networks (e.g. (Watts and Dodds., 2007; Bakshy et al., 2011; Barbieri et al., 2013; Huang et al., 2012; Goyal et al., 2011; Myers et al., 2012)) by analyzing how it spreads through the network.

Bamman et al (2012) explore the effect of gender identity and homophily on how information spreads. Aral and Walker (2002) analyze the impact of demographics on influence by identifying influential people on Facebook. They find influential people by examining how a viral message spreads through the network. They found interesting patterns among demographics: Men are more influential than women, older people tend to be more influential than younger people and that people are the most influential to their peers. We have similar findings in age and gender in our analysis. In contrast to our work, they did not use the demographics to predict influence nor do they predict influence within a discussion. Similarly, Dow et al (2013) investigate how photos on Facebook are shared and which demographics are more likely to share a particular photo.

3 Author Trait Detection

We implemented an author trait detection system that uses lexical, and lexical-style features to automatically detect author traits such as demographics and political affiliations. We also include features related to online behavior. In particular, we include the time and day of posting, but avoid features that are not available on all online discussion forums such as number of friends, interests, comments, likes/favorites, and hashtags. Several of these features are available on the datasets used in author trait detection: LiveJournal (interests, comments, friends), Blogger (comments, friends), and Twitter (friends, favorites, hashtags). However, none of them are available in WTP discussions, the dataset we use to detect influence.

3.1 Related Work

Prior work in demographic detection has used classic features such as n-grams (1-3 words), Part-of-Speech (POS) tags (e.g. is the word a noun or verb), and stylistic features (e.g. (Schler et al., 2006; Rao et al., 2010; Mukherjee and Liu, 2010)), as well as domain specific features such as hashtags and the social network in Twitter (Nguyen and Lim, 2014; Burger et al., 2011; Conover et al., 2011; Zamal et al., 2012) and friends and interests in LiveJournal (Rosenthal and McKeown, 2011). In this work we aim to make our author trait detector as general as possible and therefore only use features available in all online discussion forums by excluding genre specific features. Thus, we compare our system's results to the results in prior work that exclude genre specific features.

Prior work in age detection has explored classification based on age groups in blogs and tweets (Schler et al., 2006; Goswami et al., 2009; Rao et al., 2010; Rosenthal and McKeown, 2011) and exact age using regression (Nguyen et al., 2011; Nguyen et al., 2013a) in blog and tweets. Gender detection too has been classified in

author trait	source	label	size
age	blogger.com	year of birth	19098
	livejournal.com	year of birth	21467
gender	blogger.com	Male	9552
		Female	9546
	livejournal.com	Male	4249
		Female	3287
political party	Twitter.com	Republican	1247
		Democrat	1200
religion	Twitter.com	Christian	5207
		Islam	1901
		Atheist	1815
		Judaism	1486

Table 1: The size (in users) of each trait corpus

blogs (Schler et al., 2006; Mukherjee and Liu, 2010; Goswami et al., 2009; Nowson and Oberlander, 2006) and Twitter (Rao et al., 2010; Burger et al., 2011; Bamman et al., 2012). Predicting political orientation or ideologies has focused on predicting political views as left-wing vs right-wing in Twitter (Conover et al., 2011; Cohen and Ruths, 2013) or debates (Iyyer et al., 2014; Gottipati et al., 2013). There is little work on predicting religion with the only known prior work found to be on the prediction of Christian vs Muslim Twitter users (Nguyen and Lim, 2014) and work on classifying documents by Islamic ideology (e.g Muslim Brotherhood) and organization (e.g. Hamas) (Koppel et al., 2009).

3.2 Data

Our author trait data comes from two different types of online sources; weblogs for age and gender and microblogs for politics and religion. All of our datasets are publicly available at `http://www.cs.columbia.edu/~sara/data.php`.

3.2.1 Age and Gender

We use the publicly available blogger.com authorship corpus (Schler et al., 2006) and the LiveJournal age corpus (Rosenthal and McKeown, 2011) to detect age and gender. The Blogger corpus is annotated for age and gender while the LiveJournal corpus provides the date of birth for each poster. We use these annotations as gold labels for predicting age and gender. For uniformity, we converted the blogger age in the authorship corpus to the date of birth based on the time of download (2004). For example, a 22 year old in 2004 was born in 1982. We then automatically generated gender labels for the Live-Journal corpus internally. We generate gender labels by looking at the first name of the blogger if it was provided. We used the Social Security Administration lists[1] to determine the appropriate gender based on the popularity of the name. If the name is predominantly male or female

at a 2:1 ratio we assign it that gender. Otherwise, we exclude the blogger from the gender corpus. The size of the age and gender corpora are shown in Table 1.

3.2.2 Politics and Religion

There are several websites that either automatically generate (tweepz.com), or allow users to self-label (twellow.com and wefollow.com) their Twitter account into categories. Previous work (Zamal et al., 2012) has used the labels from wefollow.com to automatically download Twitter users related to desired categories. We follow this approach to download Twitter users based on political party (Republican/Democrat), and religion (christian, jewish, muslim, atheist). After downloading the list of users we performed some post-processing to exclude non-English speakers based on the language in their bio. We excluded any users whose bios contained many (40%) foreign characters and non-english words. Additionally, we discarded users that appeared in more than one category within a single author trait (e.g. a person cannot be labeled as Republican *and* Democrat).

We then used the Twitter API to download the last 100 tweets of each user on 11/4/2014. Downloading on this date was desirable because it ensured that the data was rich in political information because it was election day in the US. Our political party tweets consists of Republican and Democrat. We downloaded tweets pertaining to the four most popular religions in the United States[2]: Christianity, Judaism, Islam, and Atheism. The full data statistics are provided in Table 1.

3.3 Method

We present a supervised method that draws on prior work in the area as discussed in the prior section. We experimented with several classifiers in Weka (Hall et al., 2009) and found that SVM always performs the same or better than the other methods. We use this single classifier to build several models which detect each author trait by training and testing on the relevant data (e.g. the classifier is trained using the age data to build a model to predict age). The only exception is that we use Linear Regression to predict the exact age of each user using year of birth. We apply χ^2 feature selection to all groups of features in the training data to reduce the feature set to the most useful features. The features are generated by looking at the past 100 tweets or 25 blogs per user. We also limit the text to 1000 words per user to improve processing time. We include three type of features: lexical, lexical-stylistic, and online behavior.

3.3.1 Lexical Features

We include three kinds of lexical features: n-grams, part-of-speech (POS) (using Stanford Core NLP (Man-

---

[1]http://www.ssa.gov/oact/babynames/limits.html

[2]www.census.gov/compendia/statab/cats/population/religi-on.html

Author Trait	Majority	Accuracy
Age	57.1	79.6
Gender	51.9	76.4
Political Party	51.3	75.2
Religion	50.0	78.3

Table 2: The author trait results of SVM classification using accuracy

ning et al., 2014)), and collocations which have all been found to be useful in prior work (Schler et al., 2006; Rao et al., 2010; Mukherjee and Liu, 2010; Rosenthal and McKeown, 2011). We keep the top 1000 features of each type. n-grams refers to a count of 1-2 word phrases. POS features refer to the counts of POS tags. Collocations are bigrams that take the subject/object (S/O) relationship of terms into account. We implement this using Xtract (Smadja, 1993). We ran our own implementation of Xtract on the most recent 100 blog posts or tweets per user. In the Twitter datasets we run Xtract on all the text. Due to the large size of the blog corpora, we limit it to the 2,000 most recent words per user. We include the S/O bigrams (e.g. voting Democrat), POS bigrams (e.g. we VB) and S/O POS bigrams (e.g. vote NN) generated from Xtract as features.

3.3.2 Lexical-Stylistic Features

We include two types of lexical-style features: general and social media. General features can be found in any genre, such as the number of capital words, exclamation points, and question marks. Social Media features are those common in online discussions such as word lengthening (e.g. loooooong), emoticons, and acronyms. Younger people may be more likely to use such features. We also include the Linguistic Inquiry Word Count (LIWC) categories (Tausczik and Pennebaker, 2010) as features as in prior work (Schler et al., 2006). The LIWC classifies words as belonging to one or more broad categories (e.g., work, family, religion, negative emotion). These different categories can be very indicative of author traits. For example, men may talk more about work and Atheists will be less likely to talk about religion.

3.3.3 Online Behavior

While we do exclude all features that don't occur in all datasets (e.g. comments, friends, and hashtags), there is one online behavior feature that is found in all discussions. That is a time-stamp indicating when the person posted. We use this to generate two features, the most common hour (0-24 GMT) and most common day of the week (Sunday-Saturday) that the person posts. For example this could be useful in predicting age as younger people may post later in the evening than older people.

3.4 Results

We trained our classifier on each author trait. The classifier was tuned using cross-validation and all results are shown on a held-out test set of 10% of the data. All datasets were kept unbalanced. The results are shown in Table 2. The gender, religion, and political party demographics were classified using SVM.

We classified age using two models. First, we tried to predict the exact year of birth using Linear Regression; we achieved a mean absolute error (MAE) of 5.1 from the year of birth and a .55 correlation (r) which is slightly better than the results in prior work (Nguyen et al., 2011) when avoiding blog-specific features. The next approach we took was performing binary classification using 1982 as the splitting point. This year of birth was found to be significant in prior work (Rosenthal and McKeown, 2011).

Our results on gender detection are slightly worse than leading methods (Schler et al., 2006; Mukherjee and Liu, 2010). However, we think this is due to prior work using cross-validation as opposed to a held-out test set. In fact, our cross-validation results were 82.5%, slightly better than Schler et al (2006) . It is more difficult to compare to the work of Mukherjee and Liu (Mukherjee and Liu, 2010) as the datasets are different and much smaller in size. Mukherjee and Liu have a collection of blogs from several websites (e.g. technorati.com and blogger.com) and only 3100 posts. In contrast we generate our model with blogs from livejournal.com and blogger.com (Schler et al., 2006) and over 25,000 blogs labeled with gender.

Prior work in detecting politics on tweets tends to combine Republican and conservative to "right-wing" and Democrat and liberal to"left-wing" and use Twitter-specific features such as political orientation of friends to achieve high accuracy making it difficult to compare against them. Although not directly comparable due to different datasets, our results are similar or better than the results in prior work where Twitter-specific features are excluded.

Finally, the prior work in religion is two-way classification of Muslim vs Christian, making it difficult to compare against their results.

In some cases our results are better than prior work or on a new area of classification. Our system is competitive or better than prior state-of-the-art classifiers with good accuracy in detecting each trait. In addition, we are the only one to use the same system to generate four models to predict the author traits (In the past only age and gender have been detected in this manner (Schler et al., 2006)).

4 Influence Detection

In this section we describe the data, method, and experiments in detecting influence in WTP discussions using

	Train	Dev	Test	Total
# discussions	410	47	52	509
# posts	7127	730	892	8749
# participants	2536	277	317	3130
# influencers	368	41	47	456
# files w/o influencers	62	8	6	76

Table 3: Data statistics for the Wikipedia Talk Page Influence corpus

Topic	G	A	R	P
Abortion	35	8	9	3
Catholic Church	27	9	553	7
George W. Bush	4	0	8	68
Israel	4	18	623	12
Michael Jackson	2	42	4	0

Table 4: A list of topics and the occurrence of issues associated with them in **A**ge, **G**ender, **R**eligion, and **P**olitics. An occurrence > 5 indicates it is an issue relevant to that topic.

the author traits described in the previous section.

4.1 Data

We use the author trait detector to explore the impact of social proof in detecting influencers in WTP. Each page on Wikipedia is generated by user contribution, and thus discussion is needed to avoid conflict from different contributors. This discussion occurs in the Wikipedia Talk Pages[3]. They are rich in content and argumentative in nature making it an ideal dataset for detecting influence.

Our dataset is an extension of the Wikipedia dataset described in prior work (Biran et al., 2012) and contains 509 discussions ranging over 99 different topics. It is important to note that although there may be some overlap among authors across the dataset, we find the influencer within each discussion individually. This is known as situational influence. Detecting global influence would be an interesting extension in future work. The WTP discussions were annotated for influence by four different people with an average inter annotator agreement using Cohen's κ of .61. The annotators were given guidelines similar to those described in prior work (Biran et al., 2012; Nguyen et al., 2013b): An influencer is someone who has credibility in the group, persists in attempting to convince others, and introduces topics/ideas that others pick up on or support. Typically there is one influencer in each discussion, and on rare occasion two (20/509 or 3.9%). Since our goal is detecting influence, we excluded the 76 discussions without influencers from the experiments resulting in 433 discussions. Of the 3130 participants, 456 of them were found to be influential. The data was broken down into a training (80%), development (10%), and test set (10%). The statistics for each set is shown in Table 3.

4.2 Method

Our method involves four groups of features. The first is single features related to each author trait; the second is features indicating if the author trait is the majority in the discussion, and the third is a combination of author traits. We also include features related to the issue being discussed in the Wikipedia Page. We will describe the features in greater detail in the rest of this section.

In addition, as a baseline feature we include the number of words the participant has written. This feature is

important because in addition to indicating the likelihood of someone being influential (if someone barely participates in the discussion it reduces their chances of being influential), the odds of the predicted author trait being correct decreases if the provided text is minimal.

4.2.1 Single Features

We explore the occurrence of influence in each author trait as an indication of what type of people are more influential. Each author trait is represented as a binary feature during classification. The breakdown of each feature by influence in the training set is shown in Figure 1. There tend to be more old people in Wikipedia, but there is also a clear indication that older people are more influential. We have similar findings with the male gender, the Republican political party, and the Jews and Christians in religion. We suspect that the tendency towards an author trait may be dependent on the topic of the Wikipedia article as discussed in the following section. For example, political party may play a more important role in a discussion regarding abortion and religion may play a more important role in a discussion regarding Israel. Finally, we also have a feature indicating the exact year of birth that was predicted for each author (e.g. 1983).

4.2.2 Topic Features

The topic in a discussion can indicate what kind of issues will be addressed. This in turn can indicate a stronger presence of different author traits. We use the title of each discussion to infer its topic. For example, a Wikipedia article with the title "The Catholic Church" will be more likely to be edited by religious people than an article about the pop star Michael Jackson. This in turn can indicate the author trait tendencies of the people in the WTP. In order to analyze the impact of topic on influence and author traits we automatically inferred the author traits that were likely to be related to the Wikipedia article.

We implemented this by counting the occurrence of the labels and related synonyms of each author trait within the Wikipedia article. For example, male and female are gender labels. This alone was sufficient for our task since we want high precision and care less about recall. It is important to stress, that we did not do this in the WTP

---

[3]http://en.wikipedia.org/wiki/Wikipedia:Tutorial/Talk_pages

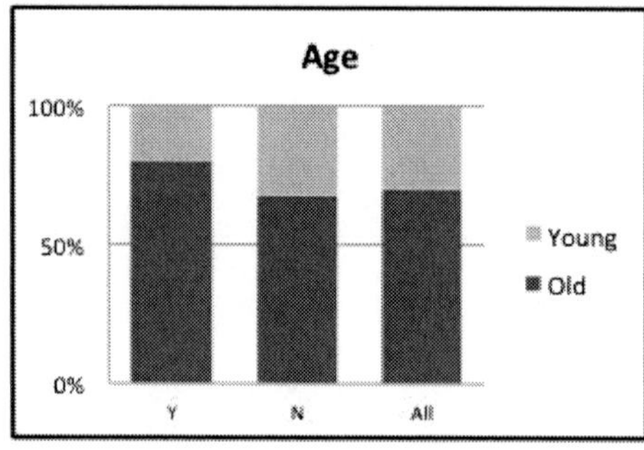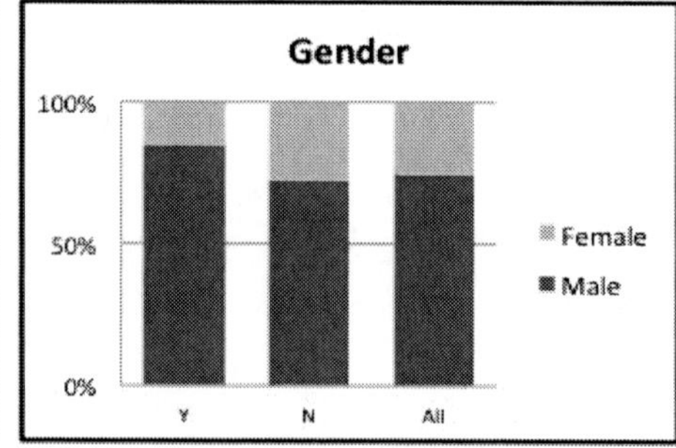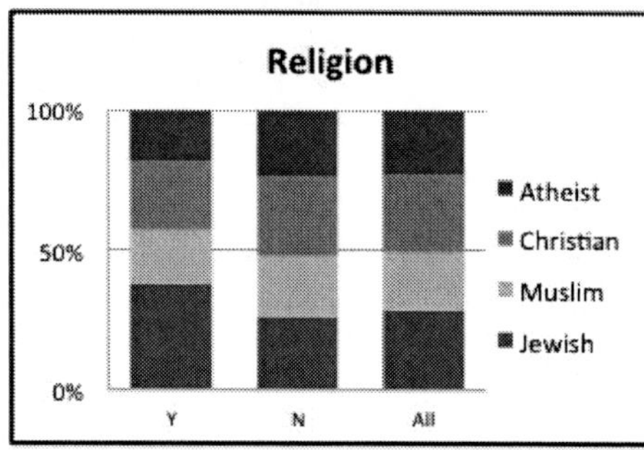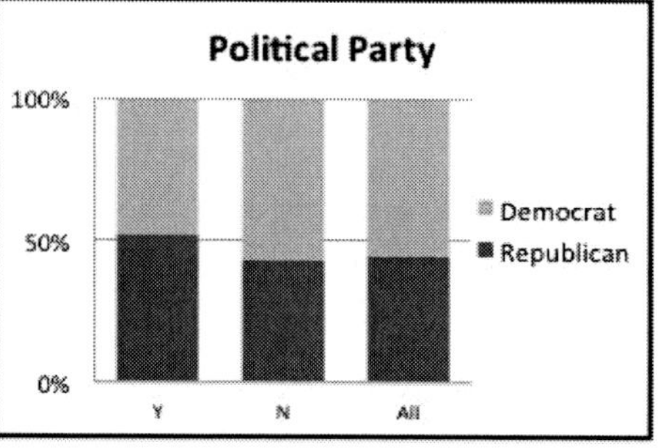

Figure 1: Breakdown of the binary features by influence (Y/N) and overall (All) in the training set.

discussions but rather in the *actual Wikipedia article*. If an author trait term occurred more than five times[4] it was considered to be an issue related to that author trait to ensure the occurrence was more than happenstance. Table 4 lists an example of topics and the occurrence of issues within the Wikipedia article. Using this method, there were 38 age, 42 gender, 66 religious, and 58 political articles. Most articles overlap on more than one author trait issue. There are a total of 99 topics with one or multiple discussions from the WTP associated to the topic.

We use each issue as a feature which is true if that topic is associated with the article and false if it is not. For example, the gender, age, and religion issues would be true for Abortion Talk Pages.

4.2.3 Majority Features

Social proof indicates that people will be influenced by those that are like them. We measure this per author trait by determining if a person is predicted to be in the majority within the discussion and have a majority feature corresponding to each author trait. For example, if the majority of the people in a discussion are predicted to be Republican, we expect that the influencer is likely to be predicted to be Republican as well. Furthermore, we expect this to be most evident when the discussion is relevant to the particular author trait. For example, a

Figure 2: The breakdown of the users being in the majority within their document for each author trait with topic being taken into account.

discussion on abortion would be relevant to religion, politics, and gender. Figure 2 illustrates that influencers are in the majority more than non-influencers when the issue is relevant in the Wikipedia article. In general all people tend to be in the majority author trait in a discussion, but there is a stronger tendency towards being in the majority when a person is an influencer. The results displayed take the topic of the document into account in that only documents applicable to each author trait are shown in the chart. For example, discussions on abortion are only included in the bars on religion, politics, and gender. We also include features to indicate whether the participant is in the majority in *all* author traits or in *no* author traits.

---

[4]The split of terms among documents is such that documents have no terms whatsoever most often and fewer than 6 terms related to an issue 48.5% times whereas 51.5% of the issues have 6 or more terms.

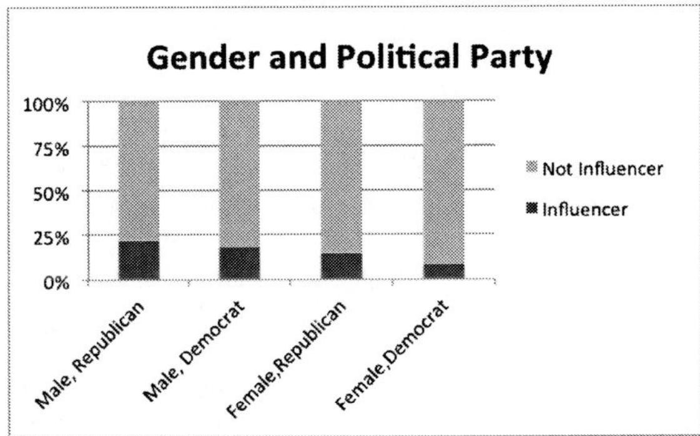

Figure 3: The breakdown of influencers and non-influencers in the training data based on the binary combination feature of gender and political party.

In order to determine whether the majority features should be useful, in addition to using the single features, we needed to verify whether there were enough cases where the overall minority author trait was still the majority author trait within a reasonable amount of discussions. We find that in the training data, in 84.1% of the discussions the majority is older people and in 88.5% of the discussions the majority is male. These percentages are in line with the trends found in the single features as shown in Figure 1. However, there still are many discussions where the majority is female (11.5%) or younger people (15.9%). In contrast to our findings in the single features shown in Figure 1, where overall there were slightly more Republicans than Democrats, we found that in 55.8% of the discussions in the training data the majority is Democrat whereas slightly more editors are Republican. In terms of religion we found that in 41.5%, 16.6%, 18.8%, and 23.2% of the discussions the majority is Jewish, Muslim, Christian, and Atheist respectively. Although Christianity is the most commonly predicted religion overall (see Figure 1), we expect that in the discussions the majority is Judaism due to the many articles that are controversial to the state of Israel (e.g. regarding Gaza and the Israeli Defense Force). This indicates that, in particular, using the majority religion feature should have a positive impact on predicting influencer in addition to the single religion features.

4.2.4 Combination Features

In addition to looking at a single author trait of a person at a time, we also explore whether combining author traits is beneficial. Many studies have shown that certain tendencies towards an issue are based on several author traits. In particular, this applies to combining demographics and politics. For example, women tend to vote for Democrats[5] and Christians tend to vote for Republicans[6].

As one example, we find that indeed in our dataset women are 53% more likely to be Democrat. However, we find that women that are Republican are more likely to be influential than women who are Democrat as shown in the breakdown of the <gender,political party> feature in the training data in Figure 3.

4.3 Experiments and Results

All results were predicted using the SVM classifier in Weka (Hall et al., 2009) built with a polynomial kernel, complexity tuned towards the development set ($C = 10$), and logistic models to provide confidence values. We experimented with other classifiers (e.g. Naive Bayes, Logistic Regression) but SVM consistently performed better or the same as other classifiers. Rather than balancing the training set using downsampling, we balance the class weights of the influencer examples based on their occurrence in the training data. This ensures that the classifier knows we are more interested in finding influencers without incurring a considerable loss in data.

Influencers are rare in discussions. Therefore, the standard measure of accuracy does not appropriately describe the success of the system. This is because predicting that no one is an influencer will have a high accuracy, but will not address our goal of finding influencers. Instead, we present results for predicting influence using F-score on the influencer class. We compare our experiments to two baselines, picking everyone as an influencer (all-yes baseline), and the number of words a person wrote in the discussion (num-words baseline).

In addition to using the results provided by the classifier, we also use the confidence of the classifier as a second prediction which we consider to be the experiment with *ranking*. Since we know that there is at least one influencer in each discussion, we choose the person given the highest confidence by the classifier as the influencer. It is important to note that it is still possible for more than one person to predicted to be the influencer. This approach only applies for discussions where no influencer was chosen. Using ranking to predict the influencer can outperform the equivalent system without ranking. In the future we would like to adjust the annotation method to rank all of the people in the discussion based on influence instead of just choosing the influencer(s).

All results are shown in Table 5. All results following the baselines include the number of words and topic features unless otherwise mentioned. The system using just the best majority features gives 2.4 points improvement in F-score compared to using just the number of

---

[5]http://www.pewresearch.org/fact-tank/2014/11/05/as-gop-celebrates-win-no-sign-of-narrowing-gender-age-gaps/

[6]http://www.pewforum.org/2014/11/05/how-the-faithful-voted-2014-preliminary-analysis/

Experiment	Conf. Matrix		P%	R%	F%
all-influencer	**47** 0	235 0	16.7	**100.0**	28.7
num words	24 46	23 189	34.3	51.0	41.0
majority best	28 54	19 181	34.1	59.6	43.4^R
single best	26 45	21 190	36.6	55.3	44.1
majority+single best	20 51	18 184	36.3	**61.7**	45.7^R
best w/o topic	27 51	20 184	34.6	57.5	43.2^R
best	**29** 50	18 185	**36.7**	**61.7**	**46.0**^{R}

Table 5: The results of all groups of features on influence detection using author traits. The confusion matrix is filled, by row, as [TP FN] and [FP TN]. ^{R} indicates that ranking was used in the results. The best results are highlighted in bold.

words in a sentence (row 3) using all of the majority features. Ranking was also useful in this system. In row 4, we show that the best system using just single features achieves a 3.1 points improvement in F-score compared to using just the number of words in the sentence. This system uses gender, religion, and political party. The best system using single and majority features combined (row 5) gave an improvement of 4.7 points in F-score overall. These features are the exact age and distance from mean age, and religion single features, and the majority, gender, religion, political party, always-the-majority, and never-the-majority features as well as using ranking. Finally, in the last row, the best set of combination and majority features had a 5.0 points improvement in F-score using the same features as in the single and majority system in addition to combination features: majority <political party, gender>, and single <religion, gender> and uses ranking. This provides evidence that homophily and social proof are both important in predicting influencers. Finally, as a comparison, we show the best system without using the topic features. In row 6, we show that excluding topic features causes a reduction in performance.

5 Discussion

Our goal in this paper is not to produce the best system for influence detection, but rather to analyze the impact of social proof in influence detection. Our results show that social proof is important in being influential. This is indicated by the usefulness of the majority features and a 5.0 boost in F-score using the best group of features.

It is interesting to note that even when the author trait of a person may be predicted incorrectly, certain tendencies are found in discussions on different issues. This in-dicates that topic is important. For example, the majority religion in most articles regarding the Catholic Church is predicted to be Christian.

We believe that the biggest drawback to our author trait predictions in the WTP discussions is due to the limited amount of text available for some people. Roughly half of the participants write less than 100 words within the discussion indicating a higher likelihood of incorrectly predicting their author traits. We included the number of words as a feature to help address this issue. The classifier should use this feature to learn that the author trait features are less reliable when the author has written less. We would like to explore combining the text written by each person throughout the entire corpus (most authors appear in more than one article) to improve the author trait predictions.

The author trait models are trained on different corpora than Wikipedia and as a result we do not know how accurate the author trait predictions on Wikipedia are. We do find that there are similar trends in our predictions in the Wikipedia training data in comparison to reported statistics of Wikipedia Editor demographics [7]. For example, in a 2013 study it was found that 83% of the Wikipedia editors were male. In Figure 1, we find that approximately 75% of the users are predicted to be male. The reported demographics on age indicate that there are more old people than young people and that the 50% split occurs somewhere between 1980-1989. Similarly, we find that the majority of users are born before 1982 (See Figure 1), indicating they are older and that 1982 is likely a good split for Wikipedia. Finally, the most popular religions of contributors on Wikipedia in 2012 are Christianity (35%), no religion (36%), Judaism (9%), and Islam (6%). In our predictions, we find that Christianity is the most common with Judaism following next. We expect the discrepancy with atheism is because it is a subset of no religion. Statistics on the political party of Wikipedia editors could not be found. The relationships between the trends in our training data and the most recent reported statistics are encouraging and indicative of positive labeling of author traits in our dataset. In the future, we would also like to have the discussions annotated for author traits to analyze the upper bound impact of author traits on influence prediction.

Finally, does being in the minority indicate that it will be harder to be influential? For example, as shown, men are more influential than women in this dataset (see Figure 1). Does this mean that women have no hope of being influential, particularly in a male dominant setting? On the surface, yes. Women may have to work harder to be influential in a male dominant setting. We, however, do not have to lose hope if we are in the minority!

---

[7] en.wikipedia.org/wiki/Wikipedia:Wikipedians#cite_note-UNU-M-6, meta.wikimedia.org/wiki/List_of_Wikimedians_by_religion

There are many traits and their importance varies across discussions. Gender may not play an important role in some discussions. For example, political party may be more important. In other words, if the majority of people in a political discussion are democrats it would be better to be a female democrat than a male republican. Social proof does, however, indicate that if a person has nothing in common with the other participants in the discussion being influential will be nearly impossible. The key then is to find something, no matter how small, that can help one relate to others in a discussion. This connection can then be exploited to become influential.

6 Conclusion

In this paper, we present an author trait detection system which predicts four different author traits: age, gender, religion, and political party. We show that influencers tend to have certain of author traits within the WTP dataset. These are particularly dependent on the issue being discussed. We also show that influencers tend to be aligned with the majority of the other participants in the conversation. This indicates that social proof is a useful measure for detecting influence. Including such features gives a 5.0 improvement compared to using the number of words of each participant in the discussion for an F-score of 46.0%.

In the future, we would like to use the different author traits to help improve each of the individual author trait results. For example, using the predicted age and gender to improve the model for predicting political party. To improve our result in influence detection, we would like to use the content per author across the corpus for author trait prediction at once. When available, the increase in content would allow us to more accurately predict the correct author traits of a person. We would also like to annotate the influencer corpus for gold author trait labels to gain a stronger grasp of the importance of author traits in influence prediction. In addition, we would like to explore the impact of detecting influence with author traits and other features used in prior work such as agreement, dialog structure, and persuasion. Finally, we would also like to explore using word embeddings and deep learning.

7 Acknowledgements

This paper is based upon work supported by the DARPA DEFT Program. The views expressed are those of the authors and do not reflect the official policy or position of the Department of Defense or the U.S. Government.

References

[Aral and Walker2012] Sinan Aral and Dylan Walker. 2012. Identifying Influential and Susceptible Members of Social Networks. *Science*, 337(6092):337–341, July.

[Bakshy et al.2011] Eytan Bakshy, Jake M. Hofman, Winter A. Mason, and Duncan J. Watts. 2011. Everyone's an influencer: quantifying influence on twitter. In *Proceedings of the fourth ACM international conference on WSDM*, WSDM '11, NY, NY, USA. ACM.

[Bamman et al.2012] David Bamman, Jacob Eisenstein, and Tyler Schnoebelen. 2012. Gender in twitter: Styles, stances, and social networks. *CoRR*.

[Barbieri et al.2013] Nicola Barbieri, Francesco Bonchi, and Giuseppe Manco. 2013. Topic-aware social influence propagation models. *Knowledge and Information Systems*, 37(3):555–584.

[Biran et al.2012] Or Biran, Sara Rosenthal, Jacob Andreas, Kathleen McKeown, and Owen Rambow. 2012. Detecting influencers in written online conversations. In *Proceedings of the LSM 2012 Workshop*, Montreal, June.

[Burger et al.2011] John D. Burger, John Henderson, George Kim, and Guido Zarrella. 2011. Discriminating gender on twitter. In *Proceedings of the Conference on EMLNP*, EMNLP '11.

[Cialdini2007] Robert B. Cialdini. 2007. *Influence: The Psychology of Persuasion (Collins Business Essentials)*. Harper Paperbacks, January.

[Cohen and Ruths2013] Raviv Cohen and Derek Ruths. 2013. Classifying political orientation on twitter: Its not easy! In *International AAAI Conference on Weblogs and Social Media*.

[Conover et al.2011] M Conover, B Gonçalves, J Ratkiewicz, A Flammini, and F Menczer. 2011. Predicting the political alignment of twitter users. In *Proceedings of 3rd IEEE Conference on Social Computing (SocialCom)*.

[Danescu-Niculescu-Mizil et al.2012] Cristian Danescu-Niculescu-Mizil, Lillian Lee, Bo Pang, and Jon Kleinberg. 2012. Echoes of power: Language effects and power differences in social interaction. In *Proceedings of the 21st International Conference on WWW*, WWW '12, pages 699–708, NYC, USA. ACM.

[Dow et al.2013] P. Alex Dow, Lada A. Adamic, and Adrien Friggeri. 2013. The anatomy of large facebook cascades. In *ICWSM*.

[Goswami et al.2009] Sumit Goswami, Sudeshna Sarkar, and Mayur Rustagi. 2009. Stylometric analysis of bloggers' age and gender. In *International AAAI Conference on Weblogs and Social Media*.

[Gottipati et al.2013] Swapna Gottipati, Minghui Qiu, Liu Yang, Feida Zhu, and Jing Jiang. 2013. Predicting user's political party using ideological stances. In *SocInfo*, volume 8238 of *Lecture Notes in Computer Science*, pages 177–191. Springer.

[Goyal et al.2011] Amit Goyal, Francesco Bonchi, and Laks V. S. Lakshmanan. 2011. A data-based approach to social influence maximization. *Proc. VLDB Endow.*, 5(1):73–84, September.

[Hall et al.2009] Mark Hall, Eibe Frank, Geoffrey Holmes, Bernhard Pfahringer, Peter Reutemann, and Ian H. Witten. 2009. The weka data mining software: An update.

[Huang et al.2012] Junming Huang, Xue-Qi Cheng, Hua-Wei Shen, Tao Zhou, and Xiaolong Jin. 2012. Exploring social influence via posterior effect of word-of-mouth recommendations. In *Proceedings of the Fifth ACM International Conference on WSDM*, WSDM '12, pages 573–582, NY, NY, USA. ACM.

[Iyyer et al.2014] Mohit Iyyer, Peter Enns, Jordan Boyd-Graber, and Philip Resnik. 2014. Political ideology detection using recursive neural networks. In *ACL*.

[Janin et al.2003] Adam Janin, Don Baron, Jane Edwards, Dan Ellis, David Gelbart, Nelson Morgan, Barbara Peskin, Thilo Pfau, Elizabeth Shriberg, Andreas Stolcke, and Chuck Wooters. 2003. The icsi meeting corpus. pages 364–367.

[Koppel et al.2009] Moshe Koppel, Navot Akiva, Eli Alshech, and Kfir Bar. 2009. Automatically classifying documents by ideological and organizational affiliation. In *ISI*, pages 176–178. IEEE.

[Manning et al.2014] Christopher D. Manning, Mihai Surdeanu, John Bauer, Jenny Finkel, Steven J. Bethard, and David McClosky. 2014. The Stanford CoreNLP natural language processing toolkit. In *Proceedings of 52nd Annual Meeting of the Association for Computational Linguistics: System Demonstrations*, pages 55–60.

[Mukherjee and Liu2010] Arjun Mukherjee and Bing Liu. 2010. Improving gender classification of blog authors. In *Proceedings of the 2010 Conference on EMLNP*, EMNLP '10, Stroudsburg, PA, USA. ACL.

[Myers et al.2012] Seth A. Myers, Chenguang Zhu, and Jure Leskovec. 2012. Information diffusion and external influence in networks. In *Proceedings of the 18th ACM SIGKDD International Conference on Knowledge Discovery and Data Mining*, KDD '12, pages 33–41, NY, NY, USA. ACM.

[Nguyen and Lim2014] Minh-Thap Nguyen and Ee-Peng Lim. 2014. On predicting religion labels in microblogging networks. In *Proceedings of the 37th International ACM SIGIR Conference*, SIGIR '14, pages 1211–1214, NY, NY, USA. ACM.

[Nguyen et al.2011] Dong Nguyen, Noah A. Smith, and Carolyn P. Rosé. 2011. Author age prediction from text using linear regression. In *Proceedings of the 5th Workshop on LaTeCH*, LaTeCH '11. ACL.

[Nguyen et al.2013a] Dong Nguyen, Rilana Gravel, Dolf Trieschnigg, and Theo Meder. 2013a. " how old do you think i am?" a study of language and age in twitter. In *ICWSM*.

[Nguyen et al.2013b] Viet-An Nguyen, Jordan Boyd-Graber, Philip Resnik, Deborah Cai, Jennifer Midberry, and Yuanxin Wang. 2013b. Modeling topic control to detect influence in conversations using nonparametric topic models. In *Machine Learning*, pages 1–41. Springer.

[Nowson and Oberlander2006] Scott Nowson and Jon Oberlander. 2006. The identity of bloggers: Openness and gender in personal weblogs. In *AAAI*. American Association for Artificial Intelligence.

[Prabhakaran and Rambow2014] Vinodkumar Prabhakaran and Owen Rambow. 2014. Predicting power relations between participants in written dialog from a single thread. In *Proceedings of the 52nd Annual Meeting of the ACL (Volume 2: Short Papers)*, pages 339–344. ACL.

[Quercia et al.2011] Daniele Quercia, Jonathan Ellis, Licia Capra, and Jon Crowcroft. 2011. In the mood for being influential on twitter. In *SocialCom/PASSAT*, pages 307–314. IEEE.

[Rao et al.2010] Delip Rao, David Yarowsky, Abhishek Shreevats, and Manaswi Gupta. 2010. Classifying latent user attributes in twitter. In *Proceedings of the 2Nd International Workshop on SMUC*, SMUC '10, pages 37–44, NY, NY, USA. ACM.

[Rosenthal and McKeown2011] Sara Rosenthal and Kathleen McKeown. 2011. Age prediction in blogs: A study of style, content, and online behavior in pre- and post-social media generations. In *proceedings of ACL-HLT*.

[Schler et al.2006] J. Schler, M. Koppel, S. Argamon, and J. Pennebaker. 2006. Effects of age and gender on blogging. In *AAAI Spring Symposium on Computational Approaches for Analyzing Weblogs*.

[Smadja1993] Frank Smadja. 1993. Retrieving collocations from text: Xtract. *Computational Linguistics*, 19:143–177.

[Strzalkowski et al.2013] Tomek Strzalkowski, Samira Shaikh, Ting Liu, George Aaron Broadwell, Jennifer Stromer-Galley, Sarah M. Taylor, Veena Ravishankar, Umit Boz, and Xiaoai Ren. 2013. Influence and power in group interactions. In *SBP*, pages 19–27.

[Tan et al.2016] Chenhao Tan, Vlad Niculae, Cristian Danescu-Niculescu-Mizil, and Lillian Lee. 2016. Winning arguments: Interaction dynamics and persuasion strategies in good-faith online discussions. In *Proceedings of WWW*.

[Tausczik and Pennebaker2010] Yla R. Tausczik and James W. Pennebaker. 2010. The psychological meaning of words: Liwc and computerized text analysis methods. *Language and Social Pyschology*.

[Watts and Dodds.2007] D. J. Watts and P. S. Dodds. 2007. Influentials, networks, and public opinion formation. *Journal of Consumer Research*, 34:441–458.

[Young et al.2011] Joel Young, Craig Martell, Pranav Anand, Pedro Ortiz, and IV Henry Gilbert. 2011. A microtext corpus for persuasion detection in dialog. In *AAAI*.

[Zamal et al.2012] Faiyaz Al Zamal, Wendy Liu, and Derek Ruths. 2012. Homophily and latent attribute inference: Inferring latent attributes of twitter users from neighbors. In *ICWSM*.

Generating Politically-Relevant Event Data

John Beieler
Human Language Technology Center of Excellence
Johns Hopkins University
jbeieler1@jhu.edu

Abstract

Automatically generated political event data is an important part of the social science data ecosystem. The approaches for generating this data, though, have remained largely the same for two decades. During this time, the field of computational linguistics has progressed tremendously. This paper presents an overview of political event data, including methods and ontologies, and a set of experiments to determine the applicability of deep neural networks to the extraction of political events from news text.

1 Introduction

Automated coding of political event data, or the record of who-did-what-to-whom within the context of political actions, has existed for roughly two decades. This type of data can prove highly useful for many types of studies. Since this data is inherently atomic, each observation is a record of a single event between a source and a target, often at the daily level, it provides a disaggregated view of political events. This means that the data enables the examination of interactions below the usual monthly or yearly levels of aggregation. This approach can be used in a manner consistent with traditional hypothesis testing that is the norm within political science (Cederman and Gleditsch, 2009; Gleditsch, 2012; Goldstein et al., 2001). Additionally, event data has proven useful in forecasting models of conflict since the finer time resolution allows analysts to gain better leverage over the prediction problem than is possible when using more highly aggregated data (Arva et al., 2013; Brandt et al., 2014; Brandt et al., 2013; Brandt et al., 2011).

The methods used to generate this data have remained largely the unchanged during the past two decades, namely using parser-based methods with text dictionaries to resolve candidate noun and verb phrases to actor and event categories. The underlying coding technologies have moved slowly in updating to reflect changes in natural language processing (NLP) technology. These NLP technologies have now advanced to such a level, and with accompanying open-source software implementations, that their inclusion in the event-data coding process comes as an obvious advancement. Given this, this paper presents the beginnings of how modern natural language processing approaches, such as deep neural networks, can work within the context of automatically generating political event data. The goal is to present a new take on generating political event data, moving from parser-based methods to classifier-based models for the identification and extraction of events. Additionally, this paper serves as an introduction to politically-relevant coding ontologies that offer a new application domain for natural language processing researchers.

2 Political Event Ontologies

Political event data has existed in various forms since the 1970s. Two of the original political event datasets were the World Event Interaction Survey (WEIS) and the Conflict and Peace Data Bank (COPDAB) (Azar, 1980; McClelland, 1976). These two datasets were eventually replaced by the projects created by Philip Schrodt and various col-

37

Proceedings of 2016 EMNLP Workshop on Natural Language Processing and Computational Social Science, pages 37–42,
Austin, TX, November 5, 2016. ©2016 Association for Computational Linguistics

laborators. In general, these projects were marked by the use of the Conflict and Mediation Event Observations (CAMEO) coding ontology and automated, machine-coding rather than human coding (Gerner et al., 2001; Schrodt et al., 2008). The CAMEO ontology is made up of 20 "top-level" categories that encompass actions such as "Make Statement" or "Protest." Each of these twenty top-level categories contains finer-grained categories in a hierarchical manner. For example, the code 14 is the top-level code for "Protest" with the sub-code 142 representing a general demonstration or rally. Under the code 141, "Demonstrate or rally," is code 1411 which codes "demonstrate or rally for leadership change." Thus, as one moves down the hierarchy of CAMEO, more fine-grained events are encountered. All told, this hierarchical scheme contains over 200 total event classifications. This ontology has served as the basis for most of the modern event datasets such as the Integrated Crisis Early Warning System (ICEWS) (O'Brien, 2010), the Global Database of Events, Language, and Tone (GDELT)[1], and the Phoenix[2] dataset.

The defining feature of the CAMEO ontology is the presence of a well-defined ontology consisting of verb phrases and noun phrases used in the coding of actions and actors. For each of the 200+ categories of event types in CAMEO, there exists a list of verb phrases that define a given category. Similarly, the scope of what is considered a valid actor within CAMEO is defined by the noun phrases contained in the actor dictionaries. Thus, CAMEO is scoped entirely by the human-defined noun and verb phrases contained within underlying text dictionaries. The creation of these dictionaries is a massively costly task in terms of human labor; to date each phrase in the dictionaries was identified, defined, and formatted for inclusion by a human coder.

2.1 Lower Resolution Ontologies

While the CAMEO ontology offers fine-grained coding of political events within the 20 top-level categories, a small but convincing set of literature suggests that this level of granularity is not necessary to answer many of the questions to which event data is

---

[1] gdeltproject.org
[2] phoenixdata.org

applied. Schrodt (2006), for example, suggests that dividing the CAMEO ontology into much lower-resolution categories, known as QuadClasses, provides enough information to perform accurate out-of-sample forecasts of relevant political events. Additionally, Schein et al. (2016) indicates that it is possible to recover this latent structure from coded events. These QuadClass variables, which are divided along conflict/cooperation and material/verbal axes, capture the information described in the above papers. As seen in Figure 1, a given event can be placed somewhere within the resultant quadrants based on what valence the event has (conflict or cooperation) and what realm the event occurred (verbal or material).

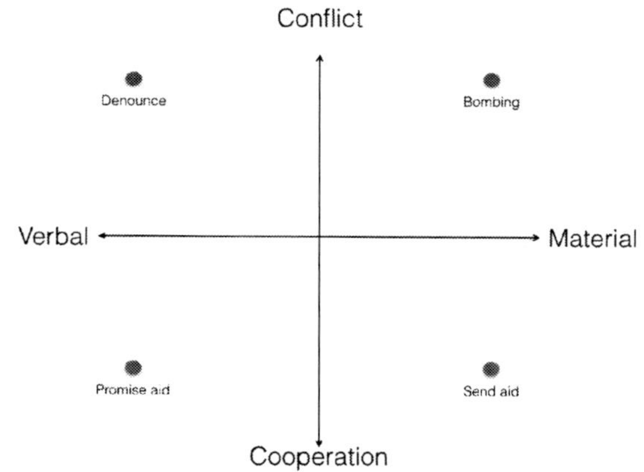

Figure 1: QuadClass Event Quadrants

Since these QuadClass variables capture much of the information necessary, the methods discussed within this paper focus on this rather than the full CAMEO coding ontology.

While the QuadClass variables lose some of the benefits of the more disaggregated, 200+ code CAMEO ontology, such as those outlined in Cederman and Gleditsch (2009), the usage of these lower-resolution categories is acceptable for a few reasons. First, as mentioned above, these categories capture a significant portion of the useful variance in the usual dependent variables of interest within political science. Second, these lower-resolution categories help resolve much of the ambiguity in the more detailed CAMEO categories. For example, the "Protest" category of CAMEO encompasses events such as demonstrations as well as political leaders verbally protesting the actions of another entity. Because of this, what seems to be a benefit of CAMEO, fine-grained differentiation between categories, becomes a possible point of confusion. Finally, and most importantly, the broad goal of the approach outlined in this paper is to enable researchers to develop application-specific ontologies that allow for categories that address the needs of a particular research question rather than attempting to make use of an ontology imperfectly suited to the task at hand. Thus, the hope is that more ontologies will proliferate to better support a researcher's specific needs.

3   Current Approaches

The current state-of-the-art for CAMEO-coded political event extraction is presented by the PETRARCH2[3] coder.[4]   The main features of PETRARCH2 include a deep reliance on information from a constituency parse tree. The default parse comes from the Stanford CoreNLP software (Manning et al., 2014). The exact operational details of PETRARCH2 are beyond the scope of this paper, with a complete explanation of the algorithm available in Norris (2016); it should suffice to say that this second version of PETRARCH makes extensive use of the actual structure of the parse tree to determine source-action-target event codings. This change to be more tightly coupled to the tree structure of the sentence, as compared to previous coders such as TABARI (Schrodt, 2001), allows for a clearer identification of actors and the assignment of role codes to the actors, and a more accurate identification of the who and whom portions of the who-did-what-to-whom equation.

At its heart, PETRARCH2 is still software to perform a lookup of terms in a set of text dictionaries. Given this, if the terms identified by the program are incorrect then the final event coding will also be incorrect. Additionally, if the terms identified by PETRARCH2 are not in the dictionaries, but would still be associated with a valid actor or event coding, then

---

[3]https://github.com/openeventdata/petrarch2

[4]Other coders exist, such as BBN's ACCENT coder, but is not currently publicly available. PETRARCH2 and ACCENT approach event coding in roughly the same manner, however.

no event is coded. This means that no matter the algorithmic design of the event coder, the output will remain constrained by the verb and actor dictionaries.

The primary issue with these methods is twofold. First, the parser-based methods rely on human-created dictionaries. As noted above, this is a labor intensive task that is not easily replicable for expansion into new ontologies; CAMEO has become the de-facto coding standard for political events largely owing to the existence of the text dictionaries created over the course of two decades. O'Connor et al. (2013) introduced a method that potentially solves the issue of developing verb patterns for the coding of political events. This method still does not address many of the other issues present with the current approaches to generating political event data, such as a reliance on syntactic parsers. The second issue, owing to the reliance on text dictionaries and parsers for the extraction of events, is the exclusively English-language nature of all available event datasets. The next section introduces an alternative to these parser-based methods that is applicable across ontologies, is tune-able for a given problem set, and is capable of working cross-lingually.

4   Statistical Approaches

In order to replace the parser-based methods for identifying an event, a new system must indentify to which of the four `QuadClass` variables, Material Conflict, Material Cooperation, Verbal Conflict, or Verbal Cooperation, the event belongs. To accomplish this, this paper makes use of convolutional neural nets.

This paper considers two neural architectures to classify a political event. The first is a 1-dimensional ConvNet with pre-trained word embedding features as described in Kim (2014). In short, it is a relatively shallow network with three parallel convolutional layers and two fully-connected layers. The fully-connected layers contain 150 and 4 units each. Dropout is applied to the two fully-connected layers so meaningful connections are learned by the model. The details of the model layers are in Table 1.

The second model is a character ConvNet based on the work by Zhang et al. (2015). The character ConvNet is a modified implementation since mul-

Layer	Frame	Kernel	Pool
1	256	3	2
2	256	4	2
3	256	5	2

Table 1: Word-based convolutional layers.

Layer	Frame	Kernel	Pool
1	256	7	3
2	256	3	N/A
3	256	3	N/A
4	256	3	3

Table 2: Character-based convolutional layers.

Dataset	Sentences
Soft-labelled English	49,296
Soft-labelled Arabic	11,466
Machine-translated Arabic	3,931

Table 3: Data source type and size

Model	Accuracy
Word-based models	
English Input	0.85
Native Arabic Input	0.25
Machine-translated Input	0.60
Character-based models	
English input	0.94
Arabic input	0.93

Table 4: Accuracy scores for Category Classifier

tiple experiments determined the full specification in Zhang et al. (2015) underperformed other specifications. The architecture for the character ConvNet consists of 3 convolutional layers and 3 fully-connected layers. The convolution layers are detailed in Table 2. The fully connected layers have 1024, 1024, and 4 output units, respectively.

5 Data

The datasets used in this paper are shown in Table 3. Each of the "soft-labelled" datasets has Quad-Class labels applied to them by PETRARCH2. The use of PETRARCH2 is necessary in order to generate enough training samples for the various classification algorithms to gain leverage over the classification task. The English corpus consists of data scraped from various online news media sites. The Arabic corpus labels are obtained via the use of a sentence-aligned English/Arabic corpus.[5] Thus, if a sentence is labelled as *Material Conflict* in the English corpus, that label is transferred to the aligned sentence in the Arabic corpus. If multiple alignments occur the label is transferred to each of the relevant sentences. The next dataset is the same set of labelled Arabic sentences that were run through the machine-translation software *Joshua* (Weese et al., 2011). These datasets provide information for three experiments: English-language, Arabic-language, and machine translated English.

[5]The specific corpus is available at https://www.ldc.upenn.edu/collaborations/past-projects/gale/data/gale-pubs.

6 Experiments

Table 4 shows the results of various models for classifying a sentence into one of four `QuadClasses`. Across the board, it is clear that the character-based ConvNets perform much better than the word-based models. The difference is less drastic for English-language inputs, a 9% difference in accuracy. For Arabic-language inputs, however, the difference is striking. The character model is over 20% more accurate than the word-based model. This is likely due to issues with tokenization and morphology when dealing with the word-based models. Even more impressive is the ability of the Arabic-language models to perform well even with a relatively small corpus of 11,466 coded sentences. These results demonstrate that character-based ConvNets are appropriate and powerful models for the classification of politically-relevant events.

7 Conclusion

This paper has demonstrated that modern approaches to natural language processing, specifically deep neural networks, offer a promising avenue for the extraction of politically-relevant events. The methods shown in this paper can work across both ontologies and languages offering a level of flexibility unseen in the realm of CAMEO-coded political event data. The implementation of these methods will allow for the exploration of languages and ontologies, as an example expanding beyond the limits of CAMEO to code events such as crime events in Spanish-language news sources, that will open new avenues of social science research.

While these methods are promising, there is still much work left to develop a fully operational event extraction pipeline. In terms of classifying events, there is still the issue of handling the many nuances of event coding. For example, if a meeting occurs between three actors that would typically lead to nine coded events when handling the various combinations of actors and binary relations. Additionally, the methods presented on this paper do not touch upon the extraction of actor information. This is another area for which modern NLP approaches, such as semantic role labelling, are highly applicable and will likely improve on the state-of-the-art.

Acknowledgments

This work was supported by the DARPA Quantitative Crisis Response program.

References

Bryan Arva, John Beieler, Ben Fisher, Gustavo Lara, Philip A. Schrodt, Wonjun Song, Marsha Sowell, and Sam Stehle. 2013. Improving forecasts of international events of interest. Paper presented at the European Political Studies Association meetings, Barcelona, June 2013.

Edward E. Azar. 1980. The conflict and peace data bank (copdab) project. *Journal of Conflict Resolution*, 24:143–152.

Patrick T Brandt, John R Freeman, and Philip A Schrodt. 2011. Real time, time series forecasting of inter-and intra-state political conflict. *Conflict Management and Peace Science*, 28(1):41–64.

Patrick T Brandt, John R Freeman, Tse min Lin, and Philip A Schrodt. 2013. Forecasting conflict in the cross-straits: Long term and short term predictions. Annual Meeting of the American Political Science Association.

Patrick T Brandt, John R Freeman, and Philip A Schrodt. 2014. Evaluating forecasts of political conflict dynamics. *International Journal of Forecasting*, 30(4):944–962.

Lars-Erik Cederman and Kristian Skrede Gleditsch. 2009. Introduction to special issue of "disaggregating civil war". *Journal of Conflict Resolution*, 24(4):590–617.

Deborah J. Gerner, Philip A. Schrodt, Omur Yilmaz, and Rajaa Abu-Jabr. 2001. Conflict and mediation event observations (cameo): A new event data framework for the analysis of foreign policy interactions. American Political Science Association, Boston, August 2002.

Nils Petter Gleditsch. 2012. Whither the weather? climate change and conflict: Introduction to whither the weather? climate change and conflict: Introduction to special issue. *Journal of Peace Research*, 49(1):3–9.

Joshua S. Goldstein, Jon C. Pevehouse, Deborah J. Gerner, and Shibley Telhami. 2001. Dynamics of middle east conflict and u.s. influence, 1979-97. *Journal of Conflict Resolution*, 45(5):594–620.

Yoon Kim. 2014. Convolutional neural networks for sentence classification. In *Proceedings of the 2014 Conference on Empirical Methods in Natural Language Processing (EMNLP)*,, pages 1746–1751, October.

Christopher D. Manning, Mihai Surdeanu, John Bauer, Jenny Finkel, Steven J. Bethard, and David McClosky. 2014. The Stanford CoreNLP natural language processing toolkit. In *Proceedings of 52nd Annual Meeting of the Association for Computational Linguistics: System Demonstrations*, pages 55–60.

Charles A. McClelland. 1976. World event/interaction survey codebook.

Sean P. O'Brien. 2010. Crisis early warning and decision support: Contemporary approaches and thoughts on future research. *International Studies Review*, 12(1):87–104.

Brendan O'Connor, Brandon Stewart, and Noah A. Smith. 2013. Learning to extract international relations from political context. In *Proceedings of the Annual Meeting of the Association for Computational Linguistics (ACL)*, pages 1094–1104.

Aaron Schein, Mingyuan Zhou, David M. Blei, and Hanna Wallach. 2016. Bayesian poisson tucker decomposition for learning the structure of international relations. In *Proceedings of the 33rd International Conference on Machine Learning*, New York, NY, USA.

Philip A. Schrodt, Omur Yilmaz, Deborah J. Gerner, and Dennis Hermrick. 2008. Coding sub-state actors using the cameo (conflict and mediation event observations) actor coding framework. In *International Studies Association, San Francisco, March 2008*.

Philip A. Schrodt. 2001. Automated coding of international event data using sparse parsing techniques. Paper presented at the International Studies Association, Chicago, 21-24 February 2001.

Philip A Schrodt. 2006. Forecasting conflict in the balkans using hidden markov models. In Robert Trappl, editor, *Programming for Peace: Computer-Aided Methods for International Conflict Resolution and Prevention*, pages 161–184. Kluwer Academic Publishers, Dordrecht, Netherlands.

Jonathan Weese, Juri Ganitkevitch, Chris Callison-Burch, Matt Post, and Adam Lopez. 2011. Joshua 3.0: Syntax-based machine translationjoshua 3.0: Syntax-based machine translation joshua 3.0: Syntax-based machine translation with the thrax grammar extractor. In *Proceedings of the 6th Workshop on Statistical Machine Translation*, pages 478–484, Edinburgh, Scotland, UK, July.

Xiang Zhang, Junbo Zhao, and Yann LeCun. 2015. Character-level convolutional networks for text classification. In *Advances in Neural Information Processing Systems 28 (NIPS 2015)*.

User profiling with geo-located posts and demographic data

Adam Poulston, Mark Stevenson and **Kalina Bontcheva**
Department of Computer Science
University of Sheffield
Sheffield S1 4DP, UK
{ARSPoulston1, k.bontcheva, mark.stevenson}@sheffield.ac.uk

Abstract

This paper presents a novel method for user profiling in social media that makes use of geo-location information associated with social media posts to avoid the need for self-reported data. These posts are combined with two publicly available sources of demographic information to automatically create data sets in which posts are labelled with socio-economic status. The data sets are linked by identifying each user's 'home location'. Analysis indicates that the nature of the demographic information is an important factor in performance of this approach.

1   Introduction

Previous research has shown that the language a person uses on-line can be indicative of a wide range of personal characteristics, including gender, age (Schler et al., 2006), personality (Schwartz et al., 2013), political ideology (Sylwester and Purver, 2015) and occupational class (Preoţiuc-Pietro et al., 2015a). Several *user profiling* models that predict these characteristics have been developed, some of which have accuracy that exceeds human performance (Burger et al., 2011; Youyou et al., 2015). User profiling models have applications such as gendered behaviour analysis (Purohit et al., 2015) and bias reduction in predictive models (Culotta, 2014).

Previous work on user profiling has traditionally relied on profiles annotated with self-reported characteristics for training data. This can be difficult to acquire in large quantities and forms a bottleneck in the development of user profiling systems.

Recently, approaches have attempted to build user profiling datasets through other means. Preoţiuc-Pietro et al. (2015a)(2015b) extracted known job titles from Twitter profile descriptions to annotate users with occupational class and income. Crowd-sourcing techniques have been used to annotate data—in Kosinski et al. (2013) users were invited to complete a personality quiz and then asked if they wanted to share their data for research purposes. In a similar fashion, Nguyen et al. (2014) provided an application which attempts to guess user's age and gender based on their Twitter profile and then asks for the correct answer afterwards. Profile information has also been collected from websites; such as blogs (Schler et al., 2006; Burger et al., 2011) or review sites (Hovy et al., 2015).

Many countries regularly conduct surveys of their population that provide large-scale demographic information, some of which is made freely available. For example, the United Kingdom conducts a mandatory census every decade. Although the full information collected is not made publicly available for a century, aggregated information is made freely available. In addition, governments are increasingly making data available for research purposes, some of which may be relevant to user profiling[1]. This data has the advantage of providing population-level information gathered using reliable methods.

This paper explores how demographic information can be used to assist with the development of user profiling models. It describes an approach to the generation of annotated training data by combining geo-located social media profiles with geo-

---

[1] e.g. http://data.gov.uk/

43

Proceedings of 2016 EMNLP Workshop on Natural Language Processing and Computational Social Science, pages 43–48,
Austin, TX, November 5, 2016. ©2016 Association for Computational Linguistics

graphically linked demographic data. This approach is applied using publicly available demographic data describing socio-economic status (Section 2). A set of geo-located tweets is collected and the 'home location' of each user identified using a clustering approach so that each profile can be mapped onto the regions in the demographic data, thereby providing labelled data (Section 4) which is used to create a user profiling system (Section 5).

2   Data Sources

This work makes use of data from two sources: demographic data provided by the UK Office for National Statistics demographic data and Twitter posts.

Demographic data provides information about characteristics of a population within a specified area. The UK government provides open datasets containing information about a range of demographic variables including highest qualification, job category and unemployment rates.

This paper makes use of *geodemographic segmentation* datasets in which an area, or individual's, demographics are generalised into a single socio-economic category. These types of data sets are often used for marketing purposes (Troy, 2008). The United Kingdom's Office for National Statistics (ONS)[2] provides a range of data sets including the Output Area Classification (OAC) and Local Authority Classification (LAC) datasets. Unlike commercial datasets, such as MOSAIC[3] and Acorn[4], the methodology used to develop the OAC and LAC datasets is fully documented.

The OAC data set is organised around output areas, regions of around 200 households in England and Wales. The OAC dataset places residents of every Output Area into a hierarchy of socio-economic groups based on responses to the 2011 UK Census. The dataset consists of a hierarchical classification scheme with three layers: supergroups (shown in Figure 1), groups and subgroups. For example, the Output Area E00124315 is associated with the '7-constrained city dwellers' supergroup , the '7a-challenged diversity' group, and the '7a2-hampered aspiration' subgroup.

1 Rural Residents
2 Cosmopolitans
3 Ethnicity Central
4 Multicultural Metropolitans
5 Urbanites
6 Suburbanites
7 Constrained City Dwellers
8 Hard-Pressed Living

Figure 1: OAC supergroups

1 English and Welsh Countryside
2 Scottish and Northern Irish Countryside
3 London Cosmopolitan
4 Suburban Traits
5 Business and Education Centres
6 Coast and Heritage
7 Prosperous England
8 Mining Heritage and Manufacturing

Figure 2: LAC supergroups

The LAC dataset is organised in a similar way to the OAC dataset, with eight supergroups (shown in Figure 2) and two layers of subgroups, but is generalized to cover Local Authorities (also provided by the UK Data service describing areas governed by a single council covering the whole of the UK), which are larger than Output Areas. Despite some similarities in names, the two datasets use different classification strategies leading to categories not being directly comparable.

Geo-located social media posts from the United Kingdom were identified using the Twitter public streaming API. The Twitter REST API was then used to retrospectively collect each user's tweets (up to 3200 per user) and any public information on their profile. Users with fewer than 50 geo-located tweets were excluded to ensure sufficient data was available for subsequent processing. Just over 135,000 profiles were initially collected, 86,262 of which had enough tweets. A small portion of profiles (3,743) not representative of the general population (e.g. profiles of celebrities, shops, spammers) were excluded using standard approaches (Chu et al., 2012; Cresci et al., 2015), leaving 82,519 profiles used for experiments described later.

[2]http://www.ons.gov.uk
[3]http://www.experian.co.uk/mosaic/
[4]http://acorn.caci.co.uk/

3 Home location identification

Demographic data provides information about individuals based on their residential address, making it important to make sure that a user is associated with that location rather than where they happened to be when sending a particular tweet. Consequently all users in the dataset were assigned a 'home location' in the form of a latitude-longitude coordinate.

Our approach assumes that each social media user commonly posts from a limited set of locations. It is further assumed that the location posted from the most often is the user's home location. The task of assigning 'home location' given a collection of geo-located posts is then approached as a clustering problem based on geo-location information associated with their tweets. Other approaches for assigning home location were considered, such as as those that consider textual (Han et al., 2014) and social network (Jurgens et al., 2015) cues, but these typically only produce accurate judgements at the city level, whereas demographic datasets often operate at a finer scale.

The coordinates of each user's geo-located posts are clustered using k-means, with k set using the 'jump' method (Sugar and James, 2011). (A range of alternative clustering algorithms were also explored but were not found to significantly improve performance.) The most populous cluster was then identified and the point closest to the cluster centroid taken as the home location. Cluster 'density' was calculated; defined as the average Vincenty distance (Vincenty, 1975) (a model of geographic distance) in miles between each data point and the cluster centroid. This provides the option to exclude users with highly uncertain home location (i.e low density home cluster).

3.1 Evaluating Home Location Assignment

Our method for home location identification was assessed by comparing self-reported locations from the 'location' field with those assigned by clustering. Only 728 of the 82,519 profiles include a self-reported location. Of these, 176 were discarded as being clearly fictitious; leaving 552 profiles for evaluation. These were further cleaned by manually removing extraneous information such as emoticons.

Varying levels of granularity were present in the declared location fields, ranging from street level to country, with the majority at town or city level, e.g. 'Edinburgh'. A number of the location fields also included a single coordinate location. The Nominatim geocoding tool[5] was used to convert the self-reported locations to geographical coordinates. Vincenty distance between these coordinates and the assigned home location was calculated.

The majority of distances (69.7%) were accurate to within 10 miles, more than half (56.9%) accurate to within 5 miles and 30.8% within 1 mile. The home location gained from the location text field is only expected to be accurate to within 5 or 10 miles because the majority of self-reported locations are towns or cities. The results given here therefore suggest that the clustering approach presented here can identify the home location of a Twitter user with reasonable accuracy.

4 Demographically Labelling Data

A data set was created in which each social media profiles were associated with their corresponding OAC and LAC supergroup. A home location was assigned to each of the 82,519 profiles identified of Section 2 using the approach described in Section 3. Point-in-polygon tests then linked each profile with its relevant Output Area and Local Authority. Once a profile was allocated an associated boundary, demographic linking is a simple look-up task.

Two user profiling datasets were created by linking users with their local demographics; users in England and Wales were labelled with one of eight OAC supergroups associated with that user's local Output Area, and users across the whole of the UK were labelled with one of eight LAC supergroups associated with their Local Authority. These datasets are referred to as 'OAC-P and 'LAC-P', respectively.

5 User demographic prediction

We approach our analysis as a classification problem, aiming to use the content of a user's tweets to predict their LAC-P and OAC-P from the eight possible classifications in each data set.

A classification pipeline was created, taking each user's corpus of tweets as input, tokenized using a

---

[5]http://openstreetmap.org/

Twitter aware tokenizer (Gimpel et al., 2011). TF-IDF transformed word n-grams (1- and 2-grams) were used as features for a multi-class Support Vector Machine (SVM) with a linear kernel. n-grams and SVMs were chosen as they have been shown to consistently perform well at user profiling tasks, both for social media (Rao and Yarowsky, 2010; Rout et al., 2013; Schwartz et al., 2013) and other types of text (Boulis and Ostendorf, 2005; Garera and Yarowsky, 2009), and are as such a useful tool to establish baseline performance. Balanced sets were extracted from the OAC-P and LAC-P datasets with 2000 members per label in both cases. 10-fold cross-validation was used for all experiments.

5.1 Results

The results of the SVM classifier are presented in Table 1, compared with results from a random baseline. Prediction of both OAC and LAC outperform the random baseline, indicating that the training dataset described in this article can be used to create valuable user profiling systems. Results for LAC are encouraging and indicate that it is possible to achieve promising results while using a simple classifier. The OAC predictions are noticeably worse than LAC but still outperform the baseline.

The large difference in performance obtained using the two data sets may be down to differences in their nature. Analysis revealed that the regions defined in the OAC-P dataset are smaller than those in the LAC-P dataset; the average length of the diagonal of the minimum bounding rectangle for each region is 0.93 miles for Output Areas, whereas it is 34.5 miles for Local Authorities. It seems probable that profiles are more likely to be mis-classified when assigned to more fine-grained regions in the OAC-P data set, resulting in a noisier data set.

Another difference between the data sets is that the OAC scheme aims to model 'geographically independent socio-economic status' in contrast to the LAC categories which are region dependent (e.g. 'London Cosmopolitan'). Examination of the highest ranked features by SVM coefficient for each LAC supergroup revealed a connection between groups and geography. The most important features for many classes are words or phrases referencing specific areas in the UK as well as several stereotypical dialect features. For example, the '3-

	OAC–P	LAC–P
Random Baseline	0.1259	0.1259
SVM classifier	0.2757	0.5047

Table 1: Accuracy for OAC–P and LAC–P prediction

London Cosmopolitan' supergroup's highest ranked features relate exclusively to London, its surrounding boroughs and public transport system. In contrast, the OAC's feature coefficients are not as location dependent; for example, '1-Rural Residents' contains features such as 'Severn' (a river), 'stables', 'mountain bike' and 'emmerdale' (a UK soap opera set in the countryside). Similarly, '4-Multicultural Metropolitans' is the only group identified that has non-English phrases and the Islamic holidays Eid and Ramadan as important features—a promising sign given the supergroup title.

6 Conclusion

This paper explored the use of population-level demographic information for user profiling. It presented a novel approach to the generation of automatically labelled data by making use of geo-located social media posts. The 'home location' for a user is identified using clustering and then combined with publicly available information from two previously unexplored demographic datasets. A simple classifier based solely on tweet content was able to predict socio-economic status with promising results for one data set.

Analysis indicated that the properties of the demographic data are important. Key factors include the granularity of the output area and degree to which the groupings are based on socio-economic, rather than geographic, characteristics rather than geographic features.

The demographic data sets used in this work have the advantages that they are large-scale and collected using sound methodologies. However, the information they contain is aggregated and is updated infrequently. Our future work will explore the extent to which these disadvantages can be overcome. Accurate identification of home location is important for the approach presented here. We will also explore its effect on overall performance and approaches for identifying home location more accurately.

Code available at `https://github.com/adampoulston/geo-user-profiling`.

References

Constantinos Boulis and Mari Ostendorf. 2005. A quantitative analysis of lexical differences between genders in telephone conversations. In *Proceedings of the 43rd Annual Meeting on Association for Computational Linguistics*, pages 435–442. Association for Computational Linguistics.

John D Burger, John Henderson, George Kim, and Guido Zarrella. 2011. Discriminating gender on twitter. In *Proceedings of the Conference on Empirical Methods in Natural Language Processing*, pages 1301–1309. Association for Computational Linguistics.

Zi Chu, Steven Gianvecchio, Haining Wang, and Sushil Jajodia. 2012. Detecting automation of twitter accounts: Are you a human, bot, or cyborg? *Dependable and Secure Computing, IEEE Transactions on*, 9(6):811–824.

Stefano Cresci, Roberto Di Pietro, Marinella Petrocchi, Angelo Spognardi, and Maurizio Tesconi. 2015. Fame for sale: efficient detection of fake twitter followers. *Decision Support Systems*, 80:56–71.

Aron Culotta. 2014. Reducing sampling bias in social media data for county health inference. In *Joint Statistical Meetings Proceedings*.

Nikesh Garera and David Yarowsky. 2009. Modeling latent biographic attributes in conversational genres. In *Proceedings of the Joint Conference of the 47th Annual Meeting of the ACL and the 4th International Joint Conference on Natural Language Processing of the AFNLP: Volume 2-Volume 2*, pages 710–718. Association for Computational Linguistics.

Kevin Gimpel, Nathan Schneider, Brendan O'Connor, Dipanjan Das, Daniel Mills, Jacob Eisenstein, Michael Heilman, Dani Yogatama, Jeffrey Flanigan, and Noah A Smith. 2011. Part-of-speech tagging for twitter: Annotation, features, and experiments. In *Proceedings of the 49th Annual Meeting of the Association for Computational Linguistics: Human Language Technologies: short papers-Volume 2*, pages 42–47. Association for Computational Linguistics.

Bo Han, Paul Cook, and Timothy Baldwin. 2014. Text-based twitter user geolocation prediction. *Journal of Artificial Intelligence Research*, pages 451–500.

Dirk Hovy, Anders Johannsen, and Anders Søgaard. 2015. User review sites as a resource for large-scale sociolinguistic studies. In *Proceedings of the 24th International Conference on World Wide Web*, pages 452–461. ACM.

David Jurgens, Tyler Finethy, James McCorriston, Yi Tian Xu, and Derek Ruths. 2015. Geolocation prediction in twitter using social networks: A critical analysis and review of current practice. In *Proceed-*

ings of the 9th International AAAI Conference on Weblogs and Social Media (ICWSM).

Michal Kosinski, David Stillwell, and Thore Graepel. 2013. Private traits and attributes are predictable from digital records of human behavior. *Proceedings of the National Academy of Sciences*, 110(15):5802–5805.

Dong Nguyen, Dolf Trieschnigg, and Theo Meder. 2014. Tweetgenie: Development, evaluation, and lessons learned. *COLING 2014*, pages 62–66.

Daniel Preoţiuc-Pietro, Vasileios Lampos, and Nikolaos Aletras. 2015a. An analysis of the user occupational class through Twitter content. *Proceedings of the 53rd Annual Meeting of the Association for Computational Linguistics and the 7th International Joint Conference on Natural Language Processing (Volume 1: Long Papers)*, pages 1754–1764.

Daniel Preoţiuc-Pietro, Svitlana Volkova, Vasileios Lampos, Yoram Bachrach, and Nikolaos Aletras. 2015b. Studying user income through language, behaviour and affect in social media. *PloS one*, 10(9):e0138717.

Hemant Purohit, Tanvi Banerjee, Andrew Hampton, Valerie L Shalin, Nayanesh Bhandutia, and Amit P Sheth. 2015. Gender-based violence in 140 characters or fewer: A# bigdata case study of twitter. *arXiv preprint arXiv:1503.02086*.

Delip Rao and David Yarowsky. 2010. Detecting latent user properties in social media. In *Proc. of the NIPS MLSN Workshop*. Citeseer.

Dominic Rout, Kalina Bontcheva, Daniel Preoţiuc-Pietro, and Trevor Cohn. 2013. Where's@ wally?: a classification approach to geolocating users based on their social ties. In *Proceedings of the 24th ACM Conference on Hypertext and Social Media*, pages 11–20. ACM.

Jonathan Schler, M Koppel, S Argamon, and J Pennebaker. 2006. Effects of age and gender on blogging. In *Proceedings of AAAI Spring Symposium on Computational Approaches for Analyzing Weblogs: Papers from the AAAI Spring Symposium*, pages 199–205.

H. Andrew Schwartz, Johannes C. Eichstaedt, Margaret L. Kern, Lukasz Dziurzynski, Stephanie M. Ramones, Megha Agrawal, Achal Shah, Michal Kosinski, David Stillwell, Martin E. P. Seligman, and Lyle H. Ungar. 2013. Personality, gender, and age in the language of social media: The open-vocabulary approach. *PLoS ONE*, 8(9):e73791, 09.

Catherine A Sugar and Gareth M James. 2011. Finding the number of clusters in a dataset. *Journal of the American Statistical Association*.

Karolina Sylwester and Matthew Purver. 2015. Twitter language use reflects psychological differences between democrats and republicans. *PLoS ONE*, 10(9):e0137422, 09.

Austin Troy. 2008. Geodemographic segmentation. In *Encyclopedia of GIS*, pages 347–355. Springer US.

T. Vincenty. 1975. Direct and inverse solutions of geodesics on the ellipsoid with application of nested equations. *Survey Review*, 23(176):88–93.

Wu Youyou, Michal Kosinski, and David Stillwell. 2015. Computer-based personality judgments are more accurate than those made by humans. *Proceedings of the National Academy of Sciences*, 112(4):1036–1040.

Gov2Vec: Learning Distributed Representations of Institutions and Their Legal Text

John J. Nay
School of Engineering
Vanderbilt University
Program on Law & Innovation
Vanderbilt Law School
Nashville, TN 37235, USA
`john.j.nay@gmail.com`
`johnjnay.com`

Abstract

We compare policy differences across institutions by embedding representations of the entire legal corpus of each institution and the vocabulary shared across all corpora into a continuous vector space. We apply our method, Gov2Vec, to Supreme Court opinions, Presidential actions, and official summaries of Congressional bills. The model discerns meaningful differences between government branches. We also learn representations for more fine-grained word sources: individual Presidents and (2-year) Congresses. The similarities between learned representations of Congresses over time and sitting Presidents are negatively correlated with the bill veto rate, and the temporal ordering of Presidents and Congresses was implicitly learned from only text. With the resulting vectors we answer questions such as: how does Obama and the 113th House differ in addressing climate change and how does this vary from environmental or economic perspectives? Our work illustrates vector-arithmetic-based investigations of complex relationships between word sources based on their texts. We are extending this to create a more comprehensive legal semantic map.

1 Introduction

Methods have been developed to efficiently obtain representations of words in $\mathbf{R}^d$ that capture subtle semantics across the dimensions of the vectors (Collobert and Weston, 2008). For instance, after sufficient training, relationships encoded in difference vectors can be uncovered with vector arithmetic:

vec("king") - vec("man") + vec("woman") returns a vector close to vec("queen") (Mikolov et al. 2013a).

Applying this powerful notion of distributed continuous vector space representations of words, we embed representations of institutions and the words from their law and policy documents into shared semantic space. We can then combine positively and negatively weighted word and government vectors into the same query, enabling complex, targeted and subtle similarity computations. For instance, which government branch is more characterized by "validity and truth," or "long-term government career"?

We apply this method, Gov2Vec, to a unique corpus of Supreme Court opinions, Presidential actions, and official summaries of Congressional bills. The model discerns meaningful differences between House, Senate, President and Court vectors. We also learn more fine-grained institutional representations: individual Presidents and Congresses (2-year terms). The method implicitly learns important latent relationships between these government actors that was not provided during training. For instance, their temporal ordering was learned from only their text. The resulting vectors are used to explore differences between actors with respect to policy topics.

2 Methods

A common method for learning vector representations of words is to use a neural network to predict a target word with the mean of its context words' vectors, obtain the gradient with back-propagation of the prediction errors, and update vectors in the direction of higher probability of observing the correct target word (Bengio et al. 2003; Mikolov et

Proceedings of 2016 EMNLP Workshop on Natural Language Processing and Computational Social Science, pages 49–54,
Austin, TX, November 5, 2016. ©2016 Association for Computational Linguistics

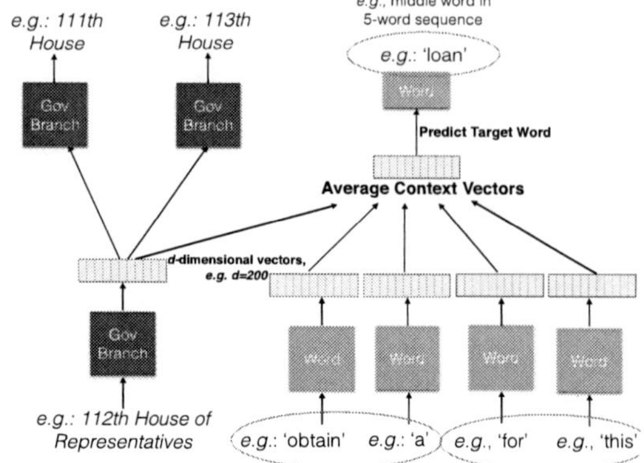

Figure 1: Gov2Vec only updates GovVecs with word prediction. For Structured Gov2Vec training, which updates GovVecs with word and Gov prediction, we set "Gov window size" to 1, e.g. a Congress is used to predict those directly before and after.

al. 2013b). After iterating over many word contexts, words with similar meaning are embedded in similar locations in vector space as a by-product of the prediction task (Mikolov et al. 2013b). Le and Mikolov (2014) extend this word2vec method to learn representations of documents. For predictions of target words, a vector unique to the document is concatenated with context word vectors and subsequently updated. Similarly, we embed institutions and their words into a shared vector space by averaging a vector unique to an institution with context word vectors when predicting that institution's words and, with back-propagation and stochastic gradient descent, update representations for institutions and the words (which are shared across all institutions).[1]

There are two hyper-parameters for the algorithm that can strongly affect results, but suitable values are unknown. We use a tree of Parzen estimators search algorithm (Bergstra et al. 2013) to sample from parameter space[2] and save all models estimated. Subsequent analyses are conducted across all models, propagating our uncertainty in hyper-parameters. Due to stochasticity in training and the uncertainty in the hyper-parameter values, patterns

robust across the ensemble are more likely to reflect useful regularities than individual models.

Gov2Vec can be applied to more fine-grained categories than entire government branches. In this context, there are often relationships between word sources, e.g. Obama after Bush, that we can incorporate into the learning process. During training, we alternate between updating GovVecs based on their use in the prediction of words in their policy corpus and their use in the prediction of other word sources located nearby in time. We model temporal institutional relationships, but any known relationships between entities, e.g. ranking Congresses by number of Republicans, could also be incorporated into the Structured Gov2Vec training process (Fig. 1).

After training, we extract $(M + S) \times d_j \times J$ parameters, where M is the number of unique words, S is the number of word sources, and d_j the vector dimensionality, which varies across the J models (we set $J = 20$). We then investigate the most cosine similar words to particular vector combinations, $\arg\max_{v* \in V_{1:N}} cos(v*, \frac{1}{W} \sum_{i=1}^{W} w_i \times s_i)$, where $cos(a, b) = \frac{\vec{a} \cdot \vec{b}}{\|\vec{a}\|\|\vec{b}\|}$, w_i is one of W WordVecs or GovVecs of interest, $V_{1:N}$ are the N most frequent words in the vocabulary of M words ($N < M$ to exclude rare words during analysis) excluding the W query words, s_i is 1 or -1 for whether we're positively or negatively weighting w_i. We repeat similarity queries over all J models, retain words with $> C$ cosine similarity, and rank the word results based on their frequency and mean cosine similarity across the ensemble. We also measure the similarity of WordVec combinations to each GovVec and the similarities between GovVecs to validate that the process learns useful embeddings that capture expected relationships.

3 Data

We created a unique corpus of 59 years of all U.S. Supreme Court opinions (1937-1975, 1991-2010), 227 years of all U.S. Presidential Memorandum, Determinations, and Proclamations, and Executive Orders (1789-2015), and 42 years of official summaries of all bills introduced in the U.S. Congress (1973-2014). We used official summaries rather than full bill text because full texts are only available from 1993 and summaries are available from

---

[1]We use a binary Huffman tree (Mikolov et al. 2013b) for efficient hierarchical softmax prediction of words, and conduct 25 epochs while linearly decreasing the learning rate from 0.025 to 0.001.

[2]vector dimensionality, uniform(100, 200), and maximum distance between the context and target words, uniform(10, 25)

1973. We scraped all Presidential Memorandum (1,465), Determinations (801), Executive Orders (5,634), and Proclamations (7,544) from the American Presidency Project website. The Sunlight Foundation downloaded official bill summaries from the U.S. Government Publishing Office (GPO), which we downloaded. We downloaded Supreme Court Decisions issued 1937–1975 (Vol. 300-422) from the GPO, and the PDFs of Decisions issued 1991–2010 (Vol. 502-561) from the Supreme Court. We removed HTML artifacts, whitespace, stop words, words occurring only once, numbers, and punctuation, and converted to lower-case.

4 Results

4.1 WordVec-GovVec Similarities

We tested whether our learned vectors captured meaningful differences between branches. Fig. 2 displays similarities between these queries and the branches, which reflect *a priori* known differences.

Gov2Vec has unique capabilities that summary statistics, e.g. word frequency, lack: it can compute similarities between any source and word as long as the word occurs at least in one source, whereas word counting cannot provide meaningful similarities when a word never occurs in a source's corpus. Most importantly, Gov2Vec can combine complex combinations of positively and negatively weighted vectors in a similarity query.

4.2 GovVec-GovVec Similarities

We learned representations for individual Presidents and Congresses by using vectors for these higher resolution word sources in the word prediction task. To investigate if the representations capture important latent relationships between institutions, we compared the cosine similarities between the Congresses over time (93rd–113th) and the corresponding sitting Presidents (Nixon–Obama) to the bill veto rate. We expected that a lower veto rate would be reflected in more similar vectors, and, indeed, the Congress-President similarity and veto rate are negatively correlated (Spearman's ρ computed on raw veto rates and similarities: -0.74; see also Fig. 3).[3]

---

[3]Leveraging temporal relationships in the learning process, Structured Gov2Vec, and just using the text, yield very similar (impressive) results on this task. Figs. 3 and 4 and the correlation reported are derived from the text-only Gov2Vec results.

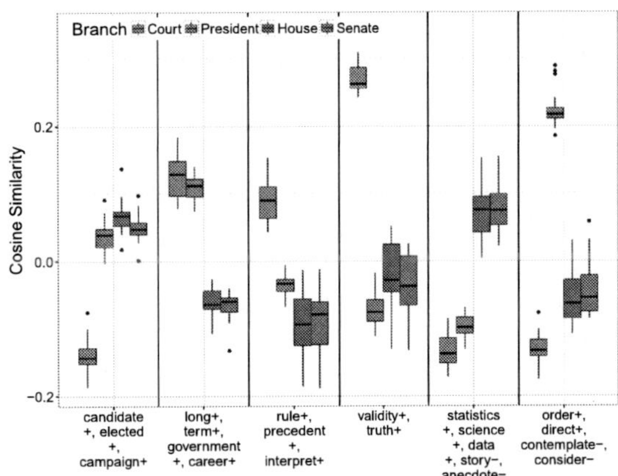

Figure 2: We compute the mean of similarities of each branch to all words and subtract this from each branch's similarity computation to normalize branches within vector space. Positive and negative weighting is noted with + and −. Compared to the Court, the President is much closer to "order and direct" than "contemplate and consider." The opposite holds for "validity and truth." The left panel reflects the fact that the House is elected most often and the Court the least (never).

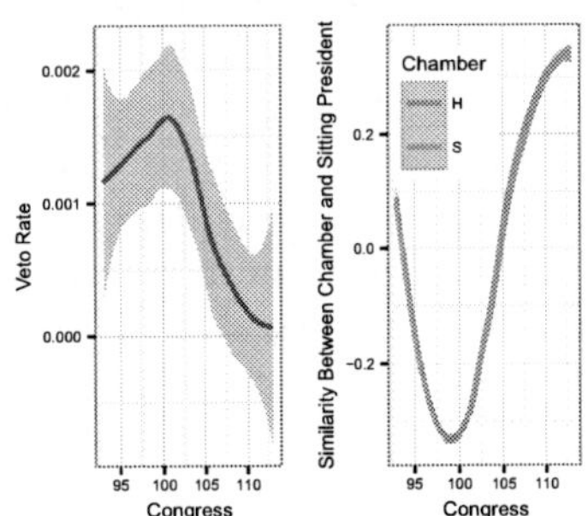

Figure 3: Loess-smoothed veto rate (left) and loess-smoothed (across ensemble) similarity of Congresses to Presidents (right).

As a third validation, we learn vectors from only text and project them into two dimensions with principal components analysis. From Fig. 4 it's evident that temporal and institutional relationships were implicitly learned.[4] One dimension (top-to-bottom) almost perfectly rank orders Presidents and Congresses by time, and another dimension (side-to-side) separates the President from Congress.

---

[4]These are the only results reported in this paper from a single model within the ensemble. We conducted PCA on other models in the ensemble and the same relationships hold.

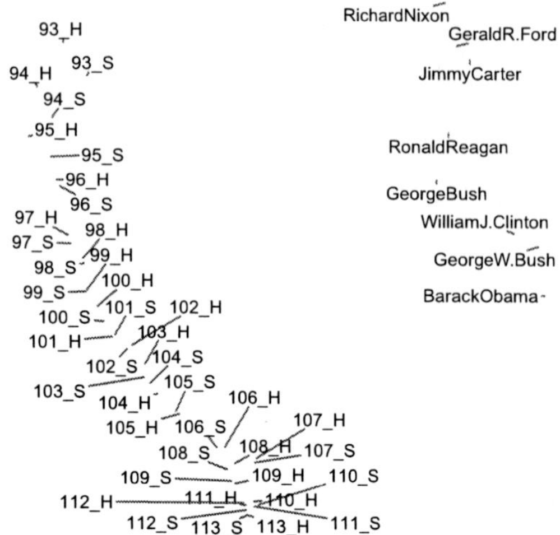

Figure 4: 2-dimensional Congresses (93-113 House and Senate) and Presidents.

4.3 GovVec-WordVec Policy Queries

Fig. 5 (top) asks: how does Obama and the 113th House differ in addressing climate change and how does this vary across environmental and economic contexts? The most frequent word across the ensemble (out of words with > 0.35 similarity to the query) for the Obama-economic quadrant is "unprecedented." "Greenhouse" and "ghg" are more frequent across models and have a higher mean similarity for Obama-Environmental than 113th House-Environmental.

Fig. 5 (bottom) asks: how does the House address war from "oil" and "terror" perspectives and how does this change after the 2001 terrorist attack.[5] Compared to the 106th, both the oil and terrorism panels in the 107th (when 9-11 occurred) have words more cosine similar to the query (further to the right) suggesting that the 107th House was closer to the topic of war, and the content changes to primarily strong verbs such as instructs, directs, requires, urges, and empowers.

____

[5]For comparisons across branches, e.g. 113th House and Obama, Structured Gov2Vec learned qualitatively more useful representations so we plot that here. For comparisons within Branch, e.g. 106th and 107th House, to maximize uniqueness of the word sources to obtain more discriminating words, we use text-only Gov2Vec.

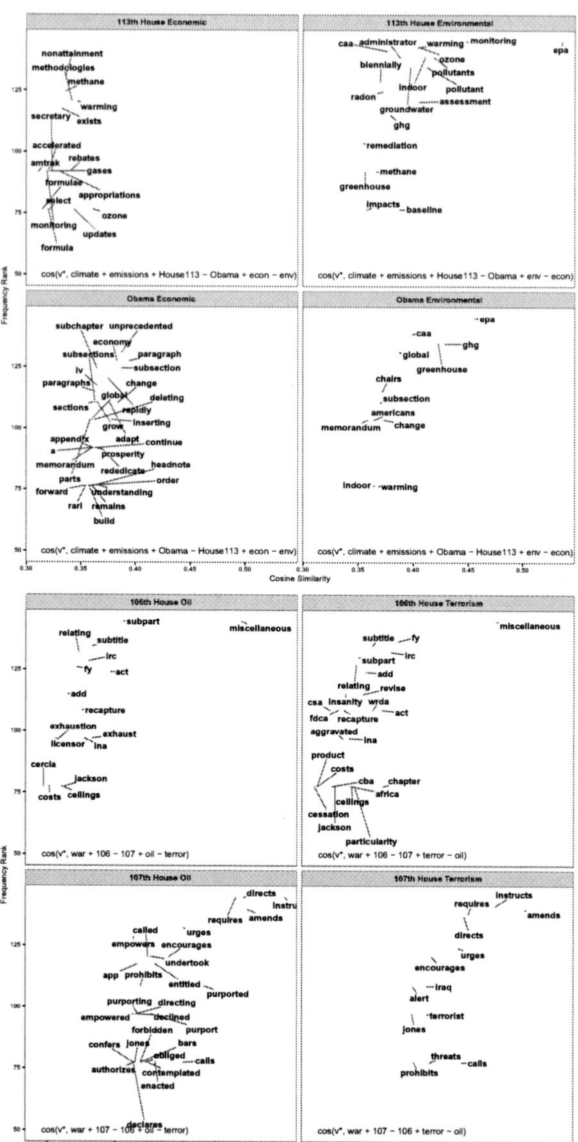

Figure 5: The top panel is the climate policy query comparing the 113th U.S. House of Representatives and President Obama: $\arg\max_{v*} cos(v*, wv(\text{climate}) + wv(\text{emissions}) + gv(G1) - gv(G2) + wv(C1) - wv(C2))$, where $G=\{113\text{ House, Obama}\}$, $G1 \in G$, $G2 \in G$, $G1 \neq G2$, $C=\{\text{economic, environmental}\}$, $C1 \in C$, $C2 \in C$, $C1 \neq C2$. The bottom panel is the war policy query for the U.S. House of Representatives before and after the 9-11 terrorist attacks: wv(war), $G=\{106\text{ House, }107\text{ House}\}$, $C=\{\text{oil, terror}\}$. The exact query used to create each quadrant is provided at the bottom of the quadrant.

5 Additional Related Work

Political scientists model text to understand political processes (Grimmer 2010; Roberts et al. 2014); however, most of this work focuses on variants of topic models (Blei et al. 2003). Djuric et al. (2015) apply a learning procedure similar to Structured Gov2Vec to streaming documents to learn representations of documents that are similar to those nearby in time. Structured Gov2Vec applies this joint hierarchical learning process (using entities to predict words *and* other entities) to non-textual entities. Kim et al. (2014) and Kulkarni et al. (2015) train neural language models for each year of a time ordered corpora to detect changes in words. Instead of learning models for distinct times, we learn a global model with embeddings for time-dependent entities that can be included in queries to analyze change. Kiros et al. (2014) learn embeddings for text attributes by treating them as gating units to a word embedding tensor. Their process is more computationally intensive than ours.

6 Conclusions and Future Work

We learned vector representations of text meta-data on a novel data set of legal texts that includes case, statutory, and administrative law. The representations effectively encoded important relationships between institutional actors that were not explicitly provided during training. Finally, we demonstrated fine-grained investigations of policy differences between actors based on vector arithmetic. More generally, the method can be applied to measuring similarity between any entities producing text, and used for recommendations, e.g. what's the closest *think-tank vector* to the *non-profit vector* representation of the Sierra Club?

Methodologically, our next goal is to explore where training on non-textual relations, i.e. Structural Gov2Vec, is beneficial. It seems to help stabilize representations when exploiting temporal relations, but political relations may prove to be even more useful. Substantively, our goal is to learn a large collection of vectors representing government actors at different resolutions and within different contexts[6] to address a range of targeted policy queries. Once we learn these representations, re-

---

[6]For instance, learn a vector for the 111th House using its

searchers could efficiently search for differences in law and policy across time, government branch, and political party.

Acknowledgments

We thank the anonymous reviewers for helpful suggestions.

References

Bengio, Yoshua, Rjean Ducharme, Pascal Vincent, and Christian Janvin. 2003. A Neural Probabilistic Language Model. *J. Mach. Learn. Res.* 3 (March): 1137–55.

Bergstra, James S., Daniel Yamins, and David Cox. 2013. Making a Science of Model Search: Hyperparameter Optimization in Hundreds of Dimensions for Vision Architectures. In *Proceedings of the 30th International Conference on Machine Learning*, 115–23.

Blei, David M., Andrew Y. Ng, and Michael I. Jordan. 2003. "Latent Dirichlet Allocation." *J. Mach. Learn. Res.* 3 (March): 993–1022.

Collobert, Ronan and Jason Weston. 2008. A Unified Architecture for Natural Language Processing: Deep Neural Networks with Multitask Learning. In *Proceedings of the 25th International Conference on Machine Learning*. 160–167. ACM.

Djuric, Nemanja, Hao Wu, Vladan Radosavljevic, Mihajlo Grbovic, and Narayan Bhamidipati. 2015. Hierarchical Neural Language Models for Joint Representation of Streaming Documents and Their Content. In *Proceedings of the 24th International Conference on World Wide Web*, 248–55. WWW '15. New York, NY, USA: ACM.

Grimmer, Justin. 2010. "A Bayesian Hierarchical Topic Model for Political Texts: Measuring Expressed Agendas in Senate Press Releases." *Political Analysis* 18 (1): 1–35.

Kim, Yoon, Yi-I. Chiu, Kentaro Hanaki, Darshan Hegde, and Slav Petrov. 2014. Temporal Analysis of Language Through Neural Language Models.

---

text and temporal relationships to other Houses, learn a vector for the 111th House using its text and political composition relationships to other Houses (e.g. ranking by number of Republicans), and then move down in temporal and institutional resolution, e.g. to individual Members. Then use press release text to gain a different perspective and iterate through the resolutions again.

In *Proceedings of the ACL 2014 Workshop on Language Technologies and Computational Social Science*, 61–65. Association for Computational Linguistics.

Kiros, Ryan, Richard Zemel, and Ruslan R Salakhutdinov. 2014. A Multiplicative Model for Learning Distributed Text-Based Attribute Representations. In *Advances in Neural Information Processing Systems 27*, edited by Z. Ghahramani, M. Welling, C. Cortes, N. D. Lawrence, and K. Q. Weinberger, 2348–56. Curran Associates, Inc.

Kulkarni, Vivek, Rami Al-Rfou, Bryan Perozzi, and Steven Skiena. 2015. Statistically Significant Detection of Linguistic Change. In *Proceedings of the 24th International Conference on World Wide Web*, 625–35. WWW '15. New York, NY, USA: ACM.

Le, Quoc, and Tomas Mikolov. 2014. Distributed Representations of Sentences and Documents. In *Proceedings of the 31st International Conference on Machine Learning*, 1188–96.

Mikolov, T., W.T. Yih, and G. Zweig. 2013a. Linguistic Regularities in Continuous Space Word Representations. In *HLT-NAACL*, 746–51.

Mikolov, Tomas, Ilya Sutskever, Kai Chen, Greg S Corrado, and Jeff Dean. 2013b. Distributed Representations of Words and Phrases and Their Compositionality. In *Advances in Neural Information Processing Systems 26*, edited by C. J. C. Burges, L. Bottou, M. Welling, Z. Ghahramani, and K. Q. Weinberger, 3111–9. Curran Associates, Inc.

Roberts, Margaret E., Brandon M. Stewart, Dustin Tingley, Christopher Lucas, Jetson Leder-Luis, Shana Kushner Gadarian, Bethany Albertson, and David G. Rand. 2014. "Structural Topic Models for Open-Ended Survey Responses." *American Journal of Political Science* 58 (4): 1064–82.

#WhoAmI in 160 Characters? Classifying Social Identities Based on Twitter Profile Descriptions

Anna Priante
Public Administation
University of Twente
a.priante@utwente.nl

Djoerd Hiemstra
Database Group
University of Twente
d.hiemstra@utwente.nl

Tijs van den Broek
NIKOS
University of Twente
t.a.vandenbroek@utwente.nl

Aaqib Saeed
Computer Science
University of Twente
a.saeed@student.utwente.nl

Michel Ehrenhard
NIKOS
University of Twente
m.l.ehrenhard@utwente.nl

Ariana Need
Public Administation
University of Twente
a.need@utwente.nl

Abstract

We combine social theory and NLP methods to classify English-speaking Twitter users' online social identity in profile descriptions. We conduct two text classification experiments. In Experiment 1 we use a 5-category online social identity classification based on identity and self-categorization theories. While we are able to automatically classify two identity categories (Relational and Occupational), automatic classification of the other three identities (Political, Ethnic/religious and Stigmatized) is challenging. In Experiment 2 we test a merger of such identities based on theoretical arguments. We find that by combining these identities we can improve the predictive performance of the classifiers in the experiment. Our study shows how social theory can be used to guide NLP methods, and how such methods provide input to revisit traditional social theory that is strongly consolidated in offline settings.

1 Introduction

Non-profit organizations increasingly use social media, such as Twitter, to mobilize people and organize cause-related collective action, such as health advocacy campaigns.

Studies in social psychology (Postmes and Brunsting, 2002; Van Zomeren et al., 2008; Park and Yang, 2012; Alberici and Milesi, 2013; Chan, 2014; Thomas et al., 2015) demonstrate that *social identity* motivates people to participate in collective action, which is the joint pursuit of a common goal or interest (Olson, 1971). *Social identity* is an individual's

self-concept derived from social roles or memberships to social groups (Stryker, 1980; Tajfel, 1981; Turner et al., 1987; Stryker et al., 2000). The use of language is strongly associated with an individual's social identity (Bucholtz and Hall, 2005; Nguyen et al., 2014; Tamburrini et al., 2015). On Twitter, profile descriptions and tweets are online expressions of people's identities. Therefore, social media provide an enormous amount of data for social scientists interested in studying how identities are expressed online via language.

We identify two main research opportunities on online identity. First, online identity research is often confined to relatively small datasets. Social scientists rarely exploit computational methods to measure identity over social media. Such methods may offer tools to enrich online identity research. For example, Natural Language Processing (NLP) and Machine Learning (ML) methods assist to quickly classify and infer vast amounts of data. Various studies investigate how to predict individual characteristics from language use on Twitter, such as age and gender (Rao et al., 2010; Burger et al., 2011; Al Zamal et al., 2012; Van Durme, 2012; Ciot et al., 2013; Nguyen et al., 2013; Nguyen et al., 2014; Preotiuc-Pietro et al., 2015), personality and emotions (Preotiuc-Pietro et al., 2015; Volkova et al., 2015; Volkova and Bachrach, 2015), political orientation and ethnicity (Rao et al., 2010; Pennacchiotti and Popescu, 2011; Al Zamal et al., 2012; Cohen and Ruths, 2013; Volkova et al., 2014), profession and interests (Al Zamal et al., 2012; Li et al., 2014).

Second, only a few studies combine social theory and NLP methods to study online identity in

Proceedings of 2016 EMNLP Workshop on Natural Language Processing and Computational Social Science, pages 55–65,
Austin, TX, November 5, 2016. ©2016 Association for Computational Linguistics

relation to collective action. One recent example uses the Social Identity Model of Collective Action (Van Zomeren et al., 2008) to study health campaigns organized on Twitter (Nguyen et al., 2015). The authors automatically identify participants' motivations to take action online by analyzing profile descriptions and tweets.

In this line, our study contributes to scale-up research on online identity. We explore automatic text classification of online identities based on a 5-category social identity classification built on theories of identity. We analyze 2633 English-speaking Twitter users' 160-characters profile description to classify their social identities. We only focus on profile descriptions as they represent the most immediate, essential expression of an individual's identity.

We conduct two classification experiments: Experiment 1 is based on the original 5-category social identity classification, whereas Experiment 2 tests a merger of three categories for which automatic classification does not work in Experiment 1. We show that by combining these identities we can improve the predictive performance of the classifiers in the experiment.

Our study makes two main contributions. First, we combine social theory on identity and NLP methods to classify English-speaking Twitter users' online social identities. We show how social theory can be used to guide NLP methods, and how such methods provide input to revisit traditional social theory that is strongly consolidated in offline settings.

Second, we evaluate different classification algorithms in the task of automatically classifying online social identities. We show that computers can perform a reliable automatic classification for most social identity categories. In this way, we provide social scientists with new tools (i.e., social identity classifiers) for scaling-up online identity research to massive datasets derived from social media.

The rest of the paper is structured as follows. First, we illustrate the theoretical framework and the online social identity classification which guides the text classification experiments (Section 2). Second, we explain the data collection (Section 3) and methods (Section 4). Third, we report the results of the two experiments (Section 5 and 6). Finally, we discuss our findings and provide recommendations for future research (Section 7).

2   Theoretical Framework: a 5-category Online Social Identity Classification Grounded in Social Theory

We define *social identity* as an individual's self-definition based on social roles played in society or memberships of social groups. This definition combines two main theories in social psychology: identity theory (Stryker, 1980; Stryker et al., 2000) and social identity, or self-categorization, theory (Tajfel, 1981; Turner et al., 1987), which respectively focus on social roles and memberships of social groups. We combine these two theories as together they provide a more complete definition of identity (Stets and Burke, 2000). The likelihood of participating in collective action does increase when individuals both identify themselves with a social group and are committed to the role(s) they play in the group (Stets and Burke, 2000).

We create a 5-category online social identity classification that is based on previous studies of offline settings (Deaux et al., 1995; Ashforth et al., 2008; Ashforth et al., 2016). We apply such classification to Twitter users' profile descriptions as they represent the most immediate, essential expression of an individual's identity (Jensen and Bang, 2013). While tweets mostly feature statements and conversations, the profile description provides a dedicated, even limited (160 characters), space where users can write about the self-definitions they want to communicate on Twitter.

The five social identity categories of our classification are:

(1) Relational identity: self-definition based on (reciprocal or unreciprocal) relationships that an individual has with other people, and on social roles played by the individual in society. Examples on Twitter are *"I am the father of an amazing baby girl!"*, *"Happily married to @John"*, *"Crazy Justin Bieber fan"*, *"Manchester United team is my family"*.

(2) Occupational identity: self-definition based on occupation, profession and career, individual vocations, avocations, interests and hobbies. Examples on Twitter are *"Manager Communication expert"*, *"I am a Gamer, YouTuber"*, *"Big fan of pizza!"*, *"Writing about my passions: love cooking traveling reading"*.

(3) Political identity: self-definition based on political affiliations, parties and groups, as well as being a member of social movements or taking part in collective action. Examples on Twitter are *"Feminist Activist"*, *"I am Democrat"*, *"I'm a council candidate in local elections for []"*, *"mobro in #movember"*, *"#BlackLivesMatter"*.

(4) Ethnic/Religious identity: self-definition based on membership of ethnic or religious groups. Examples on Twitter are *"God first"*, *"Will also tweet about #atheism"*, *"Native Washingtonian"*, *"Scottish no Australian no-both?"*.

(5) Stigmatized identity: self-definition based on membership of a stigmatized group, which is considered different from what the society defines as normal according to social and cultural norms (Goffman, 1959). Examples on Twitter are *"People call me an affectionate idiot"*, *"I know people call me a dork and that's okay with me"*. Twitter users also attach a stigma to themselves with an ironic tone. Examples are *"I am an idiot savant"*, *"Workaholic man with ADHD"*, *"I didn't choose the nerd life, the nerd life chose me'*.

Social identity categories are not mutually exclusive. Individuals may have more than one social identity and embed all identities in their definition of the self. On Twitter, it is common to find users who express more than one identity in the profile description. For example, *"Mom of 2 boys, wife and catholic conservative, school and school sport volunteer"*, *"Proud Northerner, Arsenal fan by luck. Red Level and AST member. Gamer. Sports fan. English Civic Nationalist. Contributor at HSR. Pro-#rewilding"*.

3 Data Collection

We collect data by randomly sampling English tweets. From the tweets, we retrieve the user's profile description. We remove all profiles (i.e, 30% of the total amount) where no description is provided.

We are interested in developing an automatic classification tool (i.e., social identity classifier) that can be used to study identities of both people engaged in online collective action and general Twitter users. For this purpose, we use two different sources to collect our data: (1) English tweets from two-year (2013 and 2014) Movember cancer awareness campaign[1], which aims at changing the image of men's health (i.e., prostate and testicular cancer, mental health and physical inactivity); and (2) English random tweets posted in February and March 2015 obtained via the Twitter Streaming API. We select the tweets from the UK, US and Australia, which are the three largest countries with native English speakers. For this selection, we use a country classifier, which has been found to be fairly accurate in predicting tweets' geolocation for these countries (Van der Veen et al., 2015). As on Twitter only 2% of tweets are geo-located, we decide to use this classifier to get the data for our text classification.

From these two data sources, we obtain two Twitter user populations: Movember participants and random generic users. We sample from these two groups to have a similar number of profiles in our dataset. We obtain 1,611 Movember profiles and 1,022 random profiles. Our final dataset consists of 2,633 Twitter users' profile descriptions.

4 Methods

In this study, we combine qualitative content analysis with human annotation (Section 4.1) and text classification experiment (Section 4.2).

4.1 Qualitative Content Analysis with Human Annotation

We use qualitative content analysis to manually annotate our 2,633 Twitter users' profile descriptions. Two coders are involved in the annotation. The coders meet in training and testing sessions to agree upon rules and build a codebook[2] that guides the annotation. The identity categories of our codebook are based on the 5-category social identity classification described in Section 2. In the annotation, a Twitter profile description is labeled with "Yes" or "No" for each category label, depending on whether the profile belongs to such category or not. Multiple identities may be assigned to a single Twitter user (i.e., identity categories are not mutually exclusive). We calculate the inter-rater relia-

---

[1]This data was obtained via a Twitter datagrant, see https://blog.twitter.com/2014/twitter-datagrants-selections

[2]The codebook, code and datasets used in the experiments are available at https://github.com/annapriante/identityclassifier

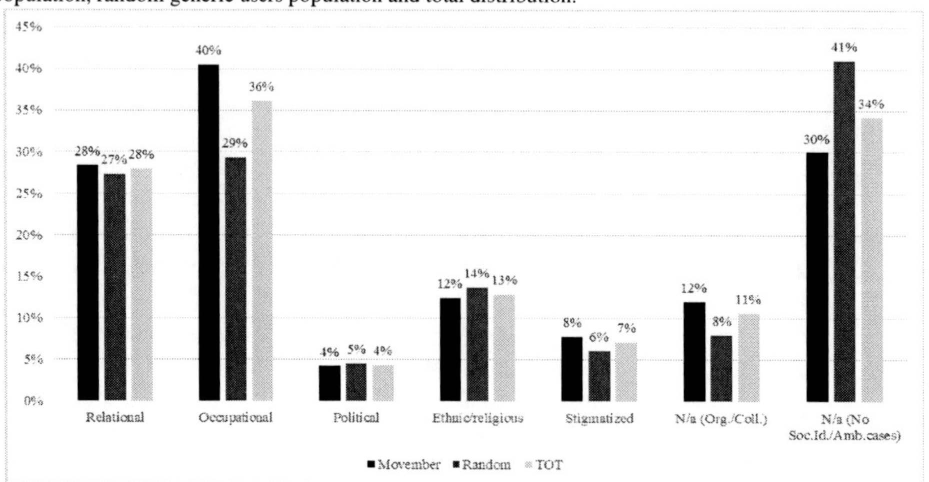

bility using Krippendorff's alpha, or Kalpha[3] (Krippendorff, 2004) based on 300 double annotations. Kalpha values are very good for all categories (Relational=0.902; Occupational=0.891; Political=0.919; Ethnic/Religious=0.891; Stigmatized=0.853).

The definition of social identity is applicable only to one individual. Accounts that belong to more than one person, or to collectives, groups, or organizations (N=280), are annotated as "Not applicable", or "N/a" (Kalpha=0.8268). Such category also includes individual profiles (N=900) for which: 1) no social identity category fits (e.g., profiles contain quote/citations/self-promotion; or individual attributes descriptions with no reference to social roles or group membership); and 2) ambiguous or incomprehensible cases[4].

Looking at the distributions of social identity categories in the annotated profile descriptions provides an overview of the types of Twitter users in our data. We check if such distributions differ in the two populations (i.e., Movember participants and random generic users). We find that each identity category is similarly distributed in the two groups (Figure 1). We conclude that the two populations are thus similar in their members' social identities.

Figure 1 shows the distributions of social identity categories over the total amount of annotated profiles (N=2,633). N/a profile descriptions are the 45% (N=1180) of the total number of profiles: organizations/collective profiles are 11% (N=280), whereas no social identity profiles/ambiguous cases are 34% (N=900). It means that only a little more than a half, i.e., the remaining 55% profiles (N=1,453), of the Twitter users in our dataset have one or more social identities. Users mainly define themselves on the basis of their occupation or interests (Occupational identities=36%), and social roles played in society or relationships with others (Relational identities=28%). By contrast, individuals do not often describe themselves in terms of political or social movement affiliation, ethnicity, nationality, religion, or stigmatized group membership. Political, Ethnic/Religious and Stigmatized identities categories are less frequent (respectively, 4%, 13% and 7%).

4.2 Automatic Text Classification

We use machine learning to automatically assign predefined identity categories to 160-character Twitter profile descriptions (N=2,633), that are manually annotated as explained in Section 4.1. For each identity category we want to classify whether the profile description belongs to a category or not. We thus

---

[3]We use Krippendorff's alpha as it is considered the most reliable inter-coder reliability statistics in content analysis.

[4]We keep N/a profiles in our dataset to let the classifiers learn that those profiles are not examples of social identities. Such choice considerably increases the number of negative examples over the positive ones that are used to detect the identity categories. However, we find that including or excluding N/a profiles does not make any significant difference in the classifiers performance.

treat the social identity classification as a binary text classification problem, where each class label can take only two values (i.e. yes or no).

We use automatic text classification and develop binary classifiers in two experiments. Experiment 1 is based on the 5-category social identity classification explained in Section 2. In Experiment 1, we compare the classifiers performance in two scenarios. First, we use a combined dataset made by both Movember participants and random generic users. Profiles are randomly assigned to a training set (Combined(1): N=2338) and a test set (Combined(2): N=295). Second, we use separated datasets, i.e., random generic users as training set (Random: N=1022) and Movember participants as test set (Movember: N=1611), and vice versa.

Experiment 2 is a follow-up of Experiment 1 and we use only combined data[5]. We test a merger of three social identity categories (i.e., Political, Ethnic/religious and Stigmatized) for which we do not obtain acceptable results in Experiment 1.

4.2.1 Features Extraction

We use TF-IDF weighting (Salton and Buckley, 1988) to extract useful features from the user's profile description. We measure how important a word, or term, is in the text. Terms with a high TF-IDF score occur more frequently in the text and provide the most of information. In addition, we adopt standard text processing techniques, such as Lowercasing and Stop words, to clean up the feature set (Sebastiani, 2002). We use the Chi Square feature selection on the profile description term matrix resulted from the TF-IDF weighting to select the terms that are mostly correlated with the specific identity category (Sebastiani, 2002).

4.2.2 Classification Algorithms

In the automatic text classification experiments, we evaluate four classification algorithms. First, we use Support Vector machine (SVM) with a linear kernel, which requires less parameters to optimize and is faster compared to other kernel functions, such as Polynomial kernel (Joachims, 1998). Balanced mode is used to automatically adjust

weights for class labels. Second, Bernoulli Naïve Bayes (BNB) is applied with the Laplace smoothing value set to 1. Third, Logistic Regression (LR) is trained with balanced subsample technique to provide weights for class labels. Fourth, the Random Forest (RF) classifier is trained with 100 trees to speed up the computation compared to a higher number of trees, for which no significant difference has been found in the classifier performance. Balanced subsample technique is used to provide weights for class labels.

4.2.3 Evaluation Measures

Experimental evaluation of the classifiers is conducted to determine their performance, i.e., the degree of correct classification. We compare the four classification algorithms on the training sets using Stratified 10-Fold Cross Validation. This technique seeks to ensure that each fold is a good representative of the whole dataset and it is considered better than regular cross validation in terms of bias-variance trade-offs (Kohavi and others, 1995). In feature selection, we check for different subsets of features (i.e., 500, 1000, 2000, 3000, 4000 and 5000) with the highest Chi Square from the original feature set, which consists of highly informative features. We find that 1000 features are the most informative.

Furthermore, we calculate precision (P), recall (R) and F-score to assess the accuracy and completeness of the classifiers. The classification algorithm that provide the best performance according to F-score in the Stratified 10-Fold Cross Validation is then tested on the test sets to get better insight into the classification results.

5   Classification Experiment 1

In this section, we present the results of Experiment 1 on automatically identifying 5 online social identities based on the annotated Twitter profile descriptions. In Section 5.1, we show the results of the Stratified 10 Fold Cross Validation in three training sets, i.e., Combined(1), Movember and Random. In Section 5.2, we illustrate and discuss the results of the best classification algorithm on the test sets.

---

[5]We conduct Experiment 2 only on the combined set because in Experiment 1 we find that classifiers trained on the combined data performs better than trained on separated sets.

Table 1: Relational and Occupational identities. Stratified 10 Fold Cross Validation in three training sets: precision (P), recall (R) and F-score.

Classifier	Training Set	RELATIONAL			OCCUPATIONAL		
		P	R	F	P	R	F
SVM	Combined(1)	0.764	0.705	0.723	0.827	0.793	0.804
	Movember	0.792	0.709	0.729	0.822	0.788	0.797
	Random	0.742	0.624	0.634	0.845	0.715	0.742
BNB	Combined(1)	0.855	0.635	0.652	0.848	0.769	0.788
	Movember	0.848	0.616	0.619	0.846	0.780	0.791
	Random	0.793*	0.524	0.471*	0.859	0.605	0.599
LR	Combined(1)	0.760	0.708	0.724	0.823	0.788	0.800
	Movember	0.786	0.718	0.735	0.817	0.789	0.796
	Random	0.717	0.627	0.637	0.848	0.721	0.748
RF	Combined(1)	0.803	0.660	0.682	0.842	0.780	0.797
	Movember	0.836	0.671	0.692	0.817	0.774	0.783
	Random	0.789	0.583	0.577	0.857	0.706	0.733

Table 2: Political, Ethnic/religious and Stigmatized identities. Stratified 10 Fold Cross Validation in three training sets: precision (P), recall (R) and F-score.

Classifier	Training Set	POLITICAL			ETHNIC/RELIGIOUS			STIGMATIZED		
		P	R	F	P	R	F	P	R	F
SVM	Combined(1)	0.646*	0.548	0.563*	0.750	0.594	0.619	0.713*	0.551	0.573*
	Movember	0.680*	0.529	0.541*	0.740	0.585	0.609	0.825	0.592	0.629
	Random	0.528*	0.510	0.505*	0.784	0.581	0.602	0.520*	0.507	0.498*
BNB	Combined(1)	0.482	0.500	0.491	0.572*	0.506	0.483*	0.478	0.500	0.488
	Movember	0.479*	0.500	0.489*	0.664	0.512	0.491	0.561*	0.507	0.494*
	Random	0.478	0.500	0.488	0.432	0.500	0.463	0.470	0.500	0.484
LR	Combined(1)	0.662	0.540	0.554	0.724	0.600	0.626	0.781	0.564	0.593
	Movember	0.655	0.536	0.550	0.720	0.603	0.628	0.742	0.589	0.621
	Random	0.528	0.509	0.505	0.751	0.592	0.613	0.52	0.506	0.498
RF	Combined(1)	0.633*	0.524	0.532*	0.856*	0.526	0.523*	0.654	0.519	0.524*
	Movember	0.479*	0.500	0.489*	0.848*	0.551	0.560*	0.884*	0.585	0.623*
	Random	0.478*	0.500	0.488*	0.672	0.524	0.508	0.470*	0.500	0.484*

5.1 Stratified 10 Fold Cross Validation Results on Five Social Identity Categories

Relational identity. All classifiers provide very precise results (P>0.700) for the Relational identity category in the all three training sets (Table 1). The most precise classification algorithm is BNB in the combined set (P=0.855). By contrast, recall is quite low (0.500<R<0.700) in all classifiers in each training set, thus affecting the final F-scores. The classification algorithm with the highest recall is LR in the Movember set (R=0.708). According to F-scores, all classifiers provide from acceptable (0.400<F<0.690) to good/excellent (F>0.700) results. Classifiers trained on the Movember set provide the highest F-scores, except for BNB where F-score is higher in the combined set. By contrast, the

Random set provides the lowest performances in all cases. Overall, LR is the most precise and complete classifier in all three training sets (combined: F=0.724; Movember: F=0.735; Random: F=0.637).

Occupational identity. All classifiers provide very high precision (P>0.800) and recall (R>0.750) for the Occupational identity category (Table 1). The most precise classification algorithm is BNB in the Random set (P=0.859), whereas the classification algorithm with the highest recall is SVM in the combined set (R=0.793). According to F-scores, all classifiers provide good and excellent performances (F>0.700), except for BNB in the Random set (F=0.599). Classifiers trained on the combined set provide the highest F-scores, except for BNB where F-score is higher in the Movember set. By contrast, the Random set provides the lowest performances. Overall, SVM and LR provide the best F-scores in all three training set.

Political, Ethnic/religious and Stigmatized identities. Classifiers perform less well in automatically classifying Political, Ethnic/religious and Stigmatized identities than in Relational and Occupational ones (Table 2). Both precision and recall are almost acceptable ($0.400 < P, R < 0.690$) in all three training sets. When training SVM, BNB and RF, we get ill-defined precision and F-score, which are consequently set to 0.0 in labels with no predicted samples (in Table 2, these values are marked with a *). As we noticed earlier in Figure 1, the low number of positive examples of Political, Ethnic/religious and Stigmatized identities in the data may cause this outcome. Classifiers trained on combined and Movember sets provide similar results, whereas the Random set provides the lowest performance. Overall, LR classifier provide the best F-scores for each category in all training sets.

5.2 LR Classifier Testing

Stratified 10 Fold Cross Validation show that the optimal classification algorithm for each identity category is LR. The LR classifier is evaluated on the test sets in order to get better insight into the classification results. Since we use three training sets, we evaluate the classifier on three different test sets as explained in Section 4.2.

According to the F-scores (Table 3), we are able to automatically classify Relational and Occupational identities in all three test sets. LR trained and tested on combined data provides the best results (Relational: F=0.699; Occupational: F=0.766). Although in the Stratified 10 Fold Cross Validation the classifier trained on the Random set has lower performance than trained on the Movember set, in the final testing the classifier performs better when we use Random as training set and Movember as test set (Relational: F=0.594; Occupational: F=0.737).

Final training and testing using LR on Political, Ethnic/religious and Stigmatized identities (Table 4) is affected by the low number of positive examples in the test sets, as these identities are less frequent in our annotated sample. Classifying Political identities is the most difficult task for the classifier in all three test sets and the performance is very low (Combined(2): F=0.300; Random: F=0.266;

Movember: F=0.098). Regarding Ethnic/religious and Stigmatized identities, LR provides almost acceptable F-scores only on the combined data (Ethnic religious: F=0.543; Stigmatized: F=0.425).

5.3 Discussion: Merging Identity Categories

In Experiment 1 we show that a classifier trained on the combined data performs better than a classifier trained on only Movember profiles or Random profiles. Our results are of sufficient quality for Relational and Occupational identities on the combined set, and thus we are able to automatically classify such social identities on Twitter using LR. Experiment 1 also shows that automatically classifying Political, Ethnic/religious and Stigmatized identities may be a challenging task. Although LR provides acceptable F-scores in the Stratified 10 Fold Cross Validation, the classifier is not able to automatically classify those three identities. This may be due to unbalanced distributions of identity categories in our data, that thus affect the text classification experiment.

Despite of the unsatisfactory classifier performances in detecting Political, Ethnic/religious and Stigmatized identities, we conduct a second experiment to find an alternative way to classify such identities because of their importance in the study of collective action. Therefore, we find that using NLP methods invites us to go back to theory and revisit our framework.

People with strong Political, Ethnic/religious and/or Stigmatized identities are often more engaged in online and offline collective action (Ren et al., 2007; Spears et al., 2002). These identities have a collective, rather than individualistic, nature as they address individual membership to one or multiple social groups. By sharing a common identity with other group members, individuals may feel more committed to the group's topic or goal. Consequently, they may engage in collective action on behalf of the group, even in cases of power struggle, i.e., individuals have a *politicized identity*, see (Klandermans et al., 2002; Simon and Klandermans, 2001). Political, Ethnic/religious and/or Stigmatized identities are indeed action-oriented (Ren et al., 2007), rather than social statuses as for Relational and Occupational identities (Deaux et al., 1995). Thus, the collective, action-oriented nature

Table 3: LR Classifier Testing on Relational and Occupational identities: precision (P), recall (R) and F-score.

Training set	Test set	RELATIONAL			OCCUPATIONAL		
		P	R	F	P	R	F
Combined(1)	Combined(2)	0.757	0.648	0.699	0.743	0.791	0.766
Movember	Random	0.649	0.491	0.559	0.722	0.693	0.707
Random	Movember	0.638	0.555	0.594	0.814	0.673	0.737

Table 4: LR Classifier Testing on Political, Ethnic/religious and Stigmatized identities: precision (P), recall (R) and F-score.

Training set	Test set	POLITICAL			ETHNIC/RELIGIOUS			STIGMATIZED		
		P	R	F	P	R	F	P	R	F
Combined(1)	Combined(2)	0.600	0.200	0.300	0.661	0.460	0.543	0.958	0.273	0.425
Movember	Random	0.571	0.173	0.266	0.531	0.300	0.383	0.360	0.145	0.206
Random	Movember	0.307	0.058	0.098	0.364	0.250	0.296	0.444	0.126	0.197

of certain Political, Ethnic/religious and Stigmatized identities show how such identities may often overlap and consequently influence human behaviors and actions.

Following these theoretical arguments, we decide to merge Political, Ethnic/religious and Stigmatized identities in one category, called PES identity (N=556). In this way, we also provide more positive examples to the classifiers. In Experiment 2, we train and test again the four classification algorithms on the PES identity using the combined data. In the next section, we present the results of this second experiment and show that by combining these identities we can improve the predictive performance of the classifiers.

6   Classification Experiment 2

Table 5 shows value of precision, recall and F-score in the Stratified 10 Fold Cross Validation on the training set (i.e., Combined (1): N=2338) to select the optimal classifier. Overall, all classifiers provide quite acceptable performances for the PES identity category (0.500<F<0.650). Only when validating the BNB classifier, we obtain an ill-defined F-score (in Table 5, this value is marked with a *). RF is the most precise classification algorithm (P=0.758), whereas LR has the highest recall (R=0.608). As in Experiment 1, LR is the optimal classifier with the highest F-score (F=0.623).

LR classifier is evaluated on the test set (i.e., Combined (2): N=295) to get better insight into the classification results. The classifier is highly precise in identifying PES identities (P=0.857). By contrast, recall is quite low (R=0.466), thus affecting

Table 5: PES identity. Stratified 10 Fold Cross Validation on combined data: precision (P), recall (R) and F-score.

Classifier	P	R	F
SVM	0.664	0.583	0.595
BNB	0.750	0.524	0.504*
LR	0.678	0.608	0.623
RF	0.758	0.543	0.540

final F-score (F=0.604). In conclusion, only if we merge political, religious and stigmatized identities, the classifier performance is acceptable.

7   Final Discussion and Conclusions

In this study, we explore the task of automatically classifying Twitter social identities of Movember participants and random generic users in two text classification experiments. We are able to automatically classify two identity categories (Relational and Occupational) and a 3-identity category merger (Political, Ethnic/religious and Stigmatized). Furthermore, we find that a classifier trained on the combined data performs better than a classifier trained on one group (e.g. Random) and test on the other one (e.g. Movember).

We make two main contributions from which both social theory on identity and NLP methods can benefit. First, by combining the two we find that social theory can be used to guide NLP methods to quickly classify and infer vast amounts of data in social media. Furthermore, using NLP methods can provide input to revisit traditional social theory that is often strongly consolidated in offline settings.

Second, we show that computers can perform a reliable automatic classification for most types of social identities on Twitter. In NLP research there is already much earlier work on inferring demographic traits, therefore it may not be surprising that at least some of these identities can be easily inferred on Twitter. Our contribution is in the second experiment, where we show that merged identities are useful features to improve the predictive performance of the classifiers. In such way, we provide social scientists with three social identity classifiers (i.e., Relational, Occupational and PES identities) grounded in social theory that can scale-up online identity research to massive datasets. Social identity classifiers may assist researchers interested in the relation between language and identity, and identity and collective action. In practice, they can be exploited by organizations to target specific audiences and improve their campaign strategies.

Our study presents some limitations that future research may address and improve. First, we retrieve the user' profile description from randomly sampled tweets. In this way, people who tweet a lot have a bigger chance of ending up in our data. Future research could explore alternative ways of profile description retrieval that avoid biases of this kind.

Second, our social identity classifiers are based only on 160-characters profile descriptions, which alone may not be sufficient features for the text classification. We plan to test the classifiers also on tweets, other profile information and network features. Furthermore, the 160-character limitation constrains Twitter users to carefully select which identities express in such a short space. In our study, we do not investigate identity salience, that is, the degree or probability that an identity is more prominent than others in the text. Future research that combine sociolinguistics and NLP methods could investigate how semantics are associated to identity salience, and how individuals select and order their multiple identities on Twitter texts.

Third, in the experiments we use standard text classification techniques that are not particularly novel in NLP research. However, they are simple, effective ways to provide input for social theory. We plan to improve the classifiers performance by including other features, such as n-grams and cluster of words. Furthermore, we will explore larger datasets and include more training data for further experimentation with more complex techniques (e.g., neural networks, World2Vec).

Acknowledgments

Thanks to Balsam Awlad Wadair for the valuable help in the manual annotation; Dong Nguyen, Robin Aly, Fons Wijnhoven, Fons Mentink, Koen Kuijpers and Mike Visser for helpful discussions and feedback; and Twitter for providing part of the tweets used in this study through the Twitter DataGrant. Thanks also to the anonymous reviewers for their helpful comments.

References

Faiyaz Al Zamal, Wendy Liu, and Derek Ruths. 2012. Homophily and latent attribute inference: Inferring latent attributes of twitter users from neighbors. *ICWSM*, 270.

Augusta Isabella Alberici and Patrizia Milesi. 2013. The influence of the internet on the psychosocial predictors of collective action. *Journal of Community & Applied Social Psychology*, 23(5):373–388.

Blake E. Ashforth, Spencer H. Harrison, and Kevin G. Corley. 2008. Identification in organizations: An examination of four fundamental questions. *Journal of Management*, 34(3):325–374.

Blake E. Ashforth, Beth S. Schinoff, and Kristie M. Rogers. 2016. i identify with her,i identify with him: Unpacking the dynamics of personal identification in organizations. *Academy of Management Review*, 41(1):28–60.

Mary Bucholtz and Kira Hall. 2005. Identity and interaction: A sociocultural linguistic approach. *Discourse studies*, 7(4-5):585–614.

John D. Burger, John Henderson, George Kim, and Guido Zarrella. 2011. Discriminating gender on twitter. In *Proceedings of the Conference on Empirical Methods in Natural Language Processing*, pages 1301–1309. Association for Computational Linguistics.

Michael Chan. 2014. Social identity gratifications of social network sites and their impact on collective action participation. *Asian Journal of Social Psychology*, 17(3):229–235.

Morgane Ciot, Morgan Sonderegger, and Derek Ruths. 2013. Gender inference of twitter users in non-english contexts. In *EMNLP*, pages 1136–1145.

Raviv Cohen and Derek Ruths. 2013. Classifying political orientation on twitter: It's not easy! In *Proceedings of the Seventh International AAAI Conference on Weblogs and Social Media*.

Kay Deaux, Anne Reid, Kim Mizrahi, and Kathleen A Ethier. 1995. Parameters of social identity. *Journal of personality and social psychology*, 68(2):280.

Erving Goffman. 1959. The presentation of self in everyday life. *Garden City, NY*.

Michael J. Jensen and Henrik P. Bang. 2013. Occupy wall street: A new political form of movement and community? *Journal of Information Technology & Politics*, 10(4):444–461.

Thorsten Joachims. 1998. Text categorization with support vector machines: Learning with many relevant features. In *European conference on machine learning*, pages 137–142. Springer.

Bert Klandermans, Jose Manuel Sabucedo, Mauro Rodriguez, and Marga De Weerd. 2002. Identity processes in collective action participation: Farmers' identity and farmers' protest in the netherlands and spain. *Political Psychology*, 23(2):235–251.

Ron Kohavi et al. 1995. A study of cross-validation and bootstrap for accuracy estimation and model selection. In *Ijcai*, volume 14, pages 1137–1145.

Klaus Krippendorff. 2004. Reliability in content analysis. *Human communication research*, 30(3):411–433.

Jiwei Li, Alan Ritter, and Eduard H Hovy. 2014. Weakly supervised user profile extraction from twitter. In *ACL (1)*, pages 165–174.

Dong Nguyen, Rilana. Gravel, Dolf Trieschnigg, and Theo Meder. 2013. "how old do you think i am?" a study of language and age in twitter. In *Proceedings of the Seventh International AAAI Conference on Weblogs and Social Media, ICWSM 2013, Cambridge, MA, USA*, pages 439–448, Palo Alto, CA, USA, July. AAAI Press.

Dong Nguyen, Dolf Trieschnigg, A. Seza Dogruoz, Rilana Gravel, Mariet Theune, Theo Meder, and Franciska de Jong. 2014. Why gender and age prediction from tweets is hard: Lessons from a crowdsourcing experiment. In *Proceedings of COLING 2014, the 25th International Conference on Computational Linguistics: Technical Papers*, page 19501961. Association for Computational Linguistics, Dublin, Ireland, August 23-29 2014.

Dong Nguyen, Tijs van den Broek, Claudia Hauff, Djoerd Hiemstra, and Michel Ehrenhard. 2015. #supportthecause: Identifying motivations to participate in online health campaigns. In *Proceedings of the 2015 Conference on Empirical Methods in Natural Language Processing, EMNLP 2015, Lisbon, Portugal*, pages 2570–2576, New York, USA, September. Association for Computational Linguistics.

Mancur Olson. 1971. *The Logic of Collective Action: Public Goods and the Theory of Groups, Second printing with new preface and appendix (Harvard Economic Studies)*. Harvard economic studies, v. 124. Harvard University Press, revised edition.

Namkee Park and Aimei Yang. 2012. Online environmental community members intention to participate in environmental activities: An application of the theory of planned behavior in the chinese context. *Computers in human behavior*, 28(4):1298–1306.

Marco Pennacchiotti and Ana-Maria Popescu. 2011. A machine learning approach to twitter user classification. *Proceedings of the Fifth International AAAI Conference on Weblogs and Social Media*, 11(1):281–288.

Tom Postmes and Suzanne Brunsting. 2002. Collective action in the age of the internet mass communication and online mobilization. *Social Science Computer Review*, 20(3):290–301.

Daniel Preotiuc-Pietro, Johannes Eichstaedt, Gregory Park, Maarten Sap, Laura Smith, Victoria Tobolsky, H Andrew Schwartz, and Lyle Ungar. 2015. The role of personality, age and gender in tweeting about mental illnesses. *NAACL HLT 2015*, page 21.

Delip Rao, David Yarowsky, Abhishek Shreevats, and Manaswi Gupta. 2010. Classifying latent user attributes in twitter. In *Proceedings of the 2nd international workshop on Search and mining user-generated contents*, pages 37–44. ACM.

Yuqing Ren, Robert Kraut, and Sara Kiesler. 2007. Applying common identity and bond theory to design of online communities. *Organization studies*, 28(3):377–408.

Gerard Salton and Christopher Buckley. 1988. Term-weighting approaches in automatic text retrieval. *Information processing & management*, 24(5):513–523.

Fabrizio Sebastiani. 2002. Machine learning in automated text categorization. *ACM computing surveys (CSUR)*, 34(1):1–47.

Bernd Simon and Bert Klandermans. 2001. Politicized collective identity: A social psychological analysis. *American psychologist*, 56(4):319.

Russell Spears, Martin Lea, Rolf Arne Corneliussen, Tom Postmes, and Wouter Ter Haar. 2002. Computer-mediated communication as a channel for social resistance the strategic side of side. *Small Group Research*, 33(5):555–574.

Jan E. Stets and Peter J. Burke. 2000. Identity theory and social identity theory. *Social psychology quarterly*, pages 224–237.

Sheldon Stryker, Timothy Joseph Owens, and Robert W White. 2000. *Self, identity, and social movements*, volume 13. University of Minnesota Press.

Sheldon Stryker. 1980. *Symbolic interactionism: A social structural version*. Benjamin-Cummings Publishing Company.

Henri Tajfel. 1981. *Human groups and social categories: Studies in social psychology*. CUP Archive.

Nadine Tamburrini, Marco Cinnirella, Vincent AA Jansen, and John Bryden. 2015. Twitter users change word usage according to conversation-partner social identity. *Social Networks*, 40:84–89.

Emma F. Thomas, Craig McGarty, Girish Lala, Avelie Stuart, Lauren J. Hall, and Alice Goddard. 2015. Whatever happened to kony2012? understanding a global internet phenomenon as an emergent social identity. *European Journal of Social Psychology*, 45(3):356–367.

John C. Turner, Michael A. Hogg, Penelope J. Oakes, Stephen D. Reicher, and Margaret S. Wetherell. 1987. *Rediscovering the social group: A self-categorization theory*. Basil Blackwell.

Han Van der Veen, Djoerd Hiemstra, Tijs van den Broek, Michel Ehrenhard, and Ariana Need. 2015. Determine the user country of a tweet. *arXiv preprint arXiv:1508.02483*.

Benjamin Van Durme. 2012. Streaming analysis of discourse participants. In *Proceedings of the 2012 Joint Conference on Empirical Methods in Natural Language Processing and Computational Natural Language Learning*, pages 48–58. Association for Computational Linguistics.

Martijn Van Zomeren, Tom Postmes, and Russell Spears. 2008. Toward an integrative social identity model of collective action: a quantitative research synthesis of three socio-psychological perspectives. *Psychological bulletin*, 134(4):504.

Svitlana Volkova and Yoram Bachrach. 2015. On predicting sociodemographic traits and emotions from communications in social networks and their implications to online self-disclosure. *Cyberpsychology, Behavior, and Social Networking*, 18(12):726–736.

Svitlana Volkova, Glen Coppersmith, and Benjamin Van Durme. 2014. Inferring user political preferences from streaming communications. In *ACL (1)*, pages 186–196.

Svitlana Volkova, Yoram Bachrach, Michael Armstrong, and Vijay Sharma. 2015. Inferring latent user properties from texts published in social media. In *AAAI*, pages 4296–4297. Citeseer.

Identifying Stance by Analyzing Political Discourse on Twitter

Kristen Johnson
Purdue University
West Lafayette, IN 47907, USA
john1187@purdue.edu

Dan Goldwasser
Purdue University
West Lafayette, IN 47907, USA
dgoldwas@purdue.edu

Abstract

Politicians often use Twitter to express their beliefs, stances on current political issues, and reactions concerning national and international events. Since politicians are scrutinized for what they choose or neglect to say, they craft their statements carefully. Thus despite the limited length of tweets, their content is highly indicative of a politician's stances. We present a weakly supervised method for understanding the stances held by politicians, on a wide array of issues, by analyzing how issues are framed in their tweets and their temporal activity patterns. We combine these components into a global model which collectively infers the most likely stance and agreement patterns.

1 Introduction

Recently the popularity of traditional media outlets such as television and printed press has decreased, causing politicians to turn their attention to social media outlets, which allow them to directly access the public, express their beliefs, and react to current events. This trend emerged during the 2008 U.S. presidential election campaign and has since moved to the mainstream – in the 2016 campaign, all candidates employ social media platforms. One of the most notable examples of this trend is the microblogging outlet Twitter, which unlike its predecessors, requires candidates to compress their ideas, political stances, and reactions into 140 character long tweets. As a result, candidates have to cleverly choose how to frame controversial issues, as well as react to events and each other (Mejova et al., 2013; Tumasjan et al., 2010).

In this work we present a novel approach for modeling the microblogging activity of presidential candidates and other prominent politicians. We look into two aspects of the problem, *stance* prediction over a wide array of issues, as well as *agreement and disagreement* patterns between politicians over these issues. While the two aspects are related, we argue they capture different information, as identifying agreement patterns reveals alliances and rivalries between candidates, across and inside their party. We show that understanding the political discourse on microblogs requires modeling both the content of posted messages as well as the social context in which they are generated, and suggest a joint model capturing both aspects.

Converse to other works predicting stance per individual tweet (SemEval, 2016), we use the *overall* Twitter behavior to predict a *politician's* stance on an issue. We argue that these settings are better suited for the political arena on Twitter. Given the limit of 140 characters, the stance relevance of a tweet is not independent of the social context in which it was generated. In an extreme case, even the lack of Twitter activity on certain topics can be indicative of a stance. Additionally, framing issues in order to create bias towards their stance is a tool often used by politicians to contextualize the discussion (Tsur et al., 2015; Card et al., 2015; Boydstun et al., 2014). Previous works exploring framing analyze text in traditional settings, such as congressional speeches or newspaper articles. To apply framing analysis to Twitter data, we allow tweets to hold multiple frames when necessary, as we find that on average many tweets are relevant to two frames per issue. This approach allows our model to make use of changing and similar framing patterns over

Proceedings of 2016 EMNLP Workshop on Natural Language Processing and Computational Social Science, pages 66–75,
Austin, TX, November 5, 2016. ©2016 Association for Computational Linguistics

(1) **Hillary Clinton (@HillaryClinton):** *We need to keep guns out of the hands of domestic abusers and convicted stalkers.*
(2) **Donald Trump (@realDonaldTrump):** *Politicians are trying to chip away at the 2nd Amendment. I won't let them take away our guns!*
(3) **Bernie Sanders (@SenSanders):** *We need sensible gun-control legislation which prevents guns from being used by people who should not have them .*

Figure 1: Tweets on the issue of gun control, highlighting issue indicators in green and different frame indicators in yellow.

politicians' timelines in order to increase our prediction accuracy.

For example, consider the issue of gun control. Figure 1 shows three issue-related tweets by three politicians. To correctly identify the stance taken by each of the politicians, our model must combine three aspects. First, the relevance of these tweets to the question can be identified using *issue* indicators (marked in green). Second, the similarity between the stances taken by two of the three politicians can be identified by observing how the issue is *framed* (marked in yellow). In this example, tweets (1) and (3) frame the issue of gun control as a matter of safety, while (2) frames it as an issue related to personal freedom, thus revealing the agreement and disagreement patterns between them. Finally, we note the strong negative sentiment of tweet (1). Notice that each aspect individually might not contain sufficient information for correct classification, but combining all three, by propagating the stance bias (derived from analyzing the negative sentiment of (1)) to politicians likely to hold similar or opposing views (derived from frame analysis), leads to a more reliable prediction.

Given the dynamic nature of this domain, we design our approach to use minimal supervision and naturally adapt to new issues. Our model builds on several weakly supervised local learners that use a small seed set of issue and frame indicators to characterize the stance of tweets (based on lexical heuristics (O'Connor et al., 2010) and framing dimensions (Card et al., 2015)) and activity statistics which capture temporally similar patterns between politicians' Twitter activity. Our final model represents agreement and stance bias by combining these weak models into a weakly supervised joint model through Probabilistic Soft Logic (PSL), a recently

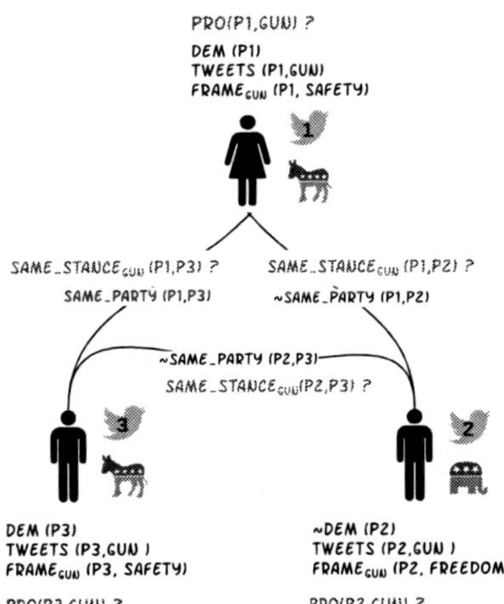

Figure 2: Relational Representation of Politicians' Twitter Activity. P1, P2, and P3 represent 3 different politicians. GUN refers to the issue of gun control; SAFETY and FREEDOM refer to different frames. Prediction target predicates are marked in red.

introduced probabilistic modeling framework (Bach et al., 2013). PSL combines these aspects declaratively by specifying high level rules over a relational representation of the politicians' activities (as shown in Figure 2), which is further compiled into a graphical model called a hinge-loss Markov random field (Bach et al., 2013), and used to make predictions about stance and agreement between politicians.

We analyze the Twitter activity of 32 prominent U.S. politicians, some of which were candidates for the U.S. 2016 presidential election. We collected their recent tweets and stances on 16 different issues, which were used for evaluation purposes. Our experiments demonstrate the effectiveness of our global modeling approach which outperforms the weak learners that provide the initial supervision.

2 Related Work

To the best of our knowledge this is the first work to use Twitter data, *specifically content, frames, and temporal activity*, to predict *politicians' stances*. Previous works (Sridhar et al., 2015; Hasan and Ng, 2014; Abu-Jbara et al., 2013; Walker et al., 2012; Abbott et al., 2011; Somasundaran and Wiebe, 2010; Somasundaran and Wiebe, 2009) have studied mining opinions and predicting stances in online debate forum data, exploiting argument and threaded conversation structures, or analyzed social interaction and group structure (Sridhar et al., 2015; Abu-Jbara et al., 2013; West et al., 2014). In our Twitter dataset, there were few "@" mention or retweet examples forming a conversation concerning the investigated issues, thus we did not have access to argument or conversation structures for analysis. Works which focus on inferring signed social networks (West et al., 2014), stance classification (Sridhar et al., 2015), social group modeling (Huang et al., 2012), and PSL collective classification (Bach et al., 2015) are closest to our work, but these typically operate in supervised settings. In this work, we use PSL *without direct supervision*, to assign *soft* values (in the range of 0 to 1) to output variables [1].

Using Twitter to analyze political discourse and influence has gained in popularity over recent years. Predicting characteristics of Twitter users, including political party affiliation has been explored (Volkova et al., 2015; Volkova et al., 2014; Conover et al., 2011). Previous works have also focused on sentiment analysis (Pla and Hurtado, 2014; Bakliwal et al., 2013), predicting ideology (Djemili et al., 2014), analyzing types of tweets and Twitter network effects around political events (Maireder and Ausserhofer, 2013), automatic polls based on Twitter sentiment and political forecasting using Twitter (Bermingham and Smeaton, 2011; O'Connor et al., 2010; Tumasjan et al., 2010), as well as uses of distant supervision (Marchetti-Bowick and Chambers, 2012).

Analyzing political tweets specifically has also attracted considerable interest. Recently, SemEval Task 6 (SemEval, 2016) aimed to detect the stance of *individual tweets*. Unlike this task and most related work on stance prediction (e.g., those mentioned above), we *do not assume that each tweet expresses a stance*. Instead, we combine tweet content and temporal indicators into a representation of a politician's overall Twitter behavior, to determine if these features are indicative of a *politician's stance*. This approach allows us to capture when politicians fail to tweet about a topic, which indicates a lack of stance as well.

To the best of our knowledge, this work is also the *first attempt to analyze issue framing in Twitter data*. To do so we used the frame guidelines developed by Boydstun et al. (2014). Issue framing is related to

---

[1]Conversely, Markov Logic Networks assign *hard* (0 or 1) values to model variables.

both analyzing biased language (Greene and Resnik, 2009; Recasens et al., 2013) and subjectivity (Wiebe et al., 2004). Several previous works have explored topic framing of public statements, congressional speeches, and news articles (Tsur et al., 2015; Card et al., 2015; Baumer et al., 2015) . Other works focus on identifying and measuring political ideologies (Iyyer et al., 2014; Bamman and Smith, 2015; Sim et al., 2013; Lewenberg et al., 2016) and policies (Gerrish and Blei, 2012; Nguyen et al., 2015; Grimmer, 2010).

Finally, unsupervised and weakly supervised models of Twitter data for several various tasks have been suggested, such as user profile extraction (Li et al., 2014b), life event extraction (Li et al., 2014a), and conversation modeling (Ritter et al., 2010). Further, Eisenstein (2013) discusses methods for dealing with the unique language used in micro-blogging platforms.

3 Data and Problem Setting

REPUBLICAN POLITICIANS
Jeb Bush, Ben Carson, Chris Christie, Ted Cruz, Carly Fiorina, Lindsey Graham, Mike Huckabee, Bobby Jindal, John Kasich, George Pataki, Rand Paul, Rick Perry, Marco Rubio, Rick Santorum, Donald Trump, Scott Walker

DEMOCRATIC POLITICIANS
Joe Biden, Lincoln Chafee, Hillary Clinton, Kirsten Gillibrand, John Kerry, Ben Lujan, Ed Markey, Martin O'Malley, Nancy Pelosi, Harry Reid, Bernie Sanders, Chuck Schumer, Jon Tester, Mark Warner, Elizabeth Warren, Jim Webb

Table 1: Politicians tracked in this study.

Collection and Pre-Processing of Tweets: We collected tweets for the 32 politicians listed in Table 1, initially beginning with those politicians participating in the 2016 U.S. presidential election (16 Republicans and 5 Democrats). To increase representation of Democrats, we collected tweets of Democrats who hold leadership roles within their party. For all 32 politicians we have a total of 99,161 tweets, with an average of 3,000 per person. There are 39,353 Democrat and 59,808 Republican tweets.

Using tweets from both parties, we compiled a set of frequently appearing keywords for each issue, with an average of seven keywords per issue. A Python script was then used on these preselected keywords to filter all tweets, keeping only those that represent our 16 political issues of interest (shown in

ISSUE	QUESTION
ABORTION	*Do you support abortion?*
ACA	*Do you support the Patient Protection and Affordable Care Act (Obamacare)?*
CONFEDERATE	*Should the federal government allow states to fly the confederate flag?*
DRUGS	*Do you support the legalization of Marijuana?*
ENVIRONMENT	*Should the federal government continue to give tax credits and subsidies to the wind power industry?*
GUNS	*Do you support increased gun control?*
IMMIGRATION	*Do you support stronger measures to increase our border security?*
IRAN	*Should the U.S. conduct targeted airstrikes on Irans nuclear weapons facilities?*
ISIS	*Should the U.S. formally declare war on ISIS?*
MARRIAGE	*Do you support the legalization of same sex marriage?*
NSA	*Do you support the Patriot Act?*
PAY	*Should employers be required to pay men and women, who perform the same work, the same salary?*
RELIGION	*Should a business, based on religious beliefs, be able to deny service to a customer?*
SOCIAL SECURITY	*Should the government raise the retirement age for Social Security?*
STUDENT	*Would you support increasing taxes on the rich in order to reduce interest rates for student loans?*
TPP	*Do you support the Trans-Pacific Partnership?*

Table 2: Issues taken from ISideWith.com and their corresponding Yes/No questions. Each issue serves as a prediction target for each politician. For example, for each politician we predict if they are for (PRO) or against ($\neg$PRO) increased gun control (GUNS), as well as if every pair of politicians shares the same stance for that issue (SAMESTANCE$_I$).

Table 2), and automatically eliminating all irrelevant tweets (e.g., those about personal issues).

Annotating Stances and Agreement: We used ISideWith.com, a popular website that matches users to politicians based on their answers to a series of 58 questions, to choose 16 of these issues (shown in Table 2) for our prediction goals. ISideWith.com uses a range of yes/no answers in their questions and provides proof of the politician's stance on that issue, *if available*, through public information such as quotes. Since we use the stances as the ground truth for evaluating our prediction, all politicians with unavailable answers or those not listed on the site were manually annotated via online searches of popular newspapers, political channels, and voting records. Since ISideWith.com does not contain answers to all questions for all politicians, especially those that are less popular, we design our approach to be generalizable to such situations by requiring minimal supervision.

Predicting Stance and Agreement: Based on the collected stances, which represent our ground truth of whether a politician is for or against an issue, we define two target predicates using PSL notation (see Section 4.1) to capture the desired output as soft truth assignments to these predicates. The first predicate, PRO(P1, ISSUE) captures the idea that politician P1 is in support of an ISSUE. Consequently, an opposing stance would be captured by the negation: $\neg$PRO(P1, ISSUE). In this work, we do not make use of stance correlations among party members (Lewenberg et al., 2016; Maddox and Lilie, 1984). For example, in U.S. politics Republicans are known to be against gun control and abortion, while Democrats support both issues. Since we are interested in determining the effectiveness of our local models (described in Section 4.2) to capture the stance of each politician, we do not encode such cross-issue information into the models. Additionally, in a weakly supervised setting, we assume we do not have access to such information.

The second target predicate, SAMESTANCE$_I$(P1, P2) classifies if two politicians share a stance for a given issue, i.e., if both are for or against an issue, where I represents 1 of the 16 issues being investigated. Although the two predicates are clearly inter-dependent, we model them as separate predicates since they can depend on different Twitter behavioral and content cues and we can often identify indicators of shared stance, without mention of the actual stance.

4 From Local to Global Models of Twitter Activity

Our approach uses a collection of weakly supervised local models to capture the similarities between stance bias, tweet content, and temporal activity patterns of users' timelines. These local models are used to provide the initial bias when learning the parameters of the global PSL model, which uses PSL to combine all of the local models together into a joint global model. In addition to the PSL local model predicates (described below), we also use directly observed information: party affiliation, denoted DEM(P1) for Democrat and ¬DEM(P1) for Republican, and SAMEPARTY(P1, P2) to denote if two politicians belong to the same party. As shown by the baseline measurements in Section 5, local information alone is not strong enough to capture stance or agreement for politicians. However, by using PSL, we are able to build connections between each local model in order to increase the overall accuracy of each global model's prediction.

4.1 Global Modeling using PSL

PSL is a recent declarative language for specifying weighted first-order logic rules. A PSL model is specified using a set of weighted logical formulas, which are compiled into a special class of graphical model, called a hinge-loss MRF, defining a probability distribution over the possible continuous value assignments to the model's random variables and allowing the model to scale easily (Bach et al., 2015). The defined probability density function has the form:

$$P(\mathbf{Y} \mid \mathbf{X}) = \frac{1}{Z} \exp\left(-\sum_{r=1}^{M} \lambda_r \phi_r(\mathbf{Y}, \mathbf{X})\right)$$

where λ is the weight vector, Z is a normalization constant, and

$$\phi_r(\mathbf{Y}, \mathbf{X}) = (\max\{l_r(\mathbf{Y}, \mathbf{X}), 0\})^{\rho_r}$$

is the hinge-loss potential corresponding to the instantiation of a rule, specified by a linear function l_r, and an optional exponent $\rho_r \in 1, 2$. The weights of the rules are learned using maximum-likelihood estimation, which in our weakly supervised setting was estimated using the Expectation-Maximization algorithm. For more details we refer the reader to Bach et al. (2015).

Specified PSL rules have the form:

$$\lambda_1 : P_1(x) \wedge P_2(x, y) \rightarrow P_3(y),$$
$$\lambda_2 : P_1(x) \wedge P_4(x, y) \rightarrow \neg P_3(y) \ .$$

where P_1, P_2, P_3, P_4 are predicates, and x, y are variables. Each rule is associated with a weight λ, which indicates its importance in the model. Given concrete constants a, b respectively instantiating the variables x, y, the mapping of the model's atoms to soft [0,1] assignments will be determined by the weights assigned to each one of the rules. For example, if $\lambda_1 > \lambda_2$, the model will prefer $P_3(b)$ to its negation. This contrasts with "classical" or other probabilistic logical models in which rules are strictly true or false. In our work, the constant symbols correspond to politicians and predicates represent party affiliation, Twitter activities, and similarities between politicians based on Twitter behaviors.

4.2 Local Models of Basic Twitter Activity

Issue: We use a keyword based heuristic, similar to the approach described in O'Connor et al. (2010), to capture which issues politicians are tweeting about. Each issue is associated with a small set of keywords, which may be mutually exclusive, such as those concerning Iran or Environment. However, some may fall under multiple issues at once (e.g., *religion* may indicate the tweet refers to ISIS, Religion, or Marriage). The majority of matching keywords determines the issue of the tweet, with rare cases of ties manually resolved. The output of this classifier is all of the issue-related tweets of a politician, which are used as input for the PSL predicate TWEETS(P1, ISSUE). This binary predicate indicates if politician P1 has tweeted about the issue or not.

Sentiment Analysis: Based on the idea that the sentiment of a tweet can help expose a politician's stance on a certain issue, we use OpinionFinder 2.0 (Wilson et al., 2005) to label each politician's issue-related tweets as positive, negative, or neutral. We observed, however, that for all politicians, a majority of tweets will be labeled as neutral. This may be caused by the difficulty of labeling sentiment for Twitter data. If a politician has no positive or negative tweets, they are assigned their party's majority sentiment assignment for that issue. This output is used as input to the PSL predicates TWEETPOS(P1, ISSUE) and TWEETNEG(P1, ISSUE).

Agreement and Disagreement: To determine how well tweet content similarity can capture stance agreement, we computed the pair-wise cosine similarity between all of the politicians. Due to the usage of similar words per issue, most politicians are grouped together, even across different parties. To overcome this noise, we compute the *frequency* of similar words within tweets about each issue. For

PSL MODEL	EXAMPLE OF PSL RULE
LOCAL BASELINE (LB)	$\text{LOCALSAMESTANCE}_I(P1, P2) \rightarrow \text{SAMESTANCE}_I(P1, P2)$
	$\text{TWEETS}(P1, \text{ISSUE}) \wedge \text{TWEETPOS}(P1, \text{ISSUE}) \rightarrow \text{PRO}(P1, \text{ISSUE})$
MODEL 1 (M1)	$\text{SAMEPARTY}(P1, P2) \wedge \text{DEM}(P1) \rightarrow \text{PRO}(P2, \text{ISSUE})$
	$\text{SAMEPARTY}(P1, P2) \rightarrow \text{SAMESTANCE}_I(P1, P2)$
MODEL 2 (M2)	$\text{TWEETS}(P1, \text{ISSUE}) \wedge \text{DEM}(P1) \rightarrow \text{PRO}(P1, \text{ISSUE})$
	$\text{TWEETPOS}(P1, \text{ISSUE}) \wedge \text{TWEETPOS}(P2, \text{ISSUE}) \rightarrow \text{SAMESTANCE}_I(P1, P2)$
MODEL 3 (M3)	$\text{LOCALSAMESTANCE}_I(P1, P2) \wedge \text{PRO}(P1, \text{ISSUE}) \rightarrow \text{PRO}(P2, \text{ISSUE})$
	$\text{SAMETEMPORALACTIVITY}_I(P1, P2) \wedge \text{SAMEPARTY}(P1, P2) \rightarrow \text{SAMESTANCE}_I(P1, P2)$
	$\text{FRAME}(P1, \text{ISSUE}) \wedge \text{FRAME}(P2, \text{ISSUE}) \rightarrow \text{SAMESTANCE}_I(P1, P2)$

Table 3: Subset of examples of the rules that are used by each PSL model. Each model also contains negated versions of rules, as well as similar rules where DEM has been replaced by ¬DEM to represent Republicans.

each issue, all of a politician's tweets are aggregated and the frequency of each word is compared to all other politicians' word frequencies. Politicians, P1 and P2, are considered to have a similar $\text{LOCALSAMESTANCE}_I(P1, P2)$ if their frequency counts per word for an issue are within the same range.

4.3 Baseline PSL Model: Using Local Models Directly

Previous stance classification works typically predict stance based on a single piece of text (e.g., forum posts or tweets) in a supervised setting, making it difficult to directly compare to our approach. To provide some comparison, we implement a baseline model which, as expected, has a weaker performance than our models. The baseline model does not take advantage of the global modeling framework, but instead learns weights over the rules listed in the first two lines of Table 3. These rules directly map the output of the local noisy models to PSL target predicates.

4.4 PSL Model 1: Party Based Agreement

The tendency of politicians to vote with their political party on most issues is encoded via the Model 1 PSL rules listed in Table 3, which aim to capture party based agreement. For some issues we initially assume Democrats (DEM) are for an issue, while Republicans (¬DEM) are against that issue, or vice versa. In the latter case, the rules of the model would change, e.g. the second rule would become: $\neg\text{DEM}(P1) \rightarrow \text{PRO}(P1, \text{ISSUE})$, and likewise for all other rules. Similarly, if two politicians are in the same party, we expect them to have the same stance, or agree, on an issue. For all PSL rules, the reverse also holds, e.g., if two politicians are not in the same

party, we expect them to have different stances.

4.5 PSL Model 2: Basic Twitter Activity

Model 2 builds upon the initial party line bias of Model 1. In addition to political party based information, we also include representations of the politician's Twitter activity, as shown in Table 3. This includes whether or not a politician tweets about an issue (TWEETS) and what sentiment is expressed in those tweets. The predicate TWEETPOS models if a politician tweets positively on the issue, whereas TWEETNEG models negative sentiment. Two different predicates are used instead of the negation of TWEETPOS, which would cause all politicians for which there are no tweets (or sentiment) on that issue to also be considered.

4.6 Local Models of High Level Twitter Activity

Temporal Activity Patterns: We observed from reading Twitter feeds that most politicians will comment on an event the day it happens. For general issues, politicians comment as often as desired to express their support or lack thereof for a particular issue. To capture patterns between politicians, we align their timelines based on days where they have tweeted about an issue. When two or more politicians tweet about the same issue on the same day, they are considered to have similar temporal activity, which may indicate stance agreement. This information is used as input for our PSL predicate $\text{SAMETEMPORALACTIVITY}_I(P1, P2)$.

Political Framing: The way politicians choose to contextualize their tweets on an issue is strongly indicative of their stance on that issue. To investigate this, we compiled a list of unique keywords for each political framing dimension as described in Boyd-stun et al. (2014) and Card et al. (2015). We use the keyword matching approach described in Section 4.2 to classify all tweets into a political frame with some tweets belonging to multiple frames. We sum over the total number of each frame type and use the frame with the maximum and second largest count as that politician's frames for that issue. In the event of a tie we assign the frame that appears most frequently within that politician's party. These frames are used as input to the PSL predicate FRAME(P1, ISSUE).

4.7 PSL Model 3: Agreement Patterns

The last three lines of Table 3 present a subset of the rules used in Model 3 to incorporate higher level Twitter information into the model. Our intuition is that politicians who tweet in a similar manner would also have similar stances on issues, which we represent with the predicate LOCALSAMESTANCE$_I$. SAMETEMPORALACTIVITY represents the idea that if politicians tweet about an issue around the same times then they also share a stance for that issue. Finally, FRAME indicates the frame used by that politician for different issues. The use of these rules allows Model 3 to overcome Model 2 inconsistencies between stance and sentiment (e.g., if someone attacks their opposition).

5   Experiments

Experimental Settings: As described in Section 4, the data generated from the local models is used as input to the PSL models. Stances collected in Section 3 are used as the ground truth for evaluation of the results of the PSL models. We initialize Model 1, as described in Section 4.4, using political party affiliation knowledge. Model 2 builds upon Model 1 by adding the results of the issue and sentiment analysis local models. Model 3 combines all previous models with higher level Twitter activities: tweet agreement, temporal activity, and frames. We implement our PSL models to have an initial bias that candidates do not share a stance and are against an issue.

Experimental Results By Issue: Table 4 presents the results of using our three proposed PSL models. Local Baseline (LB) refers to using only the weak local models for prediction with no additional information about party affiliation. We observe that for prediction of stance (PRO) LB performs better

than random chance in 11 of 16 issues; for prediction of agreement (SAMESTANCE$_I$), LB performs much lower overall, with only 5 of 16 issues predicted above chance.

Using Model 1 (M1), we improve stance prediction accuracy for 11 of the issues and agreement accuracy for all issues. Model 2 (M2) further improves the stance and agreement predictions for an additional 8 and 10 issues, respectively. Model 3 (M3) increases the stance prediction accuracy of M2 for 4 issues and the agreement accuracy for 9 issues. The final agreement predictions of M3 are significantly improved over the initial LB for all issues.

The final stance predictions of M3 are improved over all issues except Guns, Iran, and TPP. For Guns, the stance prediction remains the same throughout all models, meaning additional party information does not boost the initial predictions determined from Twitter behaviors. For Iran, the addition of M1 and M2 lower the accuracy, but the behavioral features from M3 are able to restore it to the original prediction. For TPP, this trend is likely due to the fact that all models incorporate party information and the issue of TPP is the most heavily divided within and across parties, with 8 Republicans and 4 Democrats in support of TPP and 8 Republicans and 12 Democrats opposed. Even in cases where M1 and/or M2 lowered the initial baseline result (e.g. stance for Religion or agreement for Environment), the final prediction by M3 is still higher than that of the baseline.

Framing and Temporal Information: As shown in Table 4, performance for *some* issues does not improve in Model 3. Upon investigation, we found that for all issues, except Abortion which improves in agreement, one or both of the top frames for the party are the same across party lines. For example, for ACA both Republicans and Democrats have the *Economic* and *Health and Safety* frames as their top two frames. For TPP, both parties share the *Economic* frame.

In addition to similar framing overlap, the Twitter timeline for ACA also exhibits overlap, as shown in Figure 3(a). This figure highlights one week before and after the Supreme Court ruling (seen as the peak of activity, 6/25/2015) to uphold the ACA. Conversely, Abortion, which shares no frames between parties (Democrats frame Abortion with *Constitutionality* and *Health and Safety* frames; Repub-

Issue	STANCE				AGREEMENT			
	LB	M 1	M 2	M 3	LB	M 1	M 2	M 3
ABORTION	81.25	96.88	96.88	96.88	49.31	93.75	93.75	95.36
ACA	96.88	100	100	100	51.61	100	100	100
CONFEDERATE	34.38	78.12	87.5	84.38	51.31	69.6	77.7	80.18
DRUGS	87.5	78.12	96.88	88.88	50.42	63.6	84.07	84.07
ENVIRONMENT	53.12	78.12	78.13	81.08	45.16	68.75	65.59	69.28
GUNS	93.75	93.75	93.75	93.75	48.59	68.54	99.59	99.59
IMMIGRATION	37.5	81.25	81.25	86.36	53.62	68.55	69.06	69.56
IRAN	84.38	65.62	65.63	84.38	35.57	79.73	100	100
ISIS	40.32	76.28	93.75	93.75	59.68	76.28	76.28	90.04
MARRIAGE	62.5	90.62	90.62	90.62	50.57	87.12	87.43	87.43
NSA	37.5	53.12	53.12	61.54	34.15	49.2	56.66	59.65
PAY	84.38	84.38	90.62	89.47	64.30	72.92	80.31	74.31
RELIGION	75	68.75	81.25	81.25	47.62	86.24	76.46	79.44
SOCIAL SECURITY	28.12	78.12	78.13	78.13	53.76	73.25	90.03	90.88
STUDENT	93.75	96.88	96.88	96.88	51.61	100	100	100
TPP	62.5	62.5	62.5	62.5	45.43	48.39	54.64	65.32

Table 4: Stance and Agreement Accuracy by Issue. LB uses weak local models, M1 represents party line agreement, M2 adds Twitter activity, and M3 adds higher level Twitter behaviors.

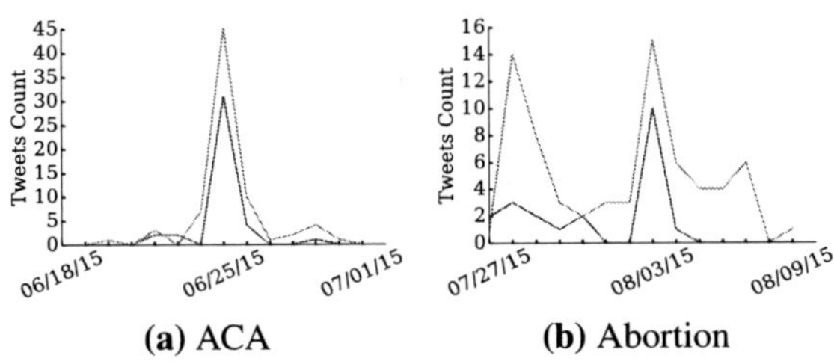

(a) ACA   **(b)** Abortion

Figure 3: Temporal Twitter Activity by Party. Republican (red) and Democrat (blue) event based temporal overlaps.

licans use *Economic* and *Capacity and Resources* frames), exhibits a timeline with greater fluctuation. The peak of Figure 3(b) is 8/3/2015, which is the day that the budget was passed to include funding for Planned Parenthood. Overall both parties have different patterns over this time range, allowing M3 to increase agreement prediction accuracy by 1.61%.

6 Conclusion

In this paper we take a first step towards understanding the dynamic microblogging behavior of politicians. Though we concentrate on a small set of politicians and issues in this work, this framework can be modified to handle additional politicians or issues, as well as those in other countries, by incorporating appropriate domain knowledge (e.g., using new keywords for different issues in other countries), which we leave as future work. Unlike previous works, which tend to focus on one aspect of this complex microblogging behavior, we build a holistic model connecting temporal behaviors, party-line bias, and issue frames into a single predictive model used to identify fine-grained policy stances and agreement. Despite having no explicit supervision, and using only intuitive "rules-of-thumb" to bootstrap our global model, our approach results in a strong prediction model which helps shed light on political discourse framing inside and across party lines.

Acknowledgements

We thank the anonymous reviewers for their thoughtful comments and suggestions.

References

Rob Abbott, Marilyn Walker, Pranav Anand, Jean E. Fox Tree, Robeson Bowmani, and Joseph King. 2011. How can you say such things?!?: Recognizing disagreement in informal political argument. In *Proc. of the Workshop on Language in Social Media*.

Amjad Abu-Jbara, Ben King, Mona Diab, and Dragomir Radev. 2013. Identifying opinion subgroups in arabic online discussions. In *Proc. of ACL*.

Stephen H. Bach, Bert Huang, Ben London, and Lise Getoor. 2013. Hinge-loss Markov random fields: Convex inference for structured prediction. In *Proc. of UAI*.

Stephen H Bach, Matthias Broecheler, Bert Huang, and Lise Getoor. 2015. Hinge-loss markov random fields and probabilistic soft logic. *arXiv preprint arXiv:1505.04406*.

Akshat Bakliwal, Jennifer Foster, Jennifer van der Puil, Ron O'Brien, Lamia Tounsi, and Mark Hughes. 2013. Sentiment analysis of political tweets: Towards an accurate classifier. In *Proc. of ACL*.

David Bamman and Noah A Smith. 2015. Open extraction of fine-grained political statements. In *Proc. of EMNLP*.

Eric Baumer, Elisha Elovic, Ying Qin, Francesca Polletta, and Geri Gay. 2015. Testing and comparing computational approaches for identifying the language of framing in political news. In *Proc. of ACL*.

Adam Bermingham and Alan F Smeaton. 2011. On using twitter to monitor political sentiment and predict election results.

Amber Boydstun, Dallas Card, Justin H. Gross, Philip Resnik, and Noah A. Smith. 2014. Tracking the development of media frames within and across policy issues.

Dallas Card, Amber E. Boydstun, Justin H. Gross, Philip Resnik, and Noah A. Smith. 2015. The media frames corpus: Annotations of frames across issues. In *Proc. of ACL*.

Michael D Conover, Bruno Gonçalves, Jacob Ratkiewicz, Alessandro Flammini, and Filippo Menczer. 2011. Predicting the political alignment of twitter users. In *Proc. of Privacy, Security, Risk and Trust (PASSAT) and SocialCom*.

Sarah Djemili, Julien Longhi, Claudia Marinica, Dimitris Kotzinos, and Georges-Elia Sarfati. 2014. What does twitter have to say about ideology? In *NLP 4 CMC: Natural Language Processing for Computer-Mediated Communication*.

Jacob Eisenstein. 2013. What to do about bad language on the internet. In *Proc. of NAACL*.

Sean Gerrish and David M Blei. 2012. How they vote: Issue-adjusted models of legislative behavior. In *Advances in Neural Information Processing Systems*, pages 2753–2761.

Stephan Greene and Philip Resnik. 2009. More than words: Syntactic packaging and implicit sentiment. In *Proc. of NAACL*.

Justin Grimmer. 2010. A bayesian hierarchical topic model for political texts: Measuring expressed agendas in senate press releases. In *Political Analysis*.

Kazi Saidul Hasan and Vincent Ng. 2014. Why are you taking this stance? identifying and classifying reasons in ideological debates. In *Proc. of EMNLP*.

Bert Huang, Stephen H. Bach, Eric Norris, Jay Pujara, and Lise Getoor. 2012. Social group modeling with probabilistic soft logic. In *NIPS Workshops*.

Mohit Iyyer, Peter Enns, Jordan L Boyd-Graber, and Philip Resnik. 2014. Political ideology detection using recursive neural networks. In *Proc. of ACL*.

Yoad Lewenberg, Yoram Bachrach, Lucas Bordeaux, and Pushmeet Kohli. 2016. Political dimensionality estimation using a probabilistic graphical model. In *Proc. of UAI*.

Jiwei Li, Alan Ritter, Claire Cardie, and Eduard H Hovy. 2014a. Major life event extraction from twitter based on congratulations/condolences speech acts. In *Proc. of EMNLP*.

Jiwei Li, Alan Ritter, and Eduard H Hovy. 2014b. Weakly supervised user profile extraction from twitter. In *Proc. of ACL*.

William Maddox and Stuart Lilie. 1984. Beyond liberal and conservative: Reassessing the political spectrum.

Axel Maireder and Julian Ausserhofer. 2013. National politics on twitter: Structures and topics of a networked public sphere. In *Information, Communication, and Society*.

Micol Marchetti-Bowick and Nathanael Chambers. 2012. Learning for microblogs with distant supervision: Political forecasting with twitter. In *Proc. of EACL*.

Yelena Mejova, Padmini Srinivasan, and Bob Boynton. 2013. Gop primary season on twitter: popular political sentiment in social media. In *WSDM*.

Viet-An Nguyen, Jordan Boyd-Graber, Philip Resnik, and Kristina Miler. 2015. Tea party in the house: A hierarchical ideal point topic model and its application to republican legislators in the 112th congress. In *Proc. of ACL*.

Brendan O'Connor, Ramnath Balasubramanyan, Bryan R Routledge, and Noah A Smith. 2010. From tweets to polls: Linking text sentiment to public opinion time series. In *Proc. of ICWSM*.

Ferran Pla and Lluís F Hurtado. 2014. Political tendency identification in twitter using sentiment analysis techniques. In *Proc. of COLING*.

Marta Recasens, Cristian Danescu-Niculescu-Mizil, and Dan Jurafsky. 2013. Linguistic models for analyzing and detecting biased language. In *Proc. of ACL*.

Alan Ritter, Colin Cherry, and Bill Dolan. 2010. Unsupervised modeling of twitter conversations. In *Proc. of NAACL*.

SemEval. 2016. Task 6. http://alt.qcri.org/semeval2016/task6/.

Yanchuan Sim, Brice DL Acree, Justin H Gross, and Noah A Smith. 2013. Measuring ideological proportions in political speeches. In *Proc. of EMNLP*.

Swapna Somasundaran and Janyce Wiebe. 2009. Recognizing stances in online debates. In *Proc. of ACL*.

Swapna Somasundaran and Janyce Wiebe. 2010. Recognizing stances in ideological on-line debates. In *Proc. of NAACL Workshops*.

Dhanya Sridhar, James Foulds, Bert Huang, Lise Getoor, and Marilyn Walker. 2015. Joint models of disagreement and stance in online debate. In *Proc. of ACL*.

Oren Tsur, Dan Calacci, and David Lazer. 2015. A frame of mind: Using statistical models for detection of framing and agenda setting campaigns. In *Proc. of ACL*.

Andranik Tumasjan, Timm Oliver Sprenger, Philipp G Sandner, and Isabell M Welpe. 2010. Predicting elections with twitter: What 140 characters reveal about political sentiment.

Svitlana Volkova, Glen Coppersmith, and Benjamin Van Durme. 2014. Inferring user political preferences from streaming communications. In *Proc. of ACL*.

Svitlana Volkova, Yoram Bachrach, Michael Armstrong, and Vijay Sharma. 2015. Inferring latent user properties from texts published in social media. In *Proc. of AAAI*.

Marilyn A. Walker, Pranav Anand, Robert Abbott, and Ricky Grant. 2012. Stance classification using dialogic properties of persuasion. In *Proc. of NAACL*.

Robert West, Hristo S Paskov, Jure Leskovec, and Christopher Potts. 2014. Exploiting social network structure for person-to-person sentiment analysis. *TACL*.

Janyce Wiebe, Theresa Wilson, Rebecca Bruce, Matthew Bell, and Melanie Martin. 2004. Learning subjective language. *Computational linguistics*.

Theresa Wilson, Paul Hoffmann, Swapna Somasundaran, Jason Kessler, Janyce Wiebe, Yejin Choi, Claire Cardie, Ellen Riloff, and Siddharth Patwardhan. 2005. Opinionfinder: A system for subjectivity analysis. In *Proc. of EMNLP*.

Learning Linguistic Descriptors of User Roles in Online Communities

Alex Wang[1], William L. Hamilton[2], Jure Leskovec[2]
[1]School of Engineering and Applied Sciences, Harvard University, Cambridge MA, 01238
[2]Computer Science Department, Stanford University, Stanford CA, 94305
`alexwang@college.harvard.edu`
`wleif,jure@stanford.edu`

Abstract

Understanding the ways in which users interact with different online communities is crucial to social network analysis and community maintenance. We present an unsupervised neural model to learn linguistic descriptors for a user's behavior over time within an online community. We show that the descriptors learned by our model capture the functional roles that users occupy in communities, in contrast to those learned via a standard topic-modeling algorithm, which simply reflect topical content. Experiments on the social media forum Reddit show how the model can provide interpretable insights into user behavior. Our model uncovers linguistic differences that correlate with user activity levels and community clustering.

1 Introduction

Social scientists and community maintainers are interested not only in the topics that users discuss in online communities, but also the manner and patterns of behavior within those discussions (Welser et al., 2007). For example, a community maintainer might be interested in knowing the proportion of users that come to the community seeking support versus the proportion of users that actively provide that support. A social scientist might be interested in how these different types of functional roles interact with different behaviors, community cohesion, user activity levels, etc.

Methods for detecting and characterizing these functional roles have had mixed results. Previous computational methods for detecting these roles required significant hand-engineering (Welser et al., 2007) or relied on non-textual features particular to one online community (Welser et al., 2011). Creating general frameworks for automatically characterizing these functional behaviors is difficult because such models must rely primarily on text from community discussions. When examining multiple communities, the social-functional aspects of language can be obscured due to differences in subject matter and jargon, and because in many communities the roles that users can occupy are not predefined or specified in any way. A key technical challenge then is automatically identifying linguistic variation that signals the varying social function of a user's posts, as opposed to variation that simply arises from topical differences across communities

In this work we explore an unsupervised neural network-based method for learning linguistic descriptors that reflect the social roles present in different communities. Unlike standard topic-modeling, we seek to learn descriptors that are independent of the subject matter of one particular community.

We apply our method to data from a collection of sub-communities from the social media forum Reddit. We find that our method is able to pick up on the abstract, functional-communicative roles that users occupy in the communities, while a baseline topic model learns concrete, topical descriptors. Analyzing the behavior of users associated with these descriptors, we find significant and intuitive differences between users of different activity levels and between users with different levels of clustering within their social network.

Proceedings of 2016 EMNLP Workshop on Natural Language Processing and Computational Social Science, pages 76–85,
Austin, TX, November 5, 2016. ©2016 Association for Computational Linguistics

2 Related Work

The idea of social roles and methods for identifying them are fairly long-standing concepts; we refer readers to Welser et al. (2007) for an in-depth review of the early history. Welser et al. (2007), analyzing Usenet forum posts, exemplifies early approaches for identifying social roles, which primarily relied on creating visualizations of authorship and reply networks then manually inspecting them to identify patterns. More recent work has leveraged more sophisticated computational models and methods such as information cascades to identify a particular role: that of social leaders and influencers (Lü et al., 2011; Tsai et al., 2014; Rosenthal, 2014). Jain et al. (2014) attempt to identify a broader set of functional roles, but their work is limited to online arguments and relies on human annotation of content. Our work attempts to provide a more general unsupervised method for identifying many functional roles in online communities, and we identify or define these roles in terms of the stylistic word choices that users make.

A separate line of work has investigated the process of "socialization" in online communities and the dynamics of multi-community engagement. Nguyen and Rosé (2011) show how users begin to use more informal language and refer more to other members as they spend more time in a community. Danescu-Niculescu-Mizil et al. (2013) build off this work and show that user lifespan can be predicted based upon the language of a user. They also characterize important linguistic differences for active long-term users, compared to inactive newer users, such as a decreased use in first-person pronouns. Tan and Lee (2015) extend this line of work to the multi-community setting, tracking thousands of users across various sub-communities on Reddit.

Lastly, for our work, we heavily draw inspiration from Iyyer et al. (2016), which presents an unsupervised neural network, called a relationship modeling network (RMN), for modeling the relationships between fictional characters in literary works. Importantly, the model is able to learn descriptors for the relationships independent of the book they appear in, which vary significantly in language due to time and geographical differences between authors. The RMN also learns the trajectory, or progression of descriptors, of the character relationships over time. Iyyer et al. (2016) provide an in-depth analysis to demonstrate the effectiveness of their model, including crowdsourced verification of the quality of the learned descriptors and relationship trajectories, thorough comparison against a hidden Markov model baseline, and quantitative analysis of results in line with previous literary scholarship.

3 Model

Given the success of the relationship modeling network (RMN), we closely follow Iyyer et al. (2016) in adapting the model to our setting. The model uses a recurrent neural network to reconstruct spans of text, represented with word vector embeddings, using a small set of interpretable embedding-based descriptors. Unlike the original RMN model which learns linguistic descriptors of relationships between character dyads in novels, we seek to model the relationship between users and online communities. In particular, whereas their method learns embeddings of characters and books, we replace them with embeddings of users and communities, respectively. The intuition in applying this model to our setting is that these embeddings should function as offsets that account for idiosyncratic or superficial variation between the language of different users or communities. By "subtracting" away this superficial variation, the system can pick up on the core variation that corresponds to different social functional roles.

Figure 1 provides a high-level overview of the model. The technical details of the model largely follow that of Iyyer et al. (2016). For completeness, we provide a formal description here.

Formally, we have a corpus of N users and M communities where each user u_i makes a sequence of posts $P_{ij} = [p_{ij}^{(1)}, p_{ij}^{(2)}, \ldots, p_{ij}^{(t)}, \ldots]$ to community c_j, where each post is a fixed-length sequence of l word tokens drawn from a vocabulary $\mathcal{V}$; i.e., $p_{ij}^{(t)} = [w_1, w_2, \ldots w_l]$ with possibly some padding. During training, the model learns K descriptors, which are represented as d_{word}-dimensional vectors $\{r_k\}_{k=1}^K$, and a function for assigning each post a score for each of the descriptors. Representing the descriptors as d_{word}-dimensional vectors allows us to interpret the descriptors by looking at their nearest word embedding neighbors. This representation

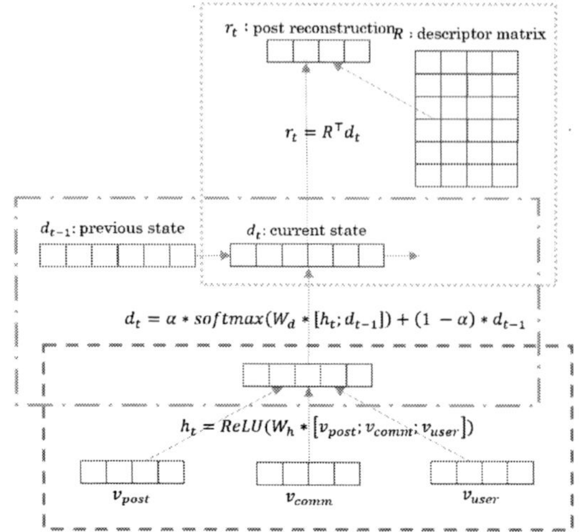

Figure 1: RMN architecture. For each post, the post text, user, and community are first embedded, concatenated, and passed through a linear and nonlinear layer (red). Next, a recurrent layer computes a distribution over descriptors using the previous distribution and a softmax (blue). Finally, to train we create a reconstruction vector and compare against the original text embedding (green).

differs from a topic learned by a topic model, where a topic is a probability distribution over words. The model represents the descriptors as rows of a descriptor matrix $R \in \mathbb{R}^{K \times d_{word}}$.

For each post, the model computes a bag-of-words representation as an average of word vector embeddings from embedding matrix E_{word}:

$$v_{post} = \frac{1}{l} \sum_{i=1}^{l} E_{word}[w_i]. \tag{1}$$

We also obtain embeddings v_{user}, v_{comm} for the user and the community via respective embedding matrices $E_{user} \in \mathbb{R}^{N \times d_{user}}$ and $E_{comm} \in \mathbb{R}^{M \times d_{comm}}$, also learned throughout training. Following Iyyer et al. (2016) we concatenate these embeddings and pass them through a linear layer parameterized by $W_h \in \mathbb{R}^{(d_{word} + d_{user} + d_{comm}) \times d_{hid}}$, followed by a nonlinear ReLU layer:

$$h_t = ReLU(W_h \cdot [v_{post}; v_{user}; v_{comm}]). \tag{2}$$

To convert h_t to scores over the descriptors, the model then computes a softmax[1]. However, in order

to also make use of information from previous posts between the user and the community, the distribution is computed by also using the distribution from the previous post:

$$d_t = \alpha \cdot softmax(W_d \cdot [h_t; d_{t-1}]) + (1 - \alpha) \cdot d_{t-1}, \tag{3}$$

where $W_d \in \mathbb{R}^{(d_{hid} + K) \times K}$. This recurrent aspect allows the model to consider the previous state of the relationship and also lets us track the progression of the relationship. The parameter α controls the degree that d_t depends on the previous distribution and can either be a hyperparameter or a learned parameter.

To train the model, we have it act as an autoencoder, where for each post we would like the post's scores for the descriptors to accurately capture the meaning of the original post. We formalize this into a training objective $J(\theta)$ by defining a reconstruction vector r_t and attempting to make it similar in terms of cosine distance to the original post v_{post}:

$$r_t = R^\top d_t, \tag{4}$$

$$J_{ij}(\theta) = \sum_{t=0}^{|P_{ij}|} \sum_{n \in S} \max(0,$$
$$1 - \cos\_sim(r_t, v_{post}) + \cos\_sim(r_t, v_n)), \tag{5}$$

where $\cos\_sim(v, w)$ is the cosine similarity between vectors v, w and S is a set of averaged bag-of-words representations v_n for a randomly sampled subset of posts from the entire dataset. $J(\theta)$ seeks to minimize the cosine distance between the reconstructed post and original post while maximizing the cosine distance between the reconstruction and the negative samples. Finally, to encourage the model to learn distinct descriptors, Iyyer et al. (2016) add an orthogonality penalty $X(\theta) = ||RR^\top - I||$ where I is the identity matrix. Then the final training objective is

$$L(\theta) = \sum_{i \in N} \sum_{j \in M} J_{ij}(\theta) + \lambda X(\theta), \tag{6}$$

where λ is a hyperparameter controlling the degree to which the model is penalized for learning semantically similar descriptors.

---

[1] see Iyyer et al. (2016) for a discussion on the use of a softmax versus other nonlinear functions

parameters	value
d_{word}	300
d_{comm}	300
d_{user}	100
d_{hid}	300
λ	1.0
α	.5
K	50
$|S|$	100

Table 1: Model parameters in experiments

4 Experimental Setup

For our experiments we use text data from user comments on Reddit (reddit.com), a social media forum with over 200 million unique users as of June, 2016.[2] Reddit allows users to post and comment in multiple sub-communities, known as subreddits, that cover a wide array of subject matter from current events to specific video games to cooking.

4.1 Data

To prevent our model from being mislead by structurally abnormal subreddits and to provide scope to our domain of inquiry, we chose to focus our experiments on a subset of video game related subreddits, using all publicly available comments from 2014. We manually selected 75 subreddits, where each community is dedicated to the discussion of a particular videogame (e.g., r/Halo3). Limiting to subreddits that discuss specific videogames has the benefit of providing a sample of subreddits that are all similar in both social structure and scope.

4.2 Preprocessing

To build our dataset, we consider all users that have made at least 50 comments to a subreddit, and we sample up to 50 users from each subreddit. Then for each subreddit-user pair, we sample at most 100 of their comments. For the vocabulary, we lowercase, filter out conjunctions and articles, then remove words that do not appear in at least 20% of the subreddits. We found that restricting the vocabulary this way removed words that are concentrated to a few subreddits, thereby encouraging the model to learn more general descriptors.

For the word embedding matrix E_{word}, we pretrain 300-dimensional word vectors using a skip-gram word2vec model trained on all subreddit data from 2014[3] and do not fine-tune these embeddings during training. User and community embeddings are initialized randomly and fine-tuned during training. To summarize, our final dataset consisted of 3.3×10^5 comments, 75 subreddits, 2575 users, and a $\sim 10^4$ word vocabulary. See Table 1 for experimental parameters.

5 Results

Our analysis (see Section 5.1) reveals that the descriptors (or topics[4]) learned via the RMN model are qualitatively different than those produced by latent Dirichlet allocation (LDA; Blei et al. (2003)) and that the RMN descriptors more effectively capture functional or stylistic aspects of language that (at least intuitively) correspond to the communication patterns of stereotypical social roles.

We then show how the unsupervised RMN model can be used to gain insights into user behavior: Section 5.2 shows how the descriptors are differentially expressed by users of varying activity levels and who have varying amounts of clustering in their local social network. Finally, Section 5.3 explores the latent dimensionality of the space of functional user roles using the learned RMN descriptor distributions.

5.1 Descriptors learned

We present a subset of the learned RMN descriptors in Table 2. For comparison, we also trained an LDA model[5] on the same data (with identical pre-processing) and present the topics learned. In the case of LDA, the words describing each topic are simply the words with the highest within-topic probabilities; in contrast, the words corresponding to the RMN descriptors are selected by finding the closest words to the descriptor vectors in terms of cosine similarity. From the examples shown, we

---

[2]http://expandedramblings.com/index.php/reddit-stats/

[3]Vectors were trained using the Gensim framework with default settings (Řehůřek and Sojka, 2010)

[4]Following Iyyer et al. (2016) we use the term *descriptors* when referring to the RMN model, but will use the standard term *topics* when discussing LDA.

[5]Using the Mallet toolbox with default hyperparameters (McCallum, 2002).

ID	RMN	LDA
1	themselves, tend, their, they, them	fire, shot, gun, range, weapons
2	ftfy, bro, hahaha, bitches, fuckin	dark, dragon, kill, souls, boss
3	competitive, matchmaking, teamspeak, skilled, player	map, area, room, make, place
4	suggestions, advice, appreciate, helpful, appreciated	level, gear, drop, loot, quest
5	restart, manually, fix, update, reset	damage, health, attack, speed, skill
6	ah, ahh, alright, thanks, haha	server, issue, problem, servers, account
7	criticizing, disagreeing, downvoting, criticize, agreeing	character, level, spell, party, make
8	nobody, thinks, clue, care, fuck	team, bet, win, game, lost
9	he, i, be, it, as	love, video, great, good, watch
10	un, <SPECIAL >, de, en, que	game, make, change, balance, scrolls

Table 2: : Eight examples coherent descriptors/topics from the RMN and LDA models (top) and two examples that were judged to be largely incoherent/non-useful (bottom). The coherent LDA topics correspond to superficial subreddit-specific topical content, while the coherent RMN descriptors capture functional aspects of language user (e.g., a user asking for advice, or providing positive acknowledgment). The incoherent LDA topics consist of mixtures of (somewhat) semantically related concrete terms. The RMN model tends to fail by producing either difficult-to-interpret sets of stopwords or interpretable, but uninteresting, sets of functionally related words (e.g., Spanish stopwords).

can see that descriptors learned by the RMN seem to be more abstract and functional—capturing concepts such as asking for advice—while the topics learned via LDA are more concrete and subreddit specific; for example, the first LDA topic shown in Table 2 is specific to "shooter"-type games, while the second is specific to fantasy role-playing games.

The learned RMN descriptors also have some intuitive mappings to standard user roles. Some correspond to anti-social or "troll"-like behavior, such as example descriptors 2 and 8 in Table 2; similarly, example descriptor 5 corresponds to "maven"-like behavior (providing technical advice), while 4 likely represents the language of inexperienced, or so-called "newbie", users—a point which we confirm in Section 5.2.

Not all the learned descriptors have such intuitive mappings, but this does not imply that they are not informative with respect to the functional roles users play in communities. Example RMN descriptor 1, which contains language discussing "the other" (e.g., "them", "they") does not map to one of these well-known categories; however, it might still have functional relevance (e.g., in the social process of outgroup derogation (Tajfel et al., 1971)).

Of course, not all the descriptors learned by the RMN are perfect. In addition to the non-functional descriptors learned, a small number of descriptors (1-3) lack a clear coherent interpretation (e.g., ex-

ample 9 in Table 2). Furthermore, some descriptors did indeed seem to capture some more topical information (e.g., example 3 in Table 2 is specific to competitive gaming). We note, however, that all of these behaviors were also observed in the LDA topics. Table 5 in the appendix lists the full set of descriptors and topics learned by both methods.

5.1.1 Descriptor quality

Previous work applying the RMN framework to fictional novels has shown that humans judge the generated RMN descriptors to be more coherent compared to topics generated by LDA (Iyyer et al., 2016). Manual inspection of the 50 descriptors/topics learned by each model in our study supported this finding, though we found the majority produced by both methods were reasonably coherent. That said, the top-10 words for LDA topics contained a large number of repeated terms. Of the 500 top-10 words generated by LDA (10 each for 50 topics), 241, or 48%, occur in more than one topic. The word "game", for example, occurs as a top-word in 16 out of the 50 topics for LDA.[6] In contrast, only 7% of the top-10 descriptor words appeared in more than one descriptor for the RMN model.

---

[6]This issue for LDA is certainly exacerbated by our preprocessing, which removes words that occur in < 20% subreddits; however, keeping these words only makes the LDA topics more subreddit specific.

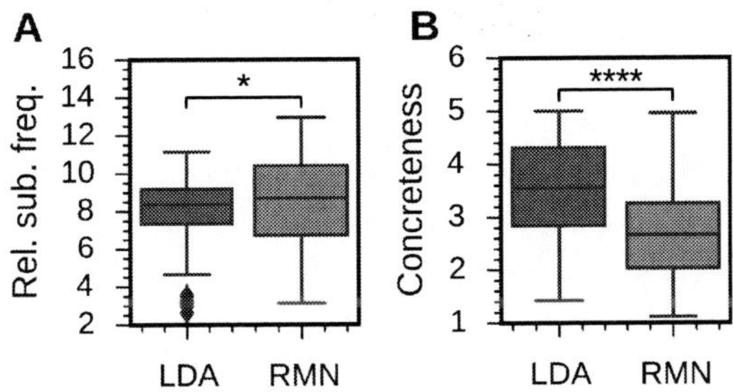

Descriptors	$\hat{\beta}$
them, tend, they, typically	85.8
ftfy, bro, hahaha, fuckin	67.0
increase, higher, lower, increases	86.2
sacrifice, peoples, humanity, damage	-127.1
additional, combine, abilities, each	-77.5
suggestions, advice, appreciate, helpful	-49.3

Table 3: Descriptors that are most predictive of activity levels. The top-3 correspond to the most positively predictive descriptors, while the bottom-3 correspond to the most negatively predictive.

Figure 2: A, The RMN role descriptor words have significantly ($p < 0.05$) higher relative subreddit frequencies compared to the top words from and LDA topics model. **B**, The RMN descriptors are significantly ($p < 0.0001$) more abstract.

5.1.2 Functional vs. topical descriptors

A key qualitative trend evident in the learned descriptors (Table 2) is that the RMN role descriptors appear to capture more functional aspects of language use, e.g., asking for advice or discussions of agreement/disagreement, while the LDA topics capture more concrete, topical, and subreddit-specific language, e.g., "guns" or "dragons".

We quantify this qualitative insight in two ways. First, we note that the RMN descriptors are less subreddit-specific and occur in a greater diversity of subreddits (after controlling for absolute frequency). In particular, we compute the *relative subreddit frequency* of a word w_i as

$$s_r(w_i) = \frac{s(w_i)}{\log(f(w_i))},\qquad(7)$$

where $s(w_i)$ is the number of subreddits w_i occurs in and $f(w_i)$ is its absolute frequency. We found that $s_r(w_i)$ was significantly higher for the 500 RMN descriptor words compared to those from LDA (Figure 2.A; $p < 0.05$, Mann-Whitney U-test). Normalizing by the logarithm of the absolute frequency in (7) is necessary because higher frequency words will simply occur in more subreddits by chance, and the median LDA descriptor-word frequency is $\sim 10\times$ higher than that of the RMN model.[7]

We also found that the RMN descriptor words were significantly more *abstract* (Figure 2.B; $p < 0.0001$, Mann-Whitney U-test), as judged by human ratings from the Brysbaert et al. (2014) concreteness lexicon. The relative abstractness of the RMN descriptor-words highlights the functional nature of the descriptors learned by the RMN model. This finding is further reinforced by the fact that the RMN descriptor words contain far more verbs compared to those from LDA: the RMN descriptors are equally balanced between verbs and nouns (132 verbs, 134 nouns) while the LDA descriptors are overwhelming nouns (98 verbs, 258 nouns).

5.2 Examining user behavior

We now show how the learned RMN descriptors reveal valuable insights into users' behaviors.

5.2.1 Describing active vs. non-active users

First, we investigated the extent to which user activity levels are associated with differential language use by regressing the number of comments a user made in the year 2014 on their average RMN descriptor distribution. We employed a negative binomial regression model since the comment counts are integer valued and heavy-tailed (McCullagh and Nelder, 1989).[8]

Table 3 shows the top-3 most positive and negative predictive descriptors (according to Wald z-statistics), all of which are significant at $p < 0.01$ by Wald's z-tests. Interestingly, we see that one of the most positive predictors of high activity levels is the topic that contains terms used to refer to "the other" (e.g., "them", "they"); this topic also contains words such as "tend" and "typically", in-

---

[7]The use of a logarithm in the denominator is motivated by the power-law scaling between type and token counts in a corpus (Egghe, 2007).

[8]Regularization is not necessary since the descriptor axes are constrained to be orthogonal during learning.

Descriptors	$\hat{\beta}$
realized, wished, refused, hoped	36.9
hours, evening, day, busy	44.6
tricking, awfully, excessively, shy	41.1
grabbed, walked, picked, bought	-80.0
medium, amazing, surprisingly, fantastic	-71.4
desktop, hardware, optimized, pcs	-60.0

Table 4: Descriptors that are most predictive of social network clustering. The top-3 correspond to the most positively predictive descriptors, while the bottom-3 correspond to the most negatively predictive.

dicating that it captures users references to a stereotyped out-group. This has important social implications, as it potentially highlights the tendency for highly active users to engage in in-group/out-group dynamics. The other topics predictive of high activity levels include one filled with informal "bro" language and a topic related to increasing/decreasing (for which a social interpretation is unclear).

In contrast, the topics most associated with low-activity levels include one related to asking for advice or suggestions, along with a topic related to discussions of "humanity" and "sacrifice". This is in line with anthropological theories of social roles such as legitimate peripheral participation (Lave and Wenger, 1991), which states that new users in a community initially participate via simple and low-risk tasks in order to become familiar with the community jargon and norms. On Reddit, engaging in the in-group/out-group behavior could be costly if users do not have a good understanding of the community-specific norms behind those behaviors. The low-risk actions on Reddit often take the form of question-asking, as newcomers are encouraged to ask questions and seek the advice of more veteran members of the community.

5.2.2 Associating network structure with descriptors

In addition to user activity levels, we also examined how a user's position in their social network is associated with use of different RMN role descriptors. For this experiment, we constructed social networks by attaching all users who commented together within the same comment-chain and whose comments were separated by at most two other comments. We then computed the users' degrees and local clustering coefficients (Watts and Strogatz, 1998) within these networks.

We performed regression analysis via ordinary least squares to relate the different RMN descriptors to the logarithm of a user's clustering coefficient. As with the analysis on activity levels, we performed regression with a vector of RMN descriptor weights for each user that is averaged over all their comments in the dataset. We also controlled for user degree and their activity level in the regression (both log-transformed).

Table 4 shows the top-3 most positive and negative predictors in this regression (according to their t-statistics), all of which are significant at the $p < 0.01$ level. We see that users with highly clustered interactions are more likely to express subjective attitudes (e.g., "realized", "wished", "hope") and are more likely to discuss temporal aspects of their lives (e.g., "day", "busy", "evenings"), perhaps indicating that high clustering during interactions is associated with more personal or in-depth discussions. In contrast, the most predictive topics in the negative direction were more focused on material aspects of gaming, including a topic discussing the purchasing of video games ("grabbed", "bought") and one discussing video game hardware ("desktop", "hardware", "optimized").

5.3 Number of types of users

Given that we found the learned RMN role descriptors to be related to social aspects of user behavior in informative ways, it is natural to investigate how much user variation there is along the learned role descriptor axes. In other words, how many types of users are there?

We investigated this question by performing principal components analysis on the set of user-descriptor vectors, where each user is assigned a vector corresponding to the weight of their average comment along the RMN role descriptor axes (as was done in the regression analysis). We also performed an identical analysis on average subreddit-descriptor vectors.

Figure 3.A shows the proportion of variance explained by the top-k principal components for both users and subreddits. We see that it takes ~6 latent dimensions to explain 80% of the variance across

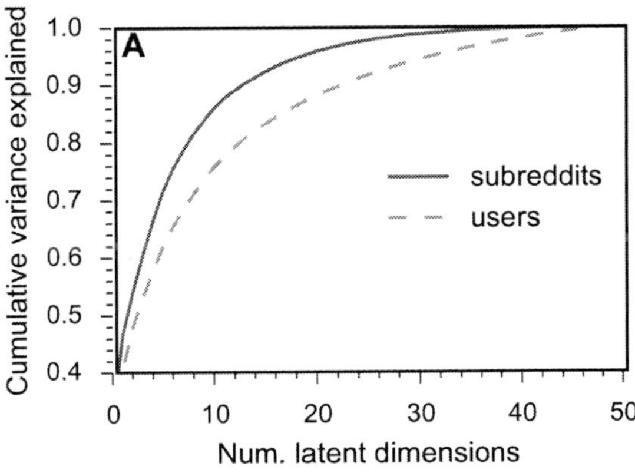
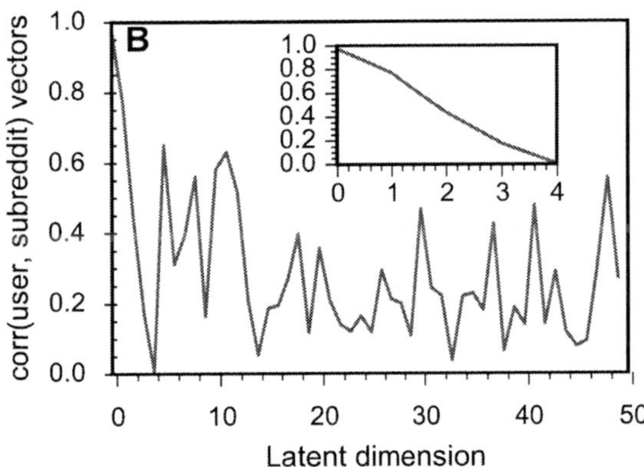

Figure 3: A, Approximately 6 latent dimensions explain 80% of the variance between subreddits in usage of the different RMN descriptors, while it takes ~12 dimensions to explain the same amount of variance in users' linguistic behavior. **B,** The principal components for users and subreddits are highly correlated for the first two principal components, but this correlation quickly drops off and becomes noise.

subreddits, while it takes ~12 latent-dimensions to explain the same amount of variance in user behavior. This indicates that despite the fact the descriptor axes are regularized to be orthogonal during learning, they still contain redundant information and users cluster in predictable ways. However, we also see that there is far more variation at the user-level compared to the subreddit-level, which indicates that the RMN descriptors are not simply recapitulating subreddit distinctions.

We also formally tested the extent to which the descriptors of users are simply determined by the language of subreddits. Figure 3.B shows the absolute Pearson correlation between the principal components of users and subreddits. This correlation is extremely high for the first two principal components but quickly drops off and becomes noise by the fifth principal component. This indicates that a large proportion of variance in user behavior is not simply explained by their being active in certain subreddits and reinforces the notion that RMN topics capture community-independent aspects of user's linguistic behavior that correspond to functional social roles.

6   Conclusion

We adapted a neural network model to learn functional descriptors of how users behave and interact in online communities, and we showed that these descriptors better captured the abstract or functional properties of language use compared to descriptors learned by a standard topic model. We then showed that the learned descriptors are useful for providing interpretable linguistic characterizations of different user behaviors. Our results highlight the usefulness of the RMN framework as an unsupervised, quantitative tool for uncovering and characterizing user roles in online communities.

This unsupervised approach to discovering stereotypical communication patterns offers a powerful compliment to social network and interaction-based methods of discovering social roles. However, one limitation of this study is that we do not formally map the learned descriptors to more traditional social role categories, and this is an important direction for future work.

An interesting extension of the model would be to take into account the immediate context in which a post is made. Because the function of a post is partially determined by what it is responding to, additional context may lead to more salient descriptors.

Acknowledgements

The authors thank R. Sosic for his helpful comments. This research has been supported in part by NSF IIS-1149837, NIH BD2K, ARO MURI, Stanford Data Science Initiative, Stanford CSLI Summer Internship Grant, SAP Stanford Graduate Fellowship, NSERC PGS-D, Boeing, Lightspeed, and Volkswagen.

Appendix

ID	RMN	LDA
0	sideways, hangs, dragging, tapping, protip	n't, server, issue, problem, servers
1	ps, weapons, dmg, weapon, shields	n't, <QUOTE >, wrong, thought, edit
2	me, have, i, my, had	n't, team, good, medic, demo
3	countered, attacking, taunting, retaliate, nullify	team, bet, win, n't, game
4	finest, go-to, funniest, glorious, favorites	story, n't, character, characters, big
5	medium, amazing, surprisingly, fantastic, warm	game, games, n't, halo, play
6	quests, npc, game, playthrough, player	hit, n't, jump, back, time
7	en, <SPECIAL>, de, en, que	build, base, units, army, gas
8	re, tricking, awfully, excessively, shy	world, life, n't, link, time
9	themselves, tend, their, they, them	character, level, n't, spell, party
10	prolly, cuz, tho, prob, legit	people, players, play, group, join
11	opponent, activates, protip, activate, combos	mod, game, mods, n't, save
12	desktop, hardware, optimized, pcs, os	tank, n't, good, tanks, tier
13	playable, considerably, usable, redundant, afaik	pc, version, n't, game, fps
14	suggestions, advice, appreciate, helpful, appreciated	war, empire, army, troops, units
15	hours, hour, evenings, day, week	city, n't, turn, cities, great
16	ah, ahh, thanks, alright, haha	team, n't, hp, set, good
17	job, incredibly, work, terribly, task	game, n't, hard, mission, missions
18	grabbed, walked, picked, bought, went	dps, n't, tank, class, healing
19	kinda, imo, looks, liked, meh	team, game, good, n't, hero
20	invalidate, exists, argument, hypothetical, valid	n't, ca, wo, wait, remember
21	additional, combine, abilities, combined, each	time, 've, hours, ago, playing
22	me, my, doge, paypal, his	ship, n't, crew, weapons, ships
23	restart, manually, fix, update, reset	post, read, question, thread, link
24	leftover, eventual, adding, pour, announcing	shit, fucking, fuck, god, man
25	no, continuity, commas, whatsoever, inconsistencies	level, gear, drop, loot, quest
26	explored, explore, approached, discuss, alliance	n't, point, make, people, fact
27	swarmed, shotted, snuck, taunting, one-shotting	play, players, player, games, game
28	criticizing, disagreeing, downvoting, criticize, agreeing	car, cars, race, sims, drive
29	nobody, thinks, clue, cares, fuck	damage, health, attack, speed, skill
30	sacrifice, peoples, humanity, damage, aura	fire, shot, gun, range, weapons
31	increased, increase, increases, higher, lower	'll, add, time, check, day
32	of, creations, purchasable, forge, workshop	map, area, room, make, place
33	ty, thx, mvp, mlg, gj	kill, back, time, run, fight
34	ftfy, bro, hahaha, hahahaha, fuckin	good, 'll, lot, things, time
35	link, links, post, posted, page	money, buy, pay, free, price
36	stop, release, waiting, pc, start	weapon, armor, weapons, set, good
37	he, i, be, it, as	game, release, n't, patch, content
38	focuses, fictional, introduction, memorable, relation	screen, click, button, n't, left
39	k, e, f, h, r	dark, dragon, kill, souls, boss
40	anticipated, progressed, progressively, hasnt, timeframe	<SPECIAL >, space, amp, make, orbit
41	war, during, fought, played, era	pretty, yeah, good, makes, cool
42	know, what, ca, yourself, you	dont, im, good, lol, yeah
43	hopefully, visit, find, will, places	black, red, blue, white, color
44	<number >, skew, variance, rarer, tended	love, video, great, good, watch
45	conquest, buildings, largest, infantry, round	na, gon, items, gold, buy
46	realised, wished, refused, hoped, relieved	n't, game, people, play, fun
47	is, s, in, level, of	n't, people, post, guy, comment
48	gorgeous, appearance, lovely, outfit, sexy	've, n't, back, time, times
49	competitive, matchmaking, teamspeak, skilled, players	game, n't, make, change, balance

Table 5: Full list of descriptors/topics for each model.

References

David M Blei, Andrew Y Ng, and Michael I Jordan. 2003. Latent dirichlet allocation. *Journal of machine Learning research*, 3(Jan):993–1022.

Marc Brysbaert, Amy Beth Warriner, and Victor Kuperman. 2014. Concreteness ratings for 40 thousand generally known english word lemmas. *Behavior Research Methods*, 46(3):904–911.

Cristian Danescu-Niculescu-Mizil, Robert West, Dan Jurafsky, Jure Leskovec, and Christopher Potts. 2013. No country for old members: User lifecycle and linguistic change in online communities. In *Proc. WWW*.

Leo Egghe. 2007. Untangling herdan's law and heaps' law: Mathematical and informetric arguments. *Journal of the American Society for Information Science and Technology*, 58(5):702–709.

Mohit Iyyer, Anupam Guha, Snigdha Chaturvedi, Jordan Boyd-Graber, and Hal Daumé III. 2016. Feuding families and former friends: Unsupervised learning for dynamic fictional relationships. In *NAACL*.

Siddharth Jain, Archna Bhatia, Angelique Rein, and Eduard H Hovy. 2014. A corpus of participant roles in contentious discussions. In *LREC*, pages 1751–1756.

Jean Lave and Etienne Wenger. 1991. *Situated learning: Legitimate peripheral participation*. Cambridge university press.

Linyuan Lü, Yi-Cheng Zhang, Chi Ho Yeung, and Tao Zhou. 2011. Leaders in social networks, the delicious case. *PloS one*, 6(6):e21202.

Andrew Kachites McCallum. 2002. Mallet: A machine learning for language toolkit. http://mallet.cs.umass.edu.

Peter McCullagh and John A Nelder. 1989. *Generalized linear models*, volume 37. CRC press.

Dong Nguyen and Carolyn P Rosé. 2011. Language use as a reflection of socialization in online communities. In *Proceedings of the Workshop on Languages in Social Media*, pages 76–85. Association for Computational Linguistics.

Radim Řehůřek and Petr Sojka. 2010. Software Framework for Topic Modelling with Large Corpora. In *Proceedings of the LREC 2010 Workshop on New Challenges for NLP Frameworks*, pages 45–50, Valletta, Malta, May. ELRA. http://is.muni.cz/publication/884893/en.

Sara Rosenthal. 2014. Detecting influencers in social media discussions. *XRDS: Crossroads, The ACM Magazine for Students*, 21(1):40–45.

Henri Tajfel, Michael G Billig, Robert P Bundy, and Claude Flament. 1971. Social categorization and intergroup behaviour. *European Journal of Social Psychology*, 1(2):149–178.

Chenhao Tan and Lillian Lee. 2015. All who wander: On the prevalence and characteristics of multi-community engagement. In *Proceedings of the 24th International Conference on World Wide Web*, pages 1056–1066. ACM.

Ming-Feng Tsai, Chih-Wei Tzeng, Zhe-Li Lin, and Arbee LP Chen. 2014. Discovering leaders from social network by action cascade. *Social Network Analysis and Mining*, 4(1):1–10.

Duncan J Watts and Steven H Strogatz. 1998. Collective dynamics of small-worldnetworks. *Nature*, 393(6684):440–442.

Howard T Welser, Eric Gleave, Danyel Fisher, and Marc Smith. 2007. Visualizing the signatures of social roles in online discussion groups. *Journal of Social Structure*, 8(2):1–32.

Howard T Welser, Dan Cosley, Gueorgi Kossinets, Austin Lin, Fedor Dokshin, Geri Gay, and Marc Smith. 2011. Finding social roles in wikipedia. In *Proceedings of the 2011 iConference*, pages 122–129. ACM.

The Effects of Data Collection Methods in Twitter

Sunghwan Mac Kim, Stephen Wan, Cécile Paris, Brian Jin and **Bella Robinson**
Data61, CSIRO, Sydney, Australia
{Mac.Kim, Stephen.Wan, Cecile.Paris, Brian.Jin, Bella.Robinson}@csiro.au

Abstract

There have been recent efforts to use social media to estimate demographic characteristics, such as age, gender or income, but there has been little work on investigating the effect of data acquisition methods on producing these estimates. In this paper, we compare four different Twitter data acquisition methods and explore their effects on the prediction of one particular demographic characteristic: occupation (or profession). We present a comparative analysis of the four data acquisition methods in the context of estimating occupation statistics for Australia. Our results show that the social network-based data collection method seems to perform the best. However, we note that each different data collection approach has its own benefits and limitations.

1 Introduction

Over the last decade, social media platforms have become prominent online channels for community interaction and communication. As a public data source, social media offers the potential to provide a cheap and large volume of real-time data to assist with social science research. Consequently, there have been several recent efforts to estimate aggregate demographic characteristics from social media (Sloan et al., 2015; Preoţiuc-Pietro et al., 2015) or to understand public views on topics like vaccination (Broniatowski et al., 2016). In such work, social media can supplement traditional data sources for social science research, such as interview and questionnaire data.

While different approaches to estimating demographic characteristics have been proposed, for example, for age and gender (Filippova, 2012) and for occupation (as these are useful as surrogates for income bracket) (Preoţiuc-Pietro et al., 2015), the effects of different data collection methods have been less studied. Twitter, as a source of predominantly public broadcast social media, allows for different methods for capturing user profile data, ranging from: (i) geolocation-based queries, (ii) word-based queries, (iii) Twitter's 1% sample stream, and (iv) social network-based crawling.

In this paper, we compare these four different Twitter data collection methods and explore their effects on estimating demographic characteristics. For this preliminary study, we focus on estimates of occupation groups for an Australian cohort and compare estimates to Australian 2011 census data.

We vary only the data collection method but use the same occupation statistic estimation throughout. We follow the methodology of Sloan et al. (2015), who use social media to estimate the United Kingdom (UK) occupation classes. This method requires an occupation taxonomy as the underlying resource for a keyword-spotting approach to compute the estimates. Sloan et al. (2015) used a resource called the *Standard Occupational Classification (SOC) 2010*[1], which was used to organise UK 2011 census data. As our estimates are for an Australian context, we use the corresponding *Australian*

---

[1] `http://www.ons.gov.uk/ons/`
`guide-method/classifications/`
`current-standard-classifications/soc2010/`
`index.html`

Proceedings of 2016 EMNLP Workshop on Natural Language Processing and Computational Social Science, pages 86–91,
Austin, TX, November 5, 2016. ©2016 Association for Computational Linguistics

and New Zealand Standard Classification of Occupations Version 1.2 (2013) or *ANZSCO*, published by the Australian Bureau of Statistics (ABS).[2] The ABS used this resource to organise statistics from the 2011 census.

2 Data Collection Methods

This section describes the four data collection approaches employed to acquire sets of Australian Twitter user profiles: (i) Geo-location queries, (ii) word-based queries, (iii) Twitter's 1% sample, and (iv) social network-based crawling. The first three methods use data sourced from existing projects that collect Twitter posts. To remove time as a confounding factor, we used the largest intersection of collection periods, from April 1 to October 30, 2014.[3]

Geo-located data was sourced from the CSIRO Data61 Emergency Situation Awareness project (Cameron et al., 2012). In this project, we took Twitter data collected for the Australia and New Zealand region. The system, which focuses on event-detection for natural disasters, uses a series of latitude/longitude coordinates and a radius with Twitter's location-based Search API to define collection boundaries that cover the heavily populated regions in Australia and New Zealand. This system relies on Twitter's built-in functionality to infer location based on Twitter metadata. We refer to data collected via this method as the *Geo-location* method.

For **word-based queries**, the data collection was based on queries curated by the State Library of New South Wales (SLNSW) as described in (Barwick et al., 2014). The SLNSW has a mandate to collect and archive data about daily life in the Australian state of New South Wales (NSW). Since 2012, their collection has extended beyond traditional media (e.g., print newspapers) to include social media. Library staff curate a set of queries on a daily basis, reacting to the salient NSW-specific news of the day. This can thus span any news topic, including politics, government, arts, festivals, sports. To date, over 1000 queries have been curated in this fashion since 2012, including general hashtags for politics (e.g. "#auspol"), event specific queries (e.g. "Vivid Festival"), and personalities. We refer to data collected via this method as the *Word-based* method.

For the third method, we used the **1% Twitter sample** which was collected as part of the CSIRO Data61 WeFeel project (Larsen et al., 2015). This sample, colloquially known as the Spritzer stream, was used for studying the emotion content in Twitter to further research in mental health. We refer to data collected via this method as the *Spritzer* method.

The **social network-based crawling** method starts with a seed set of known Australian Twitter user profiles and crawls the social network multigraph of followers to find other Australian user profiles (Dennett et al., 2016). The seed set consisted of public celebrities, politicians, journalists, government accounts, and accounts for Australian companies and institutions. Each new user profile encountered during the crawling process was automatically labelled as being Australian using the location and timezone metadata together with a gazeteer of known Australian locations, and a label propagation method. For all discovered Australian accounts, the crawling process continued. A crawling depth of 3-hops was used from the seed accounts. We refer to data collected via this method as the *Social-network* method.

2.1 Data Pre-processing

For methods (i) to (iii), the corresponding user profiles for the authors of the collected tweets were also obtained using the Twitter API. All user profiles, regardless of method were filtered as follows. We first filtered accounts using an in-house text classifier on the profile user name and description to determine if the account represented an individual or an organisation, where it is the former that is of most interest for estimating demographic statistics. This classifier uses a maximum entropy model (Berger et al., 1996) for the binary distinction, *individual* versus *organisation*, which has an accuracy of 95.2%. Finally, Twitter metadata was used to further filter user profiles, keeping only those with an Australian time zone and English specified as the language.

2.2 Data Descriptive Statistics

Table 1 shows the number of Twitter user profiles with a breakdown by Australian states, identified using time zone information. In Australia, each state

---

[2] www.abs.gov.au/ANZSCO

[3] This end date was chosen as Twitter's location-based Search API was not fully functional after this date.

Region	Geo-location	Word-query	Spritzer	Social-network	Population
AU	624,769	66,812	202,657	873,899	$\approx 20 \times 10^6$
ACT	14,157	2,585	6,885	39,193	357,222
NSW	240,055	25,923	60,119	264,235	6,917,658
NT	6,530	356	1,450	6,509	211,945
QLD	119,858	14,028	52,514	217,744	4,332,739
SA	31,494	3,768	13,840	58,857	1,596,572
TAS	11,027	903	2,548	11,671	495,354
VIC	162,037	15,815	47,815	210,585	5,354,042
WA	39,611	3,434	17,486	65,105	2,239,170

Table 1: Number of Twitter user profiles for Australian individuals and census population for Australia and its states. Abbreviations: Australia (AU), Australian Capital Territory (ACT), New South Wales (NSW), Northern Territory (NT), Queensland (QLD), South Australia (SA), Tasmania (TAS), Victoria (VIC), Western Australia (WA).

has a different Twitter time zone setting based on the capital city for that state. The table also shows population statistics obtained from the 2011 census.

3 The ANZSCO Hierarchy

The ANZSCO hierarchy organises occupations into five levels of occupation categories. The top level, known as the *major group*, contains 8 occupation groups: managers, professionals, technicians and trades workers, community and personal service workers, clerical and administrative workers, sales workers, machinery operators and drivers, and labourers. Each major group is divided into sub-major groups, which are further divided into minor groups. Each minor group is divided into unit groups, which contain the leaf level specific occupations. The ANZSCO hierarchy has 8 major groups, 43 sub-major groups, 97 minor groups and 358 unit groups. There are 1,034 occupation names represented at the leaf level of the hierarchy. In this work, our correlations will be based on data for the major groups.

4 Estimating Occupation Statistics

Our aim here is to calculate the proportions for each occupation class at the major group level. We use the ANZSCO resource to provide a list of keywords to spot. These are derived from the node labels at each level in the hierarchy.

For any given collection of user profiles and the descriptions contained therein, when a match is found to a word in this list, a counter for the node responsible is incremented. We refer to this as our KeyWord Spotting (KWS) method[4], which is inspired from the methods described in (Sloan et al., 2015). As our evaluation uses the highest major group level, we propagate counts up through the hierarchy and sum them at the top level of the hierarchy. Finally, frequencies are normalised by the sum of frequencies over all 8 occupation categories to provide percentages, as in the census data. For the KWS method, words that occur under multiple categories at the major group level were discarded. For words that occurred in multiple nodes within a single branch of the major group, the highest level node was chosen to increment the counter. We performed text pre-processing prior to calculating the estimates in order to mitigate the noisiness of free text Twitter user profile descriptions. We removed non-ASCII characters and stop words, and all tokens were lower-cased. It is possible that multiple occupations are listed in a single user profile description. In this work, the first occupation word found is selected under the assumption that it is likely to represent the main occupation (Sloan et al., 2015).

Finally, we assembled the subsets of the Twitter user profiles, where occupations were identified using the KWS method. The number of profiles from each data collection method with a matching occupation is as follows: Geo-location: 100,829 / 624,769 (16.14%), Word-query: 16,358 / 66,812 (24.48%), Spritzer: 36,034 / 202,657 (17.78%) and Social-network: 104,867 / 873,899 (12.00%).

5 Comparisons to Census Data

In this evaluation, we look at the ranking of major group occupation categories based on social media estimates of prevalence and compare this derived ranking to the ordering from the 2011 census data. We used Kendall's τ (Kendall, 1938), a nonparametric statistical metric for comparing different rankings.

We calculate the Kendall τ rank correlation coefficient to compare the census occupation group percentages with the corresponding Twitter-derived

---

[4]While there has been a significant work on occupation inference (Preoţiuc-Pietro et al., 2015), we take a simple KWS approach to identify user occupations. Note that the primary goal of this work is to compare different data collection methods to estimate occupation statistics.

Region	Geo-location		Word-query		Spritzer		Social-network	
	cor	p-value	cor	p-value	cor	p-value	cor	p-value
AU	0.5714	0.0610	0.5714	0.0610	0.5714	0.0610	0.5714	0.0610
ACT	**0.7857**	0.0055	**0.7638**	0.0088	**0.7857**	0.0055	**0.7638**	0.0088
NSW	**0.7143**	0.0141	**0.7857**	0.0055	**0.7857**	0.0055	**0.7143**	0.0141
NT	0.5000	0.1087	**0.6183**	0.0341	0.5714	0.0610	**0.6429**	0.0312
QLD	0.5000	0.1087	0.4286	0.1789	0.4286	0.1789	0.4286	0.1789
SA	0.5000	0.1087	0.4728	0.1051	0.5000	0.1087	0.5714	0.0610
TAS	0.3571	0.2751	0.4286	0.1789	0.4001	0.1702	0.2857	0.3988
VIC	**0.6429**	0.0312	0.5000	0.1087	0.5714	0.0610	**0.6429**	0.0312
WA	0.5000	0.1087	0.4286	0.1789	0.4286	0.1789	0.4286	0.1789

Table 2: Kendall correlations for estimates of national and state occupation statistics derived by the KWS tagger. Bold indicates statistically significant results ($p<0.05$).

percentages from each data collection method. Table 2 shows the correlation coefficients for Australia and its states with respect to the Geo-location, Word-query, Spritzer and Social-network based methods. For determining significance, we set $\alpha = 0.05$.

We observe that the correlations are almost but not quite statistically significant at national level, with $p \approx 0.06$. We note that the correlation are identical for the national level. In this case, each method is resulting in the same number of ranking mistakes. As Kendall's τ is a measurement of the number of pairwise swaps needed to convert compare two rankings, the coefficients are identical

At the state-level, we observe that the Social-network data has the most states with significant correlations: 4 out of 7 states.[5] The Geo-location and Word-query based methods both have 3 states with significant correlations, whereas the Spritzer method has 2 states. This suggests that the social network crawling method performs better than the others at producing these estimates.

6 Discussion and Future work

Our results show that, for statistics at the national level, all methods appear to perform identically. However, for statistics at the state level, differences in the different data collection methods become apparent.

The Social-network method may be superior to the Spritzer method because it acquires a far larger set of user profiles. The same can be said about the Geo-location method which also collects a large number of Australian user profiles. This extra data,

or the ability of the Social-network and Geo-location based methods to sample relevant profiles, results in significant correlations for VIC, the second most populous state in Australia, which is not captured well by the Spritzer method.

Interestingly, the Word-query method retrieves the smallest number of unique user profiles but does surprisingly well compared to the Spritzer method. We suspect this is due to the curation of queries that collect social media related to the state of NSW. Indeed, the correlation for NSW for this method is better than that of the Social-network approach. Furthermore, NSW has the highest correlation among all the states. We do note, however, that this method requires human-curated queries, a process that is time intensive.

For all methods, there are significant correlations for the ACT state. We find the ACT to be well represented in all of the social media collection methods, perhaps because it is the capital of Australia.[6] Presumably, a large volume of Twitter traffic is generated by government and industry staff located within the state. The Word-query method shows a significant correlation for the NT state. We suspect that the Word-query based method also does well for non-NSW states because the library uses some general queries like *#auspol*, which capture nation-wide discussions.

The Social-network method may have an advantage over the other data collection methods as it does not require users to actively post Twitter messages. Some Twitter users follow accounts of interest and rarely post messages themselves and therefore will be missed by the Geo-location, Word-query and Spritzer methods.

In this work, Kendall's τ coefficient does not provide deep insight at the national level of Australia. This is likely due to the number of categories being ranked. In the major group of the ANZSCO taxonomy, there are only 8 groupings of occupations. To provide further insights about the rankings at the national level, we visualise the major occupation rankings amongst the four data collection methods for Australia, as shown in Figure 1. The English letters on the X-axis correspond to 8 major occupations in

---

[5]Technically, the ACT and NT are territories, not states.

[6]Note that the ACT is geographically surrounded by the state of NSW.

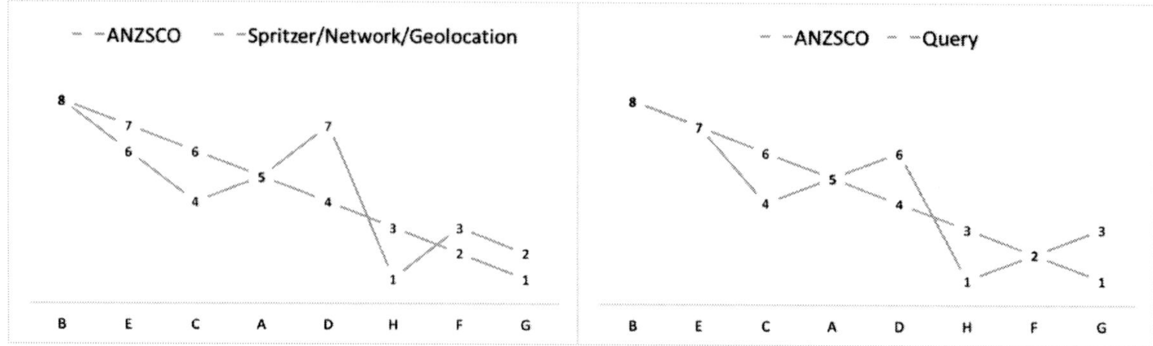

Figure 1: Comparison of major occupation rankings between ANZSCO and four data collection methods for Australia (A: Managers, B: Professionals, C: Technician and Trades Workers, D: Community and Personal Service Workers, E: Clerical and Administrative Workers, F: Sales Workers, G: Machinery Operators and Drivers, H: Labourers).

the ANZSCO hierarchy. These are listed according to ANZSCO rankings, with B at the highest rank and G at the lowest. The digits on the graph indicate the rankings produced by each data collection method. We notice that *Professionals* (B) and *Managers* (A), as the first and fourth ranked occupation groups in ANZSCO, are ranked correctly by all methods. Interestingly, the Word-query based method is the only one to correctly rank the *Clerical and Administrative Workers* (E) and *Sales Workers* (F) classes. We can only hypothesise that, because this method uses the queries capturing discussions about everyday life, it is able to better represent these subgroups.

The current study does have some limitations. One of these is that our Word-query method uses queries specific to one state in Australia, NSW, whereas the other data collection methods do not suffer from this bias. In future work, we will try to repeat our exploration of Word-query methods with a more general set of human-curated queries. We have also focused here on estimating statistics about occupation. We are also interested in examining the effects of data collection methods in estimating other demographic characteristics, such as age and gender. Finally, we would also like to replicate this work for other languages and countries outside of an Australian context.

7   Conclusion

In this paper, we see that different data collection methods have an effect on the quality of estimates of occupation classes. The question of which is best may depend on the application context requiring the estimate of occupation classes. If the aim is to produce an estimate for the current population, the Social-network approach may be best as it is able to find a large volume of user profiles, with little manual intervention. However, for many applications there may be a time-based element. For example, to study public discussion corresponding to a social event or information campaign taking place at a certain time, one may want to use posts colected using the Geo-location or Word-query based methods to better target the most relevant audience or community. Our study shows that methods based on posts can still yield good estimates.

Acknowledgments

The authors are grateful to anonymous NLPCSS@EMNLP reviewers.

References

Kathryn Barwick, Mylee Joseph, Cécile Paris, and Stephen Wan. 2014. Hunters and collectors: seeking social media content for cultural heritage collections. In *VALA 2014: Streaming With Possibilities*.

Adam L. Berger, Vincent J. Della Pietra, and Stephen A. Della Pietra. 1996. A maximum entropy approach to natural language processing. *Computational Linguistics*, 22(1):39–71.

David A Broniatowski, Mark Dredze, Karen M Hilyard, Maeghan Dessecker, Sandra Crouse Quinn, Amelia

Jamison, Michael J. Paul, and Michael C. Smith. 2016. Both mirror and complement: A comparison of social media data and survey data about flu vaccination. In *American Public Health Association*.

Mark A. Cameron, Robert Power, Bella Robinson, and Jie Yin. 2012. Emergency situation awareness from twitter for crisis management. In *Proceedings of the 21st International Conference on World Wide Web*, WWW '12 Companion, pages 695–698, New York, NY, USA. ACM.

Amanda Dennett, Surya Nepal, Cecile Paris, and Bella Robinson. 2016. Tweetripple: Understanding your twitter audience and the impact of your tweets. In *Proceedings of the 2nd IEEE International Conference on Collaboration and Internet Computing*, Pittsburgh, PA, USA, November. IEEE.

Katja Filippova. 2012. User demographics and language in an implicit social network. In *Proceedings of EMNLP-CoNLL*, pages 1478–1488, Jeju Island, Korea, July. Association for Computational Linguistics.

M. G. Kendall. 1938. A new measure of rank correlation. *Biometrika*, 30(1/2):81–93.

Mark E. Larsen, Tjeerd W. Boonstra, Philip J. Batterham, Bridianne O'Dea, Cecile Paris, and Helen Christensen. 2015. We Feel: Mapping Emotion on Twitter. *IEEE Journal of Biomedical and Health Informatics*, 19(4):1246–1252.

Daniel Preoţiuc-Pietro, Vasileios Lampos, and Nikolaos Aletras. 2015. An analysis of the user occupational class through twitter content. In *Proceedings of ACL-IJCNLP*, pages 1754–1764, Beijing, China, July. Association for Computational Linguistics.

Luke Sloan, Jeffrey Morgan, Pete Burnap, and Matthew Williams. 2015. Who tweets? deriving the demographic characteristics of age, occupation and social class from twitter user meta-data. *PLoS ONE*, 10(3):e0115545, 03.

Expressions of Anxiety in Political Texts

Ludovic Rheault

Department of Political Science, University of Toronto

Abstract

Anxiety has a special importance in politics since the emotion is tied to decision-making under uncertainty, a feature of democratic institutions. Yet, measuring specific emotions like anxiety in political settings remains a challenging task. The present study tackles this problem by making use of natural language processing (NLP) tools to detect anxiety in a corpus of digitized parliamentary debates from Canada. I rely upon a vector space model to rank parliamentary speeches based on the semantic similarity of their words and syntax with a set of common expressions of anxiety. After assessing the performance of this approach with annotated corpora, I use it to test an implementation of state-trait anxiety theory. The findings support the hypothesis that political issues with a lower degree of familiarity, such as foreign affairs and immigration, are more anxiogenic than average, a conclusion that appears robust to estimators accounting for unobserved individual traits.

1   Introduction

Of the variety of emotions experienced by humans, anxiety ranks arguably among the most relevant for politics. Put simply, anxiety means feeling worried or concerned in the face of uncertainty (LaBar, 2016). We inherited this emotion from evolutionary processes with the critical function of keeping us alert to external threats (Suomi and Harlow, 1976; LeDoux, 2012; LaBar, 2016). Scholars have tied the emotion not only to uncertainty, but also to one's lack of control over events (Mandler, 1972; Mineka

and Kelly, 1989). Of all social contexts, democratic institutions appear to combine the full set of ingredients required to rouse anxiety. Indeed, parliaments gather individuals with the specific purpose of making decisions under uncertainty, sometimes in situations of emergency. The rules of the game are collective by nature, meaning that individual concerns are at times ignored by the majority, which can exacerbate the sense of helplessness. As a result, it appears natural to associate the domain of politics with anxiety. The emotion has already gained the attention of scholars interested in politics, although empirical evidence has focused mostly on actors outside political institutions, such as voters (Marcus et al., 2000, e.g.). This paper represents a systematic attempt to automatically measure the level of anxiety in an extensive corpus of parliamentary debates.

Previous studies seeking to measure anxiety in text using methods of NLP have been sporadic, yet influential (Gilbert and Karahalios, 2010; Bollen et al., 2011). Since the task of detecting anxiety involves the recognition of rather subtle forms of expression in language, the levels of accuracy reached using machine learning classifiers are typically lower than for other tasks. More than a decade ago, Mishne (2005) released a valuable resource for the study of emotions in text, namely a corpus of blog posts from the LiveJournal website where users were invited to self-report their current mood by selecting options from a list, including *anxious*. In the original study, classifiers trained with Bag-of-Words (BoW) features reached an accuracy rate of 54.25% for the detection of the anxious mood, in balanced class problems. In a more recent study using an

Proceedings of 2016 EMNLP Workshop on Natural Language Processing and Computational Social Science, pages 92–101,
Austin, TX, November 5, 2016. ©2016 Association for Computational Linguistics

unbalanced dataset, Gilbert and Karahalios (2010) reached a very high level of accuracy for the detection of non-anxious texts, but only around 30% of correct predictions for anxious ones. Papers focusing on the related concept of fear have reported F1-scores between 0.20 and 0.74 (Strapparava and Mihalcea, 2007; Roberts et al., 2012; Mohammad, 2012).[1] It should be noted, however, that trying to map specific emotions such as anxiety into binary categories may not be the optimal approach. Feelings can be of various intensities, and binary annotations amount to losing precious information. Several modern approaches have instead relied upon emotion-specific lexicons that can be used to create continuous indicators (Tumasjan et al., 2010; Mohammad et al., 2013; Zhao et al., 2014). Using such a methodology, for instance, Bollen et al. (2011) were able to show that anxiety in social media is related to movements in the stock market.

The objective of this study is twofold. First, I seek to develop a methodology for the automatic measurement of levels of anxiety in writings, in particular, one that is adaptive to domain-specific corpora. The third section of this report describes the method and evaluates its performance using two annotated datasets: a sample of sentences from the Canadian House of Commons debates (the Hansard), annotated for anxiety using a crowd-sourcing platform, and the above-mentioned LiveJournal mood corpus. Second, my goal is to explain the prevalence of anxiety in real-life political speeches using a large section of the Hansard corpus.[2] Based on state-trait anxiety theory, which I discuss next, I implement predictive models in which some of the topics debated are expected to induce anxiety among parliamentarians.

2 Theoretical Background

I derive my expectations about the presence of anxiety in politics from the seminal state-trait anxiety theory proposed by Spielberger (1966). The theory emphasizes the distinction between anxiety as a *trait*, a more permanent feature of one's personality, and anxiety as a *state*, a temporary reaction to stressful situations. In this model, state anxiety is caused by the combination of both external events and individual predispositions. Anxiety as a trait has been the object of a voluminous literature, and corresponds to one of the "Big Five" personality traits (neuroticism) (Eysenck, 1997). In fact, other popular theories in psychology emphasize the role of factors such as personal experiences and biases in explaining anxious responses to external stimuli, for instance appraisal theory (Smith and Lazarus, 1993). Transposed to the realm of politics, this means that individual members of parliament (MPs) should exhibit various levels of anxiety in response to a situational trigger, depending on their personalities. An advantage of the Hansard corpus is that it allows to observe the same individuals repeatedly, under various situations. Thus, it becomes possible to account for individual traits, even if they are unobserved.

Regarding external factors, a central idea guiding my empirical analysis is that anxiety is more likely to occur the less an issue is known to MPs. Such an expectation directly follows from the nature of anxiety, which entails uncertainty, and parallels other theories in political psychology arguing that unfamiliar situations make individuals more anxious (Marcus, 2000; Marcus et al., 2000). In the context of a parliament, I expect subject-matters that are external to the country, such as foreign affairs and immigration, to be less familiar, hence more anxiogenic. One could view this as an argument from analogy: for individuals, strangers can be a source of anxiety since their intentions are unknown; for representatives of a state, other countries and their nationals can be a similar source of unpredictability. Of course, national issues such as natural disasters or economic downturns can also be worrisome to politicians. However, a reasonable working hypothesis is that the more foreign the object of debate, the more likely MPs are to experience anxiety.

Unlike ordinary social settings, however, members of democratic institutions have functions that may constrain the manner in which they respond to ongoing events. In particular, members face different incentives depending on the role that their political formation occupies in a legislature. Just like personality traits may predispose to anxiety, one's

---

[1]Although Freud (1920, S. 3, Ch. 25) originally made a distinction between anxiety and fear, scholars have since emphasized the close connection between the two concepts, some advocating their conflation (McReynolds, 1976; Gray and McNaughton, 2000; LaBar, 2016).

[2]The full corpus is released on the www.lipad.ca website.

partisan affiliation can affect the likelihood of expressing signs of that emotion. Parties forming the opposition are required by convention to challenge the government's decisions; in fact, a period in the daily business of the Canadian House of Commons, the Oral Question Period, is dedicated to that duty. It is natural to expect MPs from opposition parties to communicate more forcefully their worries about the problems faced by their constituents, as opposed to members of the party in power, who are expected to bring reassurance. Figure 1 is a simplified depiction of the model guiding the present study. The figure is loosely based on the state-trait anxiety model in Spielberger (1966), amended to account for the peculiarities of parliamentary life. Basically, political speeches are expected to become anxious due to external triggers (unfamiliar topics under debate), individual-level factors (mostly unobservable and deeply entrenched personality traits) and party-level functions (the government/opposition division).

3 Automated Detection of Anxiety in Text

A key challenge with the detection of anxiety in the Hansard corpus is to account for the specific language of a parliament. In contrast to the casual English used in social media, politicians in parliament may be less explicit about their mood. To illustrate, one message from the LiveJournal corpus annotated with the *anxious* mood starts with the following words:

> [I] have finals today :(I am very nervous..

In this case, the statement expresses an unfiltered feeling that can be easily detected from word usage by a computer. However, parliamentary debates are subject to a decorum and speeches are usually less personal. An efficient methodology needs to take into account the vocabulary used to communicate emotions in such a formal setting.

For this reason, I rely upon a methodology that makes use of a vector space representation— the transformation of the corpus under study into numerical vectors based on word-word co-occurrences—to identify the proximity of each new word with a small set of seed words closely related to anxiety. This approach has been used previously to perform related tasks where semantic targets can be organized as polar opposites (Turney and

Littman, 2003). I have tested the approach with different lists of seed words. Although the selection of these initial seed words may be a sensitive task, accuracy results based on the annotated corpora were not severely affected by small changes in the seed list. For this analysis, I make use of 30 lemma/part-of-speech tuples associated with anxiety on the one hand, and with the absence thereof on the other hand. In the anxiety pole, seed lemmas include *threat*, *worry*, *fear*, *danger*, *anxious* and *tension*, for instance. These are general words selected recursively from a thesaurus for their association with the concept of anxiety. In the opposite pole, seed lemmas comprise *ease*, *protect*, *confidence*, *safe*, *trust* and *calm*. Considering pairs of lemmas and parts of speech (PoS) allows to take into account the distinction between the syntactic roles of each word, for instance when being used as a verb or as a noun.

Specifically, I start by preprocessing the full Hansard Corpus between 1980 and 2015. This stage includes word and sentence segmentation, the attribution of PoS tags and lemmatization, all performed using the Stanford CoreNLP library (Manning et al., 2014). This subset of the Hansard comprises above 245 million tokens, and the period was chosen to encompass that used in the rest of the empirical analysis. The vector space model is computed on a reconstructed corpus of combined lemma and PoS pairs using the Glove program (Pennington et al., 2014), which can be trained on the entire co-occurrence matrix. I create word vectors of 300 dimensions using a symmetric window size of 15 words.

Next, for each new lemma and PoS pair in the Hansard corpus, I compute the cosine similarity between their vectors and the vectors of each lemma and PoS pairing in the seed list. The sum of similarity scores with the no-anxiety seeds is then subtracted from the sum of similarity scores obtained for the anxiety pole, and scaled back into a $[-1, 1]$ range, where 1 means the most anxious lemma and -1 the least anxious. The created lexicon comprises 14,703 lemmas occurring 200 times or more in the corpus, after excluding digits and proper nouns.

Finally, I match the numerical scores of anxiety to the lemma/PoS pairs in the original corpus and compute average values for each individual speech. The result is a continuous indicator of the level anxiety, adapted to the specific register and tone of pol-

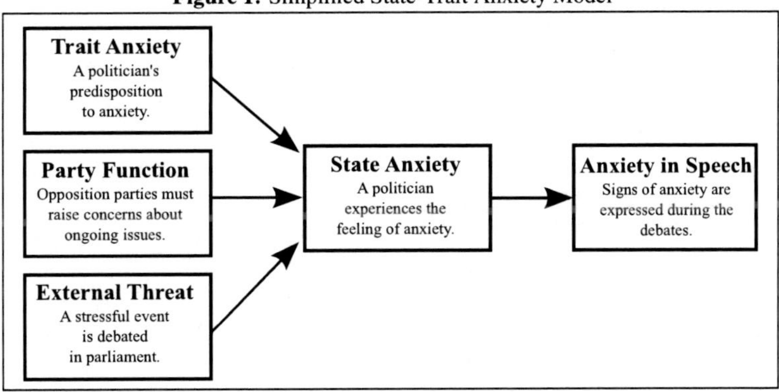

Figure 1: Simplified State-Trait Anxiety Model

itics, which can also be linked back to metadata on individual speakers, their party and the topic under debate.

To assess the performance of this approach, I retained the services of contributors from the Crowd-Flower website. I randomly selected two series of 2,000 sentences from the Hansard, respectively from the Government Orders and Oral Question Period between 1994 and 2015.[3] The decision to use sentences as a unit of annotation is justified by the large variation in the length of speeches during parliamentary debates. Preliminary assessments made with the help of a research assistant, based on entire speeches as units of analysis, revealed the task to be impractical for human coders, since full speeches may introduce several questions about how to properly code a document expressing different intensities of emotions. Shorter units of text can be more readily coded as anxious or non-anxious, and they reduce the risk of contradictory signals. I imposed the length of sentences to be above 8 tokens and removed procedural interventions (e.g. the introduction of motions). The 4,000 sentences were annotated by three different contributors via the crowd-sourcing platform, with an average pairwise agreement of 79.3%. Contributors were pre-screened with questions from a test set and their judgments considered reliable only if they reached a 70% agreement or above on these test questions. Although reliability may not reach the levels of more traditional methods, a re-

cent study suggests that crowd-sourcing yields annotations comparable to those obtained from expert surveys (Benoit et al., 2016).

The proportion of sentences coded as anxious reaches 10.7% in the 4,000 Hansard sentences, larger than in the LiveJournal corpus. To avoid an unbalanced class problem, I have matched anxious sentences with the same number of randomly selected non-anxious ones. Although this is an admittedly small sample (854 sentences), the methodology reaches appreciable levels of accuracy using support vector machines (SVMs) with a linear kernel and a penalty parameter set at 0.5. Using the anxiety indicator as a single feature, the level of accuracy is around 63% (see Table 1), already above the levels of some previously cited attempts to detect the same emotion. Performance is slightly improved when adding a BoW including unigrams and bigrams.

I achieve important gains after including a simple categorical variable identifying the speaker, as well as title annotations from the original Hansard. With these metadata as features, the rate of accuracy reaches 83.6% (with a F1-score of 0.83, after selecting the 700 best features based on chi-square tests). This result is consistent with psychology theory, which emphasizes the importance of accounting for individual-specific traits, and illustrates the role of non-textual features in classification tasks. Accuracy scores are computed with randomly assigned training and testing sets; using 3K-fold cross-validation, the percentage of accuracy reaches 82% in the best model. Additionally, I have considered grammatical features such as verb tense, after

---

[3]Those two sections of the daily business of the House are the most important ones. The Government Orders comprise the debates on the bills introduced by the government. The Oral Question Period opens the floor to the opposition, who can question the government on its agenda and decisions.

Hansard (Anxious v. Non-Anxious)

Features	Accuracy	F1-Score	Sample
Anxiety Score	62.9%	0.632	854
+BoW	69.0%	0.673	854
+Metadata	83.6%	0.830	854

LiveJournal (Anxious v. Non-Anxious Moods)

Features	Accuracy	F1-Score	Sample
Anxiety Score	57.2%	0.582	30000
+BoW	74.6%	0.745	30000

LiveJournal (Anxious v. All Others Moods)

Features	Accuracy	F1-Score	Sample
Anxiety Score	55.1%	0.565	30000
+BoW	72.9%	0.713	30000

Table 1: Accuracy Results for SVM Classifiers

identifying the verb phrase containing the root in the dependency grammar structure of each sentence. These features are significantly related to anxiety (the future tense being positively related to anxiety, and conversely for the past tense). However, they did not improve accuracy further once accounting for speaker identification.

Finally, I also assess the methodology against the LiveJournal corpus. The latter comprises over 700,000 entries associated with several moods. Since the proposed methodology is adaptive, I replicated the same steps with the LiveJournal data, creating anxiety scores using word vectors of the entire corpus and the same seed lists as before. Thus, the measure is now tailored to the specific genre of casual online discussions. To select anxious posts, I combined semantically equivalent reported moods (namely *anxious*, *stressed*, *worried* and *restless*). Following the approach in Mishne (2005), I matched a random sample of 15,000 anxious posts to the same number of non-anxious ones (merging *calm*, *relaxed*, *optimistic* and *relieved*) and to a sample of all other moods except anxiety.[4] The two bottom panels of Table 1 report the results. Accuracy using the anxiety score alone is lower than before, around 57%, still using SVMs ($C = 80$). Yet, the fact that a univariate indicator is sufficient to achieve a performance similar to that reported in previous studies using BoW models brings some additional legitimacy to the methodology. When including unigrams and

bigrams, the predictive model reaches a level of accuracy exceeding 70%. Despite the possible limitations of the two corpora discussed in this section, these results suggest that the proposed score is significantly related to anxiety, as perceived by human coders or self-reported by Internet users.

4   Application to Parliamentary Debates

To examine the prevalence of anxiety in political speeches, I rely upon the previously introduced Hansard of the Canadian House of Commons. Using the anxiety scores generated with the method described in the previous section, speeches in that corpus are now associated with a level of anxiety. The database is constructed at the speech level, each observation corresponding to one intervention, and each being associated with metadata. I removed non-substantive speeches, for instance introductory remarks, questions of procedure, and interventions from the Speaker of the House.[5] I have also removed speeches for which the MP was not identified and those comprising less than 8 tokens, to avoid a number of common brief utterances such as "Yes/No" responses.

A portion of the Canadian parliamentary debates had been manually annotated by other researchers using the Comparative Agendas Project (CAP) topic scheme, namely a set of over 40,000 questions asked during the Oral Question Period between 1983 and 2004 (Penner et al., 2006). Coders attributed a topic to each new question in a given exchange (an exchange may include a question, an answer, and sometimes follow-up questions), which means that each annotation can be matched to more than one speech in the Hansard corpus. Using variables common to both datasets, I was able to match most of those annotations back with their original text.[6] This leaves a dataset of 119,623 speeches annotated by topic, which I focus on for the empirical analysis below. The topic scheme used by the CAP team is

---

[4]I have excluded irregular postings such as lists of tracks from musical albums and messages in foreign language.

[5]In contrast to Speakers in the US House of Representatives, who are high-ranking legislators, the role of Speaker in Westminster systems is procedural. Speakers in Canada do not play a partisan role in the debates.

[6]Manual inspection after running the matching algorithm revealed a few cases of mismatch due to discrepancies in the two databases, often unresolvable. However, the large majority of annotations appear correctly attributed in the Hansard corpus.

Speech	Score
Mr. Speaker, the Prime Minister is joking about the serious and even catastrophic situation of Canada's public finances.	0.29
That this House condemn those policies of the government which, having bred a sense of insecurity, powerlessness and doubt among Canadians, are a cause of the recent increase in regional tensions and incidents of racism and bigotry in Canada.	0.27
In those capacities we have absolute confidence in the judgment of the Secretary of State for External Affairs, and we can offer that categoric assurance to the Leader of the New Democratic Party.	−0.48
Mr. Speaker, as always we will strive to protect the best interests of all Canadians.	−0.50

Table 2: Examples of Anxious and Non-Anxious Speeches

rather detailed, comprising 25 main topics and more than 200 subtopics. For the sake of this study, I have simplified the scheme to 10 categories by relabeling the original CAP annotations. These 10 topics should sound fairly intuitive to both political scientists and scholars from other disciplines: constitutional affairs, economy, education, environment, foreign affairs, health care, immigration, law and order, natural resources, and a residual category containing all other national topics such as land management and intergovernmental affairs.

Illustrating the methodology when applied to political debates, Table 2 reports two examples of speeches above the 99th percentile on the anxiety score, and two under the 1st percentile. As can be seen, the measure correctly ranks the first speech as an expression of anxiety, despite the presence of a word like *joking*, which could have been misinterpreted as indicative of a light tone. The examples may also serve to illustrate how political functions influence the emotional valence of speeches: the two anxious speeches come from members of the opposition parties, whereas the bottom two speeches of Table 2 come from the government. The large majority of speeches fall under 0 on the anxiety scale, which is consistent with the fact that the feeling remains infrequent. The average value in the full sample is −0.13. In what follows, I normalize the indicator by transforming it into a z-score with a mean of 0, which facilitates the interpretation of findings.

The main objective from now on is to test the hypotheses laid out earlier in the theoretical section.

I start by looking at the bivariate relationship between the topic under debate and the level of anxiety of MPs. Figure 2 shows the average level of anxiety by topic category (I use a weighted average with token counts as weights to account for discrepancies in speech lengths). As can be seen, immigration and foreign affairs are the topics for which Canadian MPs displayed the highest average level of anxiety between 1983 and 2004 during oral questions, which is consistent with the starting hypothesis. It shall be noted that anxiety is not bound to external topics, however. The question of natural resources—historically important for the Canadian economy, and including debates on sectors such as oil production and nuclear energy—ends up closely behind, before environment and economy. Law and order (which includes crime) and health care range somewhere in the middle, being neither the most anxious nor the least. Education and constitutional affairs rank as the least anxiogenic topics during this period.

It may be helpful to consider topic averages broken down by year to understand why immigration turns out first in the ranking during that time span. The highest levels of anxiety on the topic of immigration are observed between 1993 and 2001, period during which one of the major parties—the Conservatives—had ruptured into factions. The new parties (Reform and Bloc) began to voice a more forceful opposition on that particular topic. The period culminated with a major reform of immigration legislation in 2001, year during which the average level of anxiety reaches 0.31.

The corpus also allows for an examination of anxiety by party function, another component of the model introduced above. Table 3 reveals that members from parties in the opposition have levels of anxiety larger than the global average (+0.26), while the converse holds for parties forming the government (−0.20). The specific parties exhibiting the highest levels of anxiety in Table 3 are also those that remained in the opposition the whole time. I have also examined the link between anxiety and available biographical information on MPs. Women, for instance, appear slightly less anxious than men, still using the 1983–2004 sample of oral questions, based on a one-tailed mean comparison t-test ($p < 0.02$). Age also appears to be a significant predictor of anx-

97

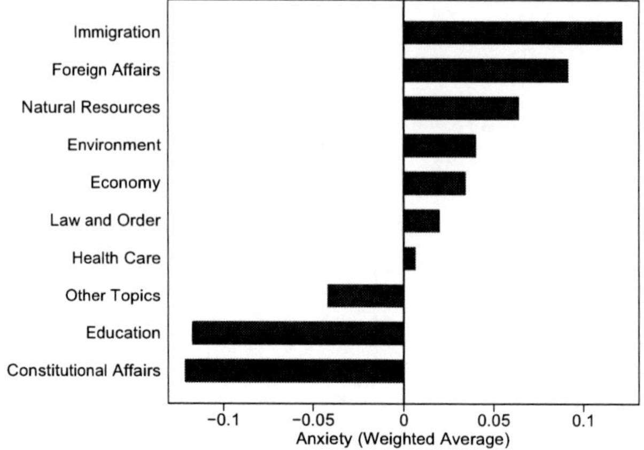

Figure 2: Anxiety by Topic in the House of Commons (1983–2004)

Political Party	Anxiety
Bloc Québécois	0.16
Canadian Alliance	0.35
Conservatives	−0.08
Liberals	−0.13
NDP	0.27
Reform	0.33
Government	−0.20
Opposition	0.26

Table 3: Weighted Average of Anxiety (Normalized Scale) by Political Group during Oral Question Period (1983–2004)

iety in speeches: older MPs are less likely to express anxiety than younger ones.

Bivariate relationships, however, ignore the fact that some of those speeches are uttered by the same individuals. As pointed out earlier in the theoretical section, individual characteristics (traits) may affect whether someone is likely to feel nervous at any given point (state). Some MPs may have a tendency to experience anxiety and express worries in the face of adversity, whereas others may have a more stoic personality. Such individual traits can represent a confounding factor, and the unexplained variance of the anxiety score may be clustered within individual MPs. For these reasons, I rely upon statistical methods accounting for individual characteristics. I first consider a "within" estimator that subtracts individual averages from each variable in the model (which amounts to including a specific intercept parameter for each MP). This is also known as a fixed effects estimator that can be expressed in the form

$$y_{ij} = a_j + \mathbf{x}'_{ij}\boldsymbol{\beta} + \varepsilon_{ij}, \qquad (1)$$

where y_{ij} is the measured anxiety of a speech i uttered by MP j, the a_j are MP-specific intercepts, $\mathbf{x}$ is a vector of observed metadata for each speech, and ε_{ij} is an error component. The within transformation precludes the inclusion of variables that do not vary within individuals, such as gender. On the other hand, this transformation implies that the estimator accounts for all unobserved MP characteristics, such as personality traits. Note that the government-opposition status varies for some MPs, and can be included among observed covariates. The second estimator is a hierarchical model with random intercepts at the party and individual levels. The model corresponds to:

$$y_{ij} = \alpha + \mathbf{x}'_{ij}\boldsymbol{\beta} + \lambda_j + \theta_k + \epsilon_{ij} \qquad (2)$$

where λ_j and θ_k are random intercepts for MP j and party k. This estimator allows for the inclusion of variables such as age and gender.

Table 4 reports estimates from both these models. Starting with the fixed effects model in the left column, estimated by OLS ($F = 40.04; p = 0.000$), the results are consistent with several of the findings stressed earlier about the relation between topics and anxiety. Since the topic variable is categorical, estimates are to be interpreted with respect to a base category, in this case the residual category "other topics". As can be seen, the estimates suggest that foreign affairs and immigration are significantly more

	Fixed Effects		Hierarchical	
Variable	**Est.**	**p**	**Est.**	**p**
Topic				
Constitutional	−0.079	0.008	−0.079	0.000
Economy	0.075	0.000	0.076	0.000
Education	−0.041	0.057	−0.045	0.011
Environment	0.065	0.072	0.071	0.000
Foreign Affairs	0.125	0.000	0.129	0.000
Health Care	0.070	0.033	0.067	0.000
Immigration	0.145	0.000	0.150	0.000
Law and Order	0.077	0.001	0.081	0.000
Nat. Resources	0.145	0.000	0.143	0.000
Party Status				
Government	−0.360	0.000	−0.357	0.000
Obs.		119,623		117,704

Table 4: Multivariate Models of Anxiety in Parliament. Both models include year, month and day of the week dummies as well as a control variable for the length of speeches in tokens. The hierarchical model is reported with approximate p-values, and also includes age and gender as controls.

anxiogenic than the base category, supporting the results presented so far. These estimates are statistically significant, with reported p-values computed using Arellano's heteroskedasticity and autocorrelation (HAC) consistent standard errors (Arellano, 1987). However, once accounting for individual-specific factors, the topic of national resources appears to produce the same effect on anxiety than immigration, and a larger effect than foreign affairs. Education and constitutional affairs remain among the least anxious topics. Members of the government appear significantly less likely to express anxiety during their interventions, in line with the observations made previously. The last column of Table 4 reports results from the three-level hierarchical model estimated by restricted maximum likelihood. This model includes age and gender as covariates, which now turn out as non-significant predictors. A few data points on the birth dates of MPs are missing, reducing the number of observations. However, the results are very close to those obtained with the first estimator, and again support some of the key findings discussed so far.

5 Conclusion

Overall, this study illustrates the potential of NLP methods for the detection of specific emotions such as anxiety in politics. The finding that some topics are a source of anxiety may help to inform future research on legislative politics, for instance to examine the role of emotions in the formation of preferences over issues. From a methodological standpoint, the study also illustrates the importance of theory and non-textual features in predictive tasks. In particular, the results suggest that machine learning models can be improved by accounting for author identification in corpora where documents are clustered by individuals. Although the findings bring support to the proposed model, a limitation of this study is that expressions of anxiety may not reflect the true emotional state of a speaker. For example, politicians may appeal to emotions strategically, in an attempt to persuade. Disentangling the motives behind the use of language would require additional research. Nonetheless, the framework proposed in these pages appears reliable enough to derive substantive results of interest.

Looking forward, the methodology could serve to answer other important questions about the role of anxiety in politics, ones that fell beyond the scope of this study. Previous research on anxiety has shown that the emotion influences how people make decisions. The experience of anxiety may ultimately make some choices less appealing, or refrain individuals from action altogether (Raghunathan and Pham, 1999; Gray and McNaughton, 2000). Marcus et al. (2000) stressed the hypothesis that anxiety leads individuals to search for more information before making decisions. Whether this has positive effects on the quality of decisions made by anxious individuals, or whether the feeling clouds their judgment, remains a debated question, albeit an important one (Brader, 2011; Ladd and Lenz, 2008; Marcus et al., 2011). Moreover, improving computational tools for the detection of specific emotions in texts can have applications useful beyond the study of politics. Examples include the detection of health conditions such as anxiety disorders, stock market forecasting or, more generally, contributions to the development of an artificial intelligence able to accurately identify specific emotions from language.

Acknowledgments

The author thanks Andreea Musulan for research assistance as well as the Connaught Fund for financial support.

References

Manuel Arellano. 1987. Computing Robust Standard Errors for Within-Groups Estimators. *Oxford Bulletin of Economics and Statistics*, 49(4):431–434.

Kenneth Benoit, Drew Conway, Benjamin E. Lauderdale, Michael Laver, and Slava Mikhaylov. 2016. Crowd-Sourced Text Analysis: Reproducible and Agile Production of Political Data. *American Political Science Review*, 110(2):278–295.

Johan Bollen, Huina Mao, and Xiaojun Zeng. 2011. Twitter Mood Predicts the Stock Market. *Journal of Computational Science*, 2(1):1–8.

Ted Brader. 2011. The Political Relevance of Emotions: 'Reassessing' Revisited. *Political Psychology*, 32(2):337–346.

Michael W. Eysenck. 1997. *Anxiety and Cognition: A Unified Theory*. Psychology Press, Hove.

Sigmund Freud. 1920. *A General Introduction to Psychoanalysis*. Boni and Liveright, New York.

Eric Gilbert and Karrie Karahalios. 2010. Widespread Worry and the Stock Market. In *Proceedings of the International Conference on Weblogs and Social Media (ICWSM 10)*.

Jeffrey A. Gray and Neil McNaughton. 2000. *The Neuropsychology of Anxiety: An Enquiry into the Functions of the Septo-Hippocampal System*. Oxford University Press, Oxford.

Kevin S. LaBar. 2016. Fear and Anxiety. In Lisa Feldman Barrett, Michael Lewis, and Jeannette M. Haviland-Jones, editors, *Handbook of Emotions*. The Guilford Press, New York.

Jonathan McDonald Ladd and Gabriel S. Lenz. 2008. Reassessing the Role of Anxiety in Vote Choice. *Political Psychology*, 29(2):275–296.

Joseph LeDoux. 2012. Rethinking the Emotional Brain. *Neuron*, 73(4):653–676.

George Mandler. 1972. Helplessness: Theory and Research in Anxiety. In Charles D. Spielberger, editor, *Anxiety: Current Trends in Theory and Research*, pages 359–378. Academic Press, New York.

Christopher D. Manning, Mihai Surdeanu, John Bauer, Jenny Finkel, Steven J. Bethard, and David McClosky. 2014. The Stanford CoreNLP Natural Language Processing Toolkit. In *Proceedings of 52nd Annual Meeting of the Association for Computational Linguistics: System Demonstrations*, pages 55–60.

George E. Marcus, W. Russell Neuman, and Michael MacKuen. 2000. *Affective Intelligence and Political Judgment*. University of Chicago Press, Chicago.

George E. Marcus, Michael MacKuen, and W. Russell Neuman. 2011. Parsimony and Complexity: Developing and Testing Theories of Affective Intelligence. *Political Psychology*, 32(2):323–336.

George E. Marcus. 2000. Emotions in Politics. *Annual Review of Political Science*, 3:221–250.

William T. McReynolds. 1976. Anxiety as Fear: A Behavioral Approach to One Emotion. In Marvin Zuckerman and Charles D. Spielberger, editors, *Emotions and Anxiety: New Concepts, Methods, and Applications*, pages 281–316. Lawrence Elbaurm Associates, Hillsdale.

Susan Mineka and Kelly A. Kelly. 1989. The Relationship Between Anxiety, Lack of Control and Loss of Control. In Andrew Steptoe and Ad Appels, editors, *Stress, Personal Control and Health*, pages 163–191. John Wiley & Sons, Chichester.

Gilad Mishne. 2005. Experiments with Mood Classification in Blog Posts. In *Style2005: 1st Workshop on Stylistic Analysis Of Text For Information Access*.

Saif M. Mohammad, Svetlana Kiritchenko, and Xiaodan Zhu. 2013. NRC-Canada: Building the State-of-the-Art in Sentiment Analysis of Tweets. In *Proceedings of the Seventh International Workshop on Semantic Evaluation Exercises (SemEval-2013)*, Atlanta, Georgia, USA, June.

Saif Mohammad. 2012. Portable Features for Classifying Emotional Text. In *2012 Conference of the North American Chapter of the Association for Computational Linguistics: Human Language Technologies*, pages 587–591.

Erin Penner, Kelly Blidook, and Stuart Soroka. 2006. Legislative Priorities and Public Opinion: Representation of Partisan Agendas in the Canadian House of Commons. *Journal of European Public Policy*, 13(7):959–974.

Jeffrey Pennington, Richard Socher, and Christopher D. Manning. 2014. Glove: Global Vectors for Word Representation. In *Conference on Empirical Methods in Natural Language Processing (EMNLP 2014)*.

Rajagopal Raghunathan and Michel Tuan Pham. 1999. All Negative Moods Are Not Equal: Motivational Influences of Anxiety and Sadness on Decision Making. *Organizational Behavior and Human Decision Processes*, 79(1):56–77.

Kirk Roberts, Michael A. Roach, Joseph Johnson, Josh Guthrie, and Sanda M. Harabagiu. 2012. EmpaTweet: Annotating and Detecting Emotions on Twitter. In *Proceedings of the 9th Language Resources and Evaluation Conference*, pages 3806–3813.

Craig A. Smith and Richard S. Lazarus. 1993. Appraisal Components, Core Relational Themes, and the Emotions. *Cognition and Emotion*, 7(3/4):233–269.

Charles D. Spielberger. 1966. Theory and Research on Anxiety. In Charles D. Spielberger, editor, *Anxiety and Behavior*, pages 3–20. Academic Press, New York.

Carlo Strapparava and Rada Mihalcea. 2007. SemEval-2007 Task 14: Affective Text. In *Proceedings of the*

4th International Workshop on Semantic Evaluations. Association for Computational Linguistics.

Stephen J. Suomi and Harry F. Harlow. 1976. The Facts and Functions of Fear. In Marvin Zuckerman and Charles D. Spielberger, editors, *Emotions and Anxiety*, pages 3–34. Lawrence Elbaurm Associates, Hillsdale.

Andranik Tumasjan, Timm O. Sprenger, Philipp G. Sandner, and Isabell M. Welpe. 2010. Predicting Elections with Twitter: What 140 Characters Reveal about Political Sentiment. In *Proceedings of the Fourth International AAAI Conference on Weblogs and Social Media*.

Peter D. Turney and Michael L. Littman. 2003. Measuring Praise and Criticism: Inference of Semantic Orientation from Association. *ACM Trans. Inf. Syst.*, 21(4):315–346.

Jian Zhao, Liang Gou, Fei Wang, and Michelle Zhou. 2014. PEARL: An Interactive Visual Analytic Tool for Understanding Personal Emotion Style Derived from Social Media. In *Proceedings of the IEEE Symposium on Visual Analytics Science and Technology*, 203–212.

Constructing an Annotated Corpus for Protest Event Mining

Peter Makarov[†]   **Jasmine Lorenzini**[*]   **Hanspeter Kriesi**[*]

[†]Institute of Computational Linguistics, University of Zurich, Switzerland
[*]Department of Political and Social Sciences, European University Institute, Italy

`makarov@cl.uzh.ch`   `{jasmine.lorenzini,hanspeter.kriesi}@eui.eu`

Abstract

We present a corpus for protest event mining that combines token-level annotation with the event schema and ontology of entities and events from protest research in the social sciences. The dataset uses newswire reports from the English Gigaword corpus. The token-level annotation is inspired by annotation standards for event extraction, in particular that of the Automated Content Extraction 2005 corpus (Walker et al., 2006). Domain experts perform the entire annotation task. We report competitive intercoder agreement results.

1 Introduction

Social scientists rely on event data to quantitatively study the behavior of political actors. Public protest (demonstrations, industrial strikes, petition campaigns, political and symbolic violence) accounts for a large part of events involving sub-state actors. Protest event data are central to the study of protest mobilization, political instability, and social movements (Hutter, 2014; Koopmans and Rucht, 2002).

To advance the machine coding[1] of protest data, we have been building a manually annotated corpus of protest events. Our protest event coding follows guidelines adapted from successful manual coding projects. All coding decisions are supported by careful token-level annotation inspired by annotation standards for event extraction. Both event cod-

ing and token-level annotation are performed by domain experts. We find that domain experts without specialist linguistic knowledge can be trained well to follow token-level annotation rules and deliver sufficient annotation quality.

Contentious politics scholars often need more fine-grained information on protest events than can be delivered by available event coding software. Our event schema includes issues—the claims and grievances of protest actors—and the number of protesters. We also code protest events that are not the main topic of the report. This is often desirable (Kriesi et al., 1995), although event coding systems would not always code them by design.

We code newswire reports from the widely used English Gigaword corpus and will release all annotations.[2]

2 Related Work

2.1 Machine coding of events

The machine coding of political event data from newswire text goes back to early 1990s and has been first applied to the study of international relations and conflicts (Gerner et al., 1994; Schrodt and Hall, 2006). Many widely used systems—e.g. TABARI (O'Brien, 2010) / PETRARCH[3], VRA-Reader[4] (King and Lowe, 2003)—have relied on pattern matching with large dictionaries of hand-crafted patterns. A system scans a news lead attempting to match an event, source and target actors—thereby extracting *who did what to whom*; the date of the event is taken

---

[1]We use the social science term *coding* to refer to information extraction. Automated extraction is *machine coding*, manual extraction is *human coding*. Event coding happens at the document level. We use the linguistic term *token-level annotation* to refer to attaching metadata to tokens in the document.

[2]`https://github.com/peter-makarov/apea_corpus`
[3]`https://github.com/openeventdata/petrarch`
[4]`http://vranet.com`

Proceedings of 2016 EMNLP Workshop on Natural Language Processing and Computational Social Science, pages 102–107,
Austin, TX, November 5, 2016. ©2016 Association for Computational Linguistics

to be the date of publication. Common ontologies CAMEO (Gerner et al., 2002) and IDEA (Bond et al., 2003) define dozens of event types and hundreds of actors. Proprietary event coder BBN ACCENT, which uses statistical entity and relation extraction and co-reference resolution, considerably outperforms a pattern matching-based coder (Boschee et al., 2013; Boschee et al., 2015). O'Connor et al. (2013) present an unsupervised Bayesian coder, which models the gradual change in the types of events between actors.

Pattern-matching coders have been found to predict event types on a par with trained human coders (King and Lowe, 2003) and sufficiently accurate for near real-time event monitoring (O'Brien, 2010). That event coding is hard and coding instructions are often not rigorous enough manifests itself in low intercoder reliability (Schrodt, 2012). Boschee et al. (2015) report an intercoder agreement of F1 45% for two human coders coding 1,000 news reports using only the top event types of the CAMEO ontology.

2.2 Machine coding of protest events

Pattern matching-based systems have been employed to assist humans in coding protest events (Imig and Tarrow, 2001; Francisco, 1996). Some (Maher and Peterson, 2008) use only machine-coded protest events. More recently, statistical learning has been applied to the coding of protest events. Hanna (2014) trains a supervised learning system leveraging the events hand-coded by the Dynamics of Collective Action[5] project (Earl et al., 2004). Nardulli et al. (2015) employ a human-in-the-loop coding system that learns from human supervision.

2.3 Corpora annotated with protest events

A major benchmark for event mining is the Automated Content Extraction (ACE) 2005 Multilingual Training Corpus (Walker et al., 2006). The corpus, distributed by the Linguistic Data Consortium, comes with token-level annotations of entities, relations, and events. Its event ontology includes the CONFLICT event type. Its sub-type ATTACK overlaps with violent protest; the other sub-type, DEMONSTRATE, is close to our understanding of demonstrative protest. Some important protest event types

e.g. petition campaign, industrial strike, symbolic protest, are not included. Unlike our project, the targets of ATTACK events are annotated (but not the targets of DEMONSTRATE events). Issues and the number of participants are not annotated.

Of some interest is the corpus of Latin American terrorism[6] used in the Message Understanding Conference evaluations 3 and 4 (Chinchor et al., 1993). It comes with a highly complex event schema that includes detailed information on the actor, human and physical targets, and distinguishes several types of terrorist acts. The corpus predates information extraction by statistical learning from annotated text and thus does not contain token-level annotation.[7]

3 Annotated Corpus of Protest Events

The main motivation for this work has been the connection of event coding, which is performed at the level of the document, to token-level annotation. In that respect, we follow the trend towards annotating for social science tasks at below the document level (Card et al., 2015; Žukov-Gregorič et al., 2016). Unlike these projects, we have chosen to train domain experts to perform careful token-level annotation. The downside of having coders annotate in a linguistically unconstrained manner—an approach sometimes advocated for annotation tasks performed by domain experts (Stubbs, 2013)—is that the resulting annotation requires extensive standardization. This is challenging in the case of a complex task like ours.

The overall coding procedure is thus twofold. The coders perform traditional event coding, which involves the identification of protest events and classification of their attributes (type, actors, etc.). In parallel, the coders carry out token-level annotation, which we motivate as a means of supporting coding decisions with the help of text. The coder connects the two by linking coded events to their mentions in the text. Figure 1 shows sample annotation.

All our coders are doctoral students in political science. All are non-native English speakers with a high command of English. One project leader is a trained linguist.

---

[5]http://web.stanford.edu/group/
collectiveaction

[6]http://www-nlpir.nist.gov/related_
projects/muc/muc_data/muc34.tar.gz
[7]DAPRA's Deep Exploration and Filtering of Text (DEFT) program has in recent years produced event extraction resources (Aguilar et al., 2014), which currently are only available for closed system evaluation. It uses the ACE event ontology.

event no	event type	location	date	actor	issue	size
1, 2, 3, 4	Occupation/Blockade	France	29.09.2003	Occupational group	For labor rights	100-999 people

(a) Coded events

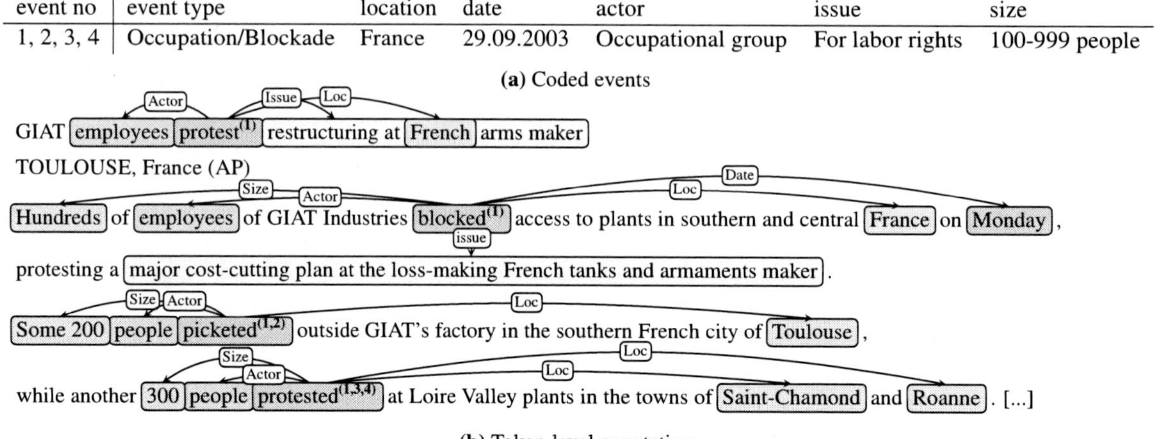

(b) Token-level annotation

Figure 1: An annotation example. **(1a)** coded events. The coder has identified four protest events—all of the same structure. Event one is a campaign event, the other events are the episode events of event one (e.g. "protested" refers to two episode events, which are differentiated based on the two distinct city-level locations). **(1b)** in-text annotations. Event mentions are in orange. In the superscript are the indices of the coded events that an event mention refers to. In the annotation interface, the coder draws links from event mentions to the mentions of event attributes (actor, location, date, etc.).

3.1 Event schema and ontology

A protest event has an event type, a date range, a country, a number of participants, a set of actor types, and a set of issue types. We distinguish ten protest event types, twenty-six issues, and twelve actor types. The types are organized hierarchically. We have not used a large ontology of entities and events that one typically finds in event coding. Our aim has been to ensure that each type occurs sufficiently often and the reliability of coding does not suffer due to codebook complexity.

The choice and definition of the types reflect our primary interest in European protest. Having examined a sample of recent European protest events coded using a larger codebook, we have selected some frequent actor types and issues and reworked the event ontology. For example, all specific issues now come with the stance on the issue fixed: *against cultural liberalism, for regionalism*, etc.

We code only asserted specific past and currently unfolding events—in contrast to the ACE 2005 corpus[8] and despite the practice of coding planned future events in manual coding work.

3.2 Token-level annotation

In devising token-level annotation guidelines, we have relied on the ACE English Annotation Guidelines for Events and Entities[9] (Doddington et al., 2004). We have borrowed many ideas, e.g. the annotation of event mentions largely as one-word triggers, which we have found to work well in practice. The ACE guidelines are written for annotators with a background in linguistics, not domain experts. We have found that it is often possible to convey more or less the same idea in less technical language, e.g. simplifying *present-participle in the nominal pre-modifier position* to *participle modifying a noun*, and by providing extensive examples.

Not all ACE rules could be adapted in this way. We do not distinguish between heads and multi-word extents, but rather annotate the one which appears easier for a given attribute. For example, we annotate collective actors ("postal workers", "left-wing protesters") as head nouns only and not full noun phrases, which would be more in line with the ACE guidelines but is challenging even for trained linguists. On the other hand, issue annotations are predominantly multi-word expressions.

The linking of coded events to token-level annotation is at the core of our approach. To consolidate

---

[8] Yet, much like the lighter-weight DEFT ERE (Entities, Relations, Events) annotation standard (Aguilar et al., 2014).

[9] https://www.ldc.upenn.edu/collaborations/past-projects/ace/annotation-tasks-and-specifications

the information about an event scattered across multiple sentences, we would need an annotated event co-reference. Yet, annotating event co-reference (as well as non-strict identity relations) is hard (Hovy et al., 2013). In the annotation interface, the coders explicitly link coded events to event mentions that refer to them, and many events can be linked to the same event mention. Thus, unlike the ACE 2005 corpus, we do not explicitly define the co-reference relation between event mentions, but read it off the explicit references. We do not annotate entity co-reference.

3.3 Workflow

We code newswire texts by the Agence France Press (AFP) and the Associated Press World (APW) of the English Gigaword Third Edition Corpus (Graff et al., 2007). We sample from two-month periods in the 2000s. For a given period, we select all documents that mention a European location in the dateline and are found protest-relevant by a classifier that we have trained, for a related project, on newswire stories including AFP and APW. For each month and agency, we randomly sample forty documents of which a project leader picks ten to twenty documents for coding. In this way, we typically get groups of documents from various dates, each group covering the same story.

Each document gets coded by at least two coders. A project leader performs adjudication. We estimate that coding one document takes an average of fifteen minutes. Our budget allows for coding up to 300 documents. In the first rounds of coding, we have not used any pre-annotation.

3.4 Intercoder reliability

We achieve competitive intercoder agreement for the first batch of documents (Table 1). During the coding of this batch, the coders received general feedback on token-level annotation (Table 1b), which partly explains the high agreement. For reference, we show the agreement achieved by the ACE coders on newswire documents annotated with events of type CONFLICT. Crucially, the ACE documents are almost twice as long on average, which drags down agreement. While the agreement on coded events is expectedly low, our coders agree substantially on coding subsets of event attributes (Table 1d).

	This work		ACE'05 nw Conflict	

a) Dual-pass statistics: number of documents coded independently by two coders, average number of tokens per document.

# docs	avg # tokens per doc	# docs	avg # tokens per doc
30	363.5	53	705.9

b) Token-level annotation: F1-score agreement for exact match ($F1_E$) and match by overlap ($F1_O$). For ACE: Location=Place, Actor=Attacker or Entity, Time=any of the Time-* types.

	avg # per doc	$F1_E$	$F1_O$	avg # per doc	$F1_E$	$F1_O$
Trigger	4.3	75.6	76.4	5.1	48.9	62.1
Location	2.7	80.2	81.5	3.0	51.9	60.0
Time	1.7	87.4	87.4	2.0	54.3	66.7
Actor	2.5	79.7	82.7	3.0	52.0	60.2
Issue	1.2	54.0	76.2	-	-	-
Size	0.7	76.9	92.3	-	-	-

c) Event co-reference: average number of coded events per document, CoNLL F1-score agreement. For our corpus, we take two event mentions to co-refer if they are linked to the same events.

avg # per doc	CoNLL F1	avg # per doc	CoNLL F1
2.0	55.39	3.4	40.11

d) Coding (this work): F1-score agreement on (event type, location, date range). Coders agree if types and locations match, and date ranges overlap. F1-score agreement on event attributes given that two events agree on type, location, date range as described.

Event type / Loc / Date		F1 58.2
	avg # unique labels per doc	F1 given type/ loc/date match
Actors	0.82	78.1
Issues	0.83	78.1
Size	0.55	93.2

Table 1: Intercoder agreement for two coders. For reference, we show agreement scores for the ACE coders on the ACE 2005 newswire reports annotated for events by both coders s.t. at least one report of each pair has CONFLICT events. We only consider specific asserted past/present events and their arguments.

4 Conclusion and Future Work

We have presented our work on a corpus of protest events, which combines event coding with careful token-level annotation. The corpus comes with coded issues and numbers of participants. Overall, we observe substantial intercoder agreement.

Little work has been done on the evaluation of event coders (Boschee et al., 2013),[10] and none on widely available data despite interest (Schrodt, 2016). We would encourage the use of our corpus as an evaluation benchmark. That would require mapping our ontology of events and entities to CAMEO categories.

As we often code groups of documents covering the same sets of events (Section 3.3), the corpus could be extended to include cross-document event co-reference annotations.

---

[10]There has been work comparing datasets of automatically coded events (Ward et al., 2013).

Acknowledgments

We would like to thank Swen Hutter, Elisa Volpi, Joldon Kutmanaliev, Chiara Milan, Daniel Schulz, and the two anonymous reviewers. This work has been supported by European Research Council Grant No. 338875.

References

[Aguilar et al.2014] Jacqueline Aguilar, Charley Beller, Paul McNamee, Benjamin Van Durme, Stephanie Strassel, Zhiyi Song, and Joe Ellis. 2014. A comparison of the events and relations across ACE, ERE, TAC-KBP, and FrameNet annotation standards. In *Proceedings of the Second Workshop on EVENTS: Definition, Detection, Coreference, and Representation*, pages 45–53.

[Bond et al.2003] Doug Bond, Joe Bond, Churl Oh, J Craig Jenkins, and Charles Lewis Taylor. 2003. Integrated data for events analysis (IDEA): An event typology for automated events data development. *Journal of Peace Research*, 40(6):733–745.

[Boschee et al.2013] Elizabeth Boschee, Premkumar Natarajan, and Ralph Weischedel. 2013. Automatic extraction of events from open source text for predictive forecasting. In *Handbook of Computational Approaches to Counterterrorism*, pages 51–67. Springer.

[Boschee et al.2015] Elizabeth Boschee, Jennifer Lautenschlager, Sean O'Brien, Steve Shellman, James Starz, and Michael Ward. 2015. BBN ACCENT Event Coding Evaluation.updated v01.pdf (ICEWS Coded Event Data). http://dx.doi.org/10.7910/DVN/28075.

[Card et al.2015] Dallas Card, Amber E Boydstun, Justin H Gross, Philip Resnik, and Noah A Smith. 2015. The media frames corpus: Annotations of frames across issues. In *ACL*, volume 2, pages 438–444.

[Chinchor et al.1993] Nancy Chinchor, David D Lewis, and Lynette Hirschman. 1993. Evaluating message understanding systems: an analysis of the third message understanding conference (muc-3). *Computational linguistics*, 19(3):409–449.

[Doddington et al.2004] George R Doddington, Alexis Mitchell, Mark A Przybocki, Lance A Ramshaw, Stephanie Strassel, and Ralph M Weischedel. 2004. The Automatic Content Extraction (ACE) Program-Tasks, Data, and Evaluation. In *LREC*, volume 2, page 1.

[Earl et al.2004] Jennifer Earl, Andrew Martin, John D McCarthy, and Sarah A Soule. 2004. The use of newspaper data in the study of collective action. *Annual review of Sociology*, pages 65–80.

[Francisco1996] Ronald A Francisco. 1996. Coercion and protest: An empirical test in two democratic states. *American Journal of Political Science*, pages 1179–1204.

[Gerner et al.1994] Deborah J Gerner, Philip A Schrodt, Ronald A Francisco, and Judith L Weddle. 1994. Machine coding of event data using regional and international sources. *International Studies Quarterly*, pages 91–119.

[Gerner et al.2002] Deborah J Gerner, Philip A Schrodt, Omür Yilmaz, and Rajaa Abu-Jabr. 2002. Conflict and mediation event observations (CAMEO): A new event data framework for the analysis of foreign policy interactions. *International Studies Association, New Orleans*.

[Graff et al.2007] David Graff, Linguistic Data Consortium, et al. 2007. *English Gigaword Third Edition LDC2007T07*. Linguistic Data Consortium.

[Hanna2014] Alex Hanna. 2014. Developing a system for the automated coding of protest event data. Available at SSRN: http://ssrn.com/abstract=2425232 or http://dx.doi.org/10.2139/ssrn.2425232.

[Hovy et al.2013] Eduard Hovy, Teruko Mitamura, Felisa Verdejo, Jun Araki, and Andrew Philpot. 2013. Events are not simple: Identity, non-identity, and quasi-identity. In *NAACL HLT*, volume 2013, page 21.

[Hutter2014] Swen Hutter. 2014. Protest event analysis and its offspring. In Donatella Della Porta, editor, *Methodological practices in social movement research*. Oxford University Press.

[Imig and Tarrow2001] Doug Imig and Sidney Tarrow. 2001. Mapping the Europeanization of contention: evidence from a quantitative data analysis. *Contentious Europeans: Protest and politics in an emerging polity*, pages 27–49.

[King and Lowe2003] Gary King and Will Lowe. 2003. An automated information extraction tool for international conflict data with performance as good as human coders: A rare events evaluation design. *International Organization*, 57(03):617–642.

[Koopmans and Rucht2002] Ruud Koopmans and Dieter Rucht. 2002. Protest event analysis. *Methods of social movement research*, 16:231–59.

[Kriesi et al.1995] Hanspeter Kriesi, Ruud Koopmans, Jan Willem Duyvendak, and Marco G Giugni. 1995. *New social movements in Western Europe: A comparative analysis*, volume 5. U of Minnesota Press.

[Maher and Peterson2008] Thomas V Maher and Lindsey Peterson. 2008. Time and country variation in contentious politics: Multilevel modeling of dissent and repression. *International Journal of Sociology*, 38(3):52–81.

[Nardulli et al.2015] Peter F Nardulli, Scott L Althaus, and Matthew Hayes. 2015. A progressive supervised-learning approach to generating rich civil strife data. *Sociological Methodology*.

[O'Brien2010] Sean P O'Brien. 2010. Crisis early warning and decision support: Contemporary approaches and thoughts on future research. *International Studies Review*, 12(1):87–104.

[O'Connor et al.2013] Brendan O'Connor, Brandon M Stewart, and Noah A Smith. 2013. Learning to extract international relations from political context. In *ACL (1)*, pages 1094–1104.

[Schrodt and Hall2006] Philip A Schrodt and Blake Hall. 2006. Twenty years of the Kansas event data system project. *The political methodologist*, 14(1):2–8.

[Schrodt2012] Philip A Schrodt. 2012. Precedents, progress, and prospects in political event data. *International Interactions*, 38(4):546–569.

[Schrodt2016] Philip A Schrodt. 2016. Comparison metrics for large scale political event data sets. `http://www.polmeth.wustl.edu/files/polmeth/schrodtepsa15eventdata.pdf`.

[Stubbs2013] Amber C Stubbs. 2013. *A Methodology for Using Professional Knowledge in Corpus*. Ph.D. thesis, Brandeis University.

[Žukov-Gregorič et al.2016] Andrej Žukov-Gregorič, Bartal Veyhe, and Zhiyuan Luo. 2016. IBC-C: A dataset for armed conflict event analysis. In *ACL*.

[Walker et al.2006] Christopher Walker, Stephanie Strassel, Julie Medero, and Kazuaki Maeda. 2006. ACE 2005 multilingual training corpus. *Linguistic Data Consortium, Philadelphia*.

[Ward et al.2013] Michael D Ward, Andreas Beger, Josh Cutler, Matt Dickenson, Cassy Dorff, and Ben Radford. 2013. Comparing GDELT and ICEWS event data. *Analysis*, 21:267–297.

Demographer: Extremely Simple Name Demographics

Rebecca Knowles
Department of Computer Science
Johns Hopkins University
Baltimore, MD 21218
`rknowles@jhu.edu`

Josh Carroll
Qntfy
Crownsville, MD 21032
`josh@qntfy.com`

Mark Dredze
Human Language Technology
Center of Excellence
Johns Hopkins University
Baltimore, MD 21211
`mdredze@cs.jhu.edu`

Abstract

The lack of demographic information available when conducting passive analysis of social media content can make it difficult to compare results to traditional survey results. We present DEMOGRAPHER,[1] a tool that predicts gender from names, using name lists and a classifier with simple character-level features. By relying only on a name, our tool can make predictions even without extensive user-authored content. We compare DEMOGRAPHER to other available tools and discuss differences in performance. In particular, we show that DEMOGRAPHER performs well on Twitter data, making it useful for simple and rapid social media demographic inference.

1 Introduction

To study the attitudes and behaviors of a population, social science research often relies on surveys. Due to a variety of factors, including cost, speed, and coverage, many studies have turned to new sources of survey data over traditional methods like phone or in-person interviews. These include web-based data sources, such as internet surveys or panels, as well as *passive analysis of social media content*. The latter is particularly attractive since it does not require active recruitment or engagement of a survey population. Rather, it builds on data that can be collected from social media platforms.

Many major social media platforms, such as Twitter, lack demographic and location characteristics available for traditional surveys. The lack of these data prevents comparisons to traditional survey results. There have been a number of attempts to *automatically* infer user attributes from available social media data, such as a collection of messages for a user. These efforts have led to author attribute, or demographic, inference (Mislove et al., 2011; Volkova et al., 2015b; Burger et al., 2011; Volkova et al., 2015a; Pennacchiotti and Popescu, 2011; Rao and Yarowsky, 2010; Rao et al., 2010; Schwartz et al., 2013; Ciot et al., 2013; Alowibdi et al., 2013; Culotta et al., 2015) and geolocation tasks (Eisenstein et al., 2010; Han et al., 2014; Rout et al., 2013; Compton et al., 2014; Cha et al., 2015; Jurgens et al., 2015; Rahimi et al., 2016).

A limitation of these content analysis methods is their reliance on multiple messages for each user (or, in the case of social network based methods, data about multiple followers or friends for each user of interest). For example, we may wish to better understand the demographics of users who tweet a particular hashtag. While having tens or hundreds of messages for each user can improve prediction accuracy, collecting more data for every user of interest may be prohibitive either in terms of API access, or in terms of the time required. In this vein, several papers have dealt with the task of geolocation from a single tweet, relying on the user's profile location, time, tweet content and other factors to make a decision (Osborne et al., 2014; Dredze et al., 2016). This includes tools like Carmen (Dredze et al., 2013) and TwoFishes.[2] For demographic prediction, several papers have explored using names to infer gender and ethnicity (Rao et al., 2011; Liu and Ruths,

---

[1] `https://bitbucket.org/mdredze/demographer`

[2] `http://twofishes.net/`

Proceedings of 2016 EMNLP Workshop on Natural Language Processing and Computational Social Science, pages 108–113,
Austin, TX, November 5, 2016. ©2016 Association for Computational Linguistics

2013; Bergsma et al., 2013; Chang et al., 2010), although there has not been an analysis of the efficacy of such tools using names alone on Twitter.

This paper surveys existing software tools for determining a user's gender based on their name. We compare these tools in terms of accuracy on annotated datasets and coverage of a random collection of tweets. Additionally, we introduce a new tool DEMOGRAPHER which makes predictions for gender based on names. Our goal is to provide a guide for researchers as to software tools are most effective for this setting. We describe DEMOGRAPHER and then provide comparisons to other tools.

2   Demographer

DEMOGRAPHER is a Python tool for predicting the gender[3] of a Twitter user based only on the name[4] of the user as provided in the profile. It is designed to be a lightweight and fast tool that gives accurate predictions when possible, and withholds predictions otherwise. DEMOGRAPHER relies on two underlying methods: name lists that associate names with genders, and a classifier that uses features of a name to make predictions. These can also be combined to produce a single prediction given a name.

The tool is modular so that new methods can be added, and the existing methods can be retrained given new data sources.

Not every first name (given name) is strongly associated with a gender, but many common names can identify gender with high accuracy. DEMOGRAPHER captures this through the use of name lists, which assign each first name to a single gender, or provide statistics on the gender breakdown for a name. Additionally, name morphology can indicate the gender of new or uncommon names (for example, names containing the string "anna" are often associated with *Female*). We use these ideas to implement the following methods for name classification.

Name list   This predictor uses a given name list to build a mapping between name and gender. We assign scores for female and male based on what fraction of times that name was associated with females and males (respectively) in the name list. This model is limited by its data source; it makes no predictions

for names not included in the name list. Other tools in our comparison also take this approach.

Classifier   We extract features based on prefix and suffix of the name (up to character 4-grams, and including whether the first and final letters are vowels) and the entire name. We train a linear SVM with L2 regularization. For training, we assume names are associated with their most frequent gender. This model increases the coverage with a modest reduction in accuracy. When combined with a threshold (below which the model would make no prediction), this model has high precision but low recall.

3   Other Tools

For comparison, we evaluate four publicly available gender prediction tools. More detailed descriptions can be found at their respective webpages.

Gender.c   We implement and test a Python version of the gender prediction tool described in Michael (2007), which uses a name list with both gender and country information. The original software is written in C and the name list contains 32,254 names and name popularity by country.

Gender Guesser   Pérez (2016) uses the same data set as Gender.c, and performs quite similarly (in terms of accuracy and coverage).

Gender Detector   Vanetta (2016) draws on US Social Security Administration data (which we also use for training DEMOGRAPHER), as well as data from other global sources, as collected by Open Gender Tracking's Global Name Data project.[5]

Genderize IO   Strømgren (2016) resolves first names to gender based on information from user profiles from several social networks. The tool is accessed via a web API, and results include gender, probability, and confidence expressed as a count. According to the website, when we ran our experiments the tool included 216,286 distinct names from 79 countries and 89 languages. It provides limited free access and larger query volumes for a fee.

Localization   Several tools include the option to provide a locale for a name to improve accuracy. For example, Jean is typically male in French and female

---

[3]We focus on gender as a social or cultural categorization.

[4]Note that we mean "name" and *not* "username."

[5]https://github.com/OpenGenderTracking/globalnamedata

in English. We excluded localization since locale is not universally available for all users. We leave it to future work to explore its impact on accuracy.

4 Data

4.1 Training Data

We train the classifier in DEMOGRAPHER and take as our name list Social Security data (Social Security Administration, 2016), which contains 68,357 unique names. The data is divided by year, with counts of the number of male and female children given each name in each year. Since it only includes names of Americans with Social Security records, it may not generalize internationally.

4.2 Evaluation Data

Wikidata We extracted 2,279,678 names with associated gender from Wikidata.[6] We use 100,000 for development, 100,000 for test, and reserve the rest for training in future work. While data for other genders is available on Wikidata, we selected only names that were associated with either *Male* or *Female*. This matches the labels available in the SSA data used for training, as well as the other gender prediction tools we compare against. This dataset is skewed heavily male (more than 4 names labeled male for every female), so we also report results on a balanced (subsampled) version.

Annotated Twitter These names are drawn from the "name" field from a subset of 58,046 still publicly tweeting users from the Burger et al. (2011) dataset (user IDs released with Volkova et al. (2013)). Of these, 30,364 are labeled *Female* and 27,682 are labeled *Male*. The gender labels are obtained by following links to Twitter users' blogger profile information (containing structured gender self-identification information).

Unannotated Twitter Since the annotated Twitter data contains predominantly English speakers (and who may not be representative of the general Twitter population who do not link to external websites), we also evaluate model coverage over a sample of Twitter data: the 1% feed from July 2016 from containing 655,963 tweets and 526,256 unique names.

---

[6]https://www.wikidata.org/wiki/Wikidata:Database_download We used the dump from 2016-08-15.

4.3 Processing

All data is lowercased for consistency. For the Twitter data, we use a regular expression to extract the first string of one or more (Latin) alphabetic characters from the name field, if one exists. This may or may not be the user's actual given name (or even a given name at all). Note that most of the tools are do not handle non-Latin scripts, which limits their usefulness in international settings.

5 Results

Table 1 reports results for Wikidata in terms of accuracy (percent of correctly predicted names only including cases where the tool made a prediction), coverage (the percent of the full test set for which the tool made a prediction), F1 (the harmonic mean of accuracy and coverage), and the number of names labeled per second. The corresponding result for the balanced version of the dataset is in parentheses.

Tools make different tradeoffs between accuracy, coverage, and speed. Both Gender.c and Gender Guesser have high accuracy and fairly high coverage at high speed (with Gender.c being the fastest of the tools evaluated). Gender Detector has slightly higher accuracy, but this comes at the cost of both coverage and speed (it is second slowest). Genderize IO has the best F1 among all name list based approaches, but stands out for lower accuracy and higher coverage. We show five settings of DEMOGRAPHER: name list only (fast, accurate, but with only fairly high coverage), classifier (slow, and either high coverage with no threshold or high accuracy with a high threshold) and the combined versions, which fall in between the name list and classifier in terms of speed, accuracy, and coverage). The combined demographer with no threshold performs best out of all tools in terms of F1.

Table 2 shows results on Twitter data. The *Coverage* column shows the percentage of the unlabeled Twitter data for which each tool was able to make a prediction. These numbers are quite a bit lower than for Wikidata and the labeled Twitter set (the names in the labeled sample contain less non-Latin alphabet text than those in the unlabeled sample). This may be due to there being many non-names in the Twitter name field, or the use of non-Latin alphabets, which many of the tools do not currently

Tool Name	Accuracy	Coverage	F1	Names/Sec
Gender.c	97.79 (96.03)	81.82 (81.72)	89.09 (88.30)	**58873.6**
Gender Guesser	97.34 (97.12)	83.02 (83.34)	89.61 (89.70)	27691.2
Gender Detector	98.43 (*98.36*)	67.55 (69.91)	80.11 (81.73)	97.8
Genderize IO	85.91 (86.69)	91.96 (92.49)	92.68 (93.11)	13.5*
Demographer: Name list	93.42 (93.74)	80.77 (82.05)	86.89 (87.98)	44445.6
Demographer: Classifier (no threshold)	87.68 (87.09)	**99.99** (*99.99*)	93.43 (93.09)	4239.0
Demographer: Classifier (0.8 threshold)	**99.15** (96.20)	39.17 (24.71)	56.16 (39.32)	
Demographer: Combined (no threshold)	90.42 (90.47)	**99.99** (99.99)	**94.97** (*94.99*)	14903.6
Demographer: Combined (0.8 threshold)	94.14 (94.44)	85.80 (85.68)	89.78 (89.84)	

Table 1: *Wikidata*: Tool performance on the test set (balanced test set in parentheses), evaluated in terms of accuracy, coverage, F1, and names per second (averaged over 3 runs). *Note that Genderize IO uses a web API (slower than running locally). In practice, caching locally and sending up to 10 names at once improves speed. This value reflects sending names individually without caching.

Tool Name	Coverage	F1
Gender.c	24.16	71.80
Gender Guesser	25.78	74.82
Gender Detector	35.47	70.56
Genderize IO	45.81	84.06
Dem.:Name list	31.22	79.35
Dem.:Classifier (no thresh.)	**69.73**	89.19
Dem.:Combined (no thresh.)	**69.73**	**90.80**

Table 2: *Twitter data*: Coverage is computed over the unlabeled Twitter data (526,256 unique names) and F1 over the gender-annotated Twitter names.

handle. DEMOGRAPHER provides the best coverage, as it can make predictions for previously unobserved names based on character-level features. For *F1* we report results on gender-annotated Twitter. DEMOGRAPHER, in its combined setting, performs best, with Genderize IO also performing fairly well.

We raise the following concerns, to be addressed in future work. The international nature of the Twitter data takes its toll on our models, as both the name list and classifier are based on US Social Security data. Clearly, more must be done to handle non-Latin scripts and to evaluate improvements based on language or localization (and appropriately localized training data). Our tool also makes the assumption that the user's given name appears first in the name field, that the name contains only characters from the Latin alphabet, and that the user's name (and their actual gender) can be classified as either *Male* or *Female*, all of which are known to be false assumptions and would need to be taken into consideration in situations where it is important to make a correct prediction (or no prediction) for an individual. We know that not all of the "name" fields actually contain names, but we do not know how the use of non-names in that field may be distributed across demographic groups. We did not evaluate whether thresholding had a uniform impact on prediction quality across demographic groups. Failing to produce accurate predictions (or any prediction at all) due to these factors could introduce bias into the sample and subsequent conclusions. One possible way to deal with some of these issues would be to incorporate predictions based on username, such as those as described in Jaech and Ostendorf (2015).

6 Conclusions

We introduce DEMOGRAPHER, a tool that can produce high-accuracy and high-coverage results for gender inference from a given name. Our tool is comparable to or better than existing tools (particularly on Twitter data). Depending on the use case, users may prefer higher accuracy or higher coverage versions, which can be produced by changing thresholds for classification decisions.

Acknowledgments

This material is based upon work supported by the National Science Foundation Graduate Research Fellowship under Grant No. DGE-1232825. We thank Adrian Benton for data collection, Svitlana Volkova for information about datasets, and the reviewers for their comments and suggestions.

References

Jalal S Alowibdi, Ugo Buy, Paul Yu, et al. 2013. Language independent gender classification on Twitter. In *Advances in Social Networks Analysis and Mining (ASONAM), 2013 IEEE/ACM International Conference on*, pages 739–743. IEEE.

Shane Bergsma, Mark Dredze, Benjamin Van Durme, Theresa Wilson, and David Yarowsky. 2013. Broadly improving user classification via communication-based name and location clustering on Twitter. In *North American Chapter of the Association for Computational Linguistics (NAACL)*.

John D Burger, John Henderson, George Kim, and Guido Zarrella. 2011. Discriminating gender on Twitter. In *Proceedings of the Conference on Empirical Methods in Natural Language Processing*, Stroudsburg, PA, USA.

Miriam Cha, Youngjune Gwon, and HT Kung. 2015. Twitter geolocation and regional classification via sparse coding. In *Ninth International AAAI Conference on Web and Social Media*.

Jonathan Chang, Itamar Rosenn, Lars Backstrom, and Cameron Marlow. 2010. epluribus: Ethnicity on social networks. In *International Conference on Weblogs and Social Media (ICWSM)*.

Morgane Ciot, Morgan Sonderegger, and Derek Ruths. 2013. Gender inference of Twitter users in non-English contexts. In *EMNLP*, pages 1136–1145.

Ryan Compton, David Jurgens, and David Allen. 2014. Geotagging one hundred million twitter accounts with total variation minimization. In *Big Data (Big Data), 2014 IEEE International Conference on*, pages 393–401. IEEE.

Aron Culotta, Nirmal Ravi Kumar, and Jennifer Cutler. 2015. Predicting the demographics of twitter users from website traffic data. In *Twenty-Ninth AAAI Conference on Artificial Intelligence*.

Mark Dredze, Michael J Paul, Shane Bergsma, and Hieu Tran. 2013. Carmen: A twitter geolocation system with applications to public health. In *AAAI Workshop on Expanding the Boundaries of Health Informatics Using AI (HIAI)*.

Mark Dredze, Miles Osborne, and Prabhanjan Kambadur. 2016. Geolocation for twitter: Timing matters. In *North American Chapter of the Association for Computational Linguistics (NAACL)*.

Jacob Eisenstein, Brendan O'Connor, Noah A Smith, and Eric P Xing. 2010. A latent variable model for geographic lexical variation. In *Empirical Methods in Natural Language Processing (EMNLP)*.

Bo Han, Paul Cook, and Timothy Baldwin. 2014. Text-based twitter user geolocation prediction. *Journal of Artificial Intelligence Research*, pages 451–500.

Aaron Jaech and Mari Ostendorf. 2015. What your username says about you. In *Proceedings of the 2015 Conference on Empirical Methods in Natural Language Processing*, pages 2032–2037, Lisbon, Portugal, September. Association for Computational Linguistics.

David Jurgens, Tyler Finethy, James McCorriston, Yi Tian Xu, and Derek Ruths. 2015. Geolocation prediction in twitter using social networks: A critical analysis and review of current practice. In *Proceedings of the 9th International AAAI Conference on Weblogs and Social Media (ICWSM)*.

Wendy Liu and Derek Ruths. 2013. What's in a name? using first names as features for gender inference in Twitter. In *AAAI Spring Symposium: Analyzing Microtext*.

J. Michael. 2007. 40000 Namen, Anredebestimmung anhand des Vornamens. http://www.heise.de/ct/ftp/07/17/182/.

Alan Mislove, Sune Lehmann, Yong-yeol Ahn, Jukka-pekka Onnela, and J Niels Rosenquist. 2011. Understanding the Demographics of Twitter Users. *Artificial Intelligence*, pages 554–557.

Miles Osborne, Sean Moran, Richard McCreadie, Alexander Von Lunen, Martin D Sykora, Elizabeth Cano, Neil Ireson, Craig Macdonald, Iadh Ounis, Yu-lan He, et al. 2014. Real-time detection, tracking, and monitoring of automatically discovered events in social media. In *Association for Computational Linguistics (ACL)*.

Marco Pennacchiotti and Ana-Maria Popescu. 2011. A machine learning approach to Twitter user classification. *ICWSM*, 11:281–288.

Israel Saeta Pérez. 2016. Gender-guesser. https://pypi.python.org/pypi/gender-guesser.

Afshin Rahimi, Trevor Cohn, and Timothy Baldwin. 2016. pigeo: A python geotagging tool. *ACL 2016*, page 127.

Delip Rao and David Yarowsky. 2010. Detecting latent user properties in social media. In *Proc. of the NIPS MLSN Workshop*. Citeseer.

Delip Rao, David Yarowsky, Abhishek Shreevats, and Manaswi Gupta. 2010. Classifying latent user attributes in Twitter. In *Proceedings of the 2nd International Workshop on Search and Mining User-generated Contents*.

Delip Rao, Michael Paul, Clay Fink, David Yarowsky, Timothy Oates, and Glen Coppersmith. 2011. Hierarchical bayesian models for latent attribute detection in social media. In *Proceedings of the Fifth International AAAI Conference on Weblogs and Social Media (ICWSM)*.

Dominic Rout, Kalina Bontcheva, Daniel Preoţiuc-Pietro, and Trevor Cohn. 2013. Where's@ wally?:

a classification approach to geolocating users based on their social ties. In *Proceedings of the 24th ACM Conference on Hypertext and Social Media*, pages 11–20. ACM.

H Andrew Schwartz, Johannes C Eichstaedt, Margaret L Kern, Lukasz Dziurzynski, Stephanie M Ramones, Megha Agrawal, Achal Shah, Michal Kosinski, David Stillwell, Martin EP Seligman, and Lyle H Ungar. 2013. Personality, gender, and age in the language of social media: The open-vocabulary approach. *PloS one*, 8(9):e73791.

The United States Social Security Administration. 2016. Baby names. http://www.socialsecurity.gov/OACT/babynames/names.zip.

Casper Strømgren. 2016. Genderize io. https://genderize.io/.

Marcos Vanetta. 2016. Gender detector. https://pypi.python.org/pypi/gender-detector/0.0.4.

Svitlana Volkova, Theresa Wilson, and David Yarowsky. 2013. Exploring demographic language variations to improve multilingual sentiment analysis in social media. In *Proceedings of the 2013 Conference on Empirical Methods in Natural Language Processing (EMNLP)*.

Svitlana Volkova, Yoram Bachrach, Michael Armstrong, and Vijay Sharma. 2015a. Inferring latent user properties from texts published in social media (demo). In *Proceedings of the Twenty-Ninth Conference on Artificial Intelligence (AAAI)*, Austin, TX, January.

Svitlana Volkova, Benjamin Van Durme, David Yarowsky, and Yoram Bachrach. 2015b. Tutorial: Social media predictive analytics. In *Conference of the North American Chapter of the Association for Computational Linguistics (NAACL), tutorial*.

Bag of What? Simple Noun Phrase Extraction for Text Analysis

Abram Handler
UMass Amherst
ahandler@cs.umass.edu

Matthew J. Denny
Penn State
matthewjdenny@gmail.com

Hanna Wallach
Microsoft Research
hanna@dirichlet.net

Brendan O'Connor
UMass Amherst
brenocon@cs.umass.edu

Abstract

Social scientists who do not have specialized natural language processing training often use a unigram bag-of-words (BOW) representation when analyzing text corpora. We offer a new phrase-based method, **NPFST**, for enriching a unigram BOW. NPFST uses a part-of-speech tagger and a finite state transducer to extract multiword phrases to be added to a unigram BOW. We compare NPFST to both n-gram and parsing methods in terms of yield, recall, and efficiency. We then demonstrate how to use NPFST for exploratory analyses; it performs well, without configuration, on many different kinds of English text. Finally, we present a case study using NPFST to analyze a new corpus of U.S. congressional bills.

For our open-source implementation, see http://slanglab.cs.umass.edu/phrases/.

1   Introduction

Social scientists typically use a unigram representation when analyzing text corpora; each document is represented as a unigram bag-of-words (BOW), while the corpus itself is represented as a document–term matrix of counts. For example, Quinn et al. (2010) and Grimmer (2010) used a unigram BOW as input to a topic model, while Monroe et al. (2008) used a unigram BOW to report the most partisan terms from political speeches. Although the simplicity of a unigram BOW is appealing, unigram analyses do not preserve meaningful multiword phrases, such as "health care" or "social security," and cannot distinguish between politically significant phrases that share a word, such as "illegal immigrant" and "undocumented immigrant." To address these limitations, we introduce **NPFST**, which extracts multiword phrases to enrich a unigram BOW as additional columns in the document–term matrix. NPFST is suitable for many different kinds of English text; it

uses modest computational resources and does not require any specialized configuration or annotations.

2   Background

We compare NPFST to several other methods in terms of yield, recall, efficiency, and interpretability. Yield refers to the number of extracted phrases—a lower yield requires fewer computational and human resources to process the phrases. Recall refers to a method's ability to recover the most relevant or important phrases, as determined by a human. A good method should have a low yield, but high recall.

2.1 n-grams

Our simplest baseline is **AllNGrams(K)**. This method extracts all n-grams, up to length K, from tokenized, sentence-segmented text, excluding n-grams that cross sentence boundaries. This method is commonly used to extract features for text classification (e.g., Yogatama et al. (2015)), but has several disadvantages in a social scientific context. First, social scientists often want to substantively interpret individual phrases, but fragmentary phrases that cross sentence constituents may not be meaningful. For example, the Affordable Care Act includes the hard-to-interpret 4-gram, "the Internet website of." Second, although AllNGrams(K) has high recall (provided that K is sufficiently large), it suffers from a higher yield and can therefore require substantial resources to process the extracted phrases.

2.2   Parsing

An alternative approach[1] is to use syntax to restrict the extracted phrases to constituents, such as noun phrases (NPs). Unlike verb, prepositional,

---

[1]Statistical collocation methods provide another approach (e.g., Dunning (1993), Hannah and Wallach (2014)). These methods focus on within-n-gram statistical dependence. In informal analyses, we found their recall unsatisfying for low-frequency phrases, but defer a full comparison for future work.

Proceedings of 2016 EMNLP Workshop on Natural Language Processing and Computational Social Science, pages 114–124,
Austin, TX, November 5, 2016. ©2016 Association for Computational Linguistics

or adjectival phrases, NPs often make sense even when stripped from their surrounding context— e.g., *[Barack Obama]$_{NP}$* vs. *[was inaugurated in 2008]$_{VP}$*. There are many methods for extracting NPs. Given the long history of constituent parsing research in NLP, one obvious approach is to run an off-the-shelf constituent parser and then retrieve all NP non-terminals from the trees.[2] We refer to this method as **ConstitParse**. Unfortunately, the major sources of English training data, such as the Penn Treebank (Marcus et al., 1993), include determiners within the NP and non-nested flat NP annotations,[3] leading to low recall in our context (see §4). Since modern parsers rely on these sources of training data, it is very difficult to change this behavior.

2.3 Part-of-Speech Grammars

Another approach, proposed by Justeson and Katz (1995), is to use part-of-speech (POS) patterns to find and extract NPs—a form of shallow partial parsing (Abney, 1997). Researchers have used this approach in a variety of different contexts (Benoit and Nulty, 2015; Frantzi et al., 2000; Kim et al., 2010; Chuang et al., 2012; Bamman and Smith, 2014). A pattern-based method can be specified in terms of a triple of parameters: (G, K, M), where G is a grammar, K is a maximum length, and M is a matching strategy. The grammar G is a non-recursive regular expression that defines an infinite set of POS tag sequences (i.e., a regular language); the maximum length K limits the length of the extracted n-grams to $n \leq K$; while the matching strategy M specifies how to extract text spans that match the grammar.

The simplest grammar that we consider is

$$(A \,|\, N) * N(PD * (A \,|\, N) * N)*$$

defined over a coarse tag set of adjectives, nouns (both common and proper), prepositions, and determiners. We refer to this grammar as SimpleNP. The constituents that match this grammar are bare NPs (with optional PP attachments), N-bars, and names. We do not include any determiners at the root NP.

We also consider three baseline matching strategies, each of which can (in theory) be used with any G and K. The first, FilterEnum, enumerates all possible strings in the regular language, up to length K, as a preprocessing step. Then, at runtime, it checks whether each n-gram in the corpus is present in this enumeration. This matching strategy is simple to implement and extracts all matches up to length K, but it is computationally infeasible if K is large. The second, FilterFSA, compiles G into a finite-state automaton (FSA) as a preprocessing step. Then, at runtime, it checks whether each n-gram matches this FSA. Like FilterEnum, this matching strategy extracts all matches up to length K; however, it can be inefficient if K is large. The third, GreedyFSA, also compiles G into an FSA, but uses a standard greedy matching approach at runtime to extract n-grams that match G. Unlike the other two matching strategies, it cannot extract overlapping or nested matches, but it can extract very long matches.[4]

In their original presentation, Justeson and Katz (1995) defined a grammar that is very similar to SimpleNP and suggested using 2- and 3-grams (i.e., $K = 3$). With this restriction, their grammar comprises seven unique patterns. They also proposed using FilterEnum to extract text spans that match these patterns. We refer to this method as **JK** = (SimpleNP, $K = 3$, FilterEnum). Many researchers have used this method, perhaps because it is described in the NLP textbook by Manning and Schütze (1999).

3 NPFST

Our contribution is a new pattern-based extraction method: **NPFST** = (FullNP, $K = \infty$, RewriteFST). In §3.1, we define the FullNP grammar, and in §3.2, we define the RewriteFST matching strategy.

3.1 FullNP Grammar

FullNP extends SimpleNP by adding coordination of pairs of words with the same tag (e.g., *(VB CC VB)* in *(cease and desist) order*); coordination of noun phrases; parenthetical post-modifiers (e.g., *401(k)*, which is a 4-gram because of common NLP tokenization conventions); numeric modifiers and nominals; and support for the Penn Treebank tag set,

---

[2] Another type of syntactic structure prediction is NP chunking. This produces a shallower, non-nested representation.

[3] The English Web Treebank (LDC2012T13) has some more nesting structure and OntoNotes (version 5, LDC2013T19) includes a variant of the Penn Treebank with Vadas and Curran (2011)'s nested NP annotations. We look forward to the availability of constituent parsers trained on these data sources.

[4] We implemented both FilterFSA and GreedyFSA using standard Python libraries—specifically, *re.match* and *re.finditer*.

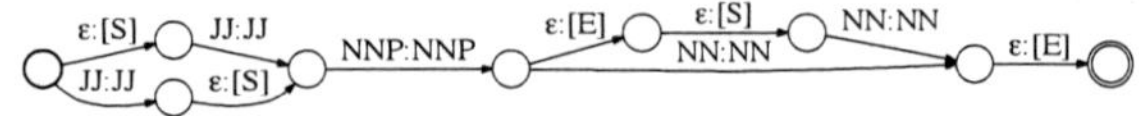

Figure 1: Composed rewrite lattice $L = I \circ P$ for input $I =$ (JJ NNP NN). Five spans are retrieved during lattice traversal.

Matching Strategy	All Matches?	Large K?
FilterEnum	yes	infeasible
FilterFSA	yes	can be inefficient
GreedyFSA	no	yes
RewriteFST	yes	yes

Table 1: RewriteFST versus the matching strategies described in §2.3. Like FilterEnum and FilterFSA, RewriteFST extracts all matches up to length K; in contrast, GreedyFSA cannot extract overlapping or nested matches. Like GreedyFSA, RewriteFST can extract long matches; in contrast, FilterEnum and is infeasible and FilterFSA can be inefficient if K is large.

the coarse universal tag set (Petrov et al., 2011), and Gimpel et al. (2011)'s Twitter-specific coarse tag set. We provide the complete definition in the appendix.

3.2 RewriteFST Matching Strategy

RewriteFST uses a finite-state transducer (FST) to rapidly extract text spans that match G—including overlapping and nested spans. This matching strategy is a form of finite-state NLP (Roche and Schabes, 1997), and therefore builds on an extensive body of previous work on FST algorithms and tools.

The input to RewriteFST is a POS-tagged[5] sequence of tokens I, represented as an FSA. For a simple tag sequence, this FSA is a linear chain, but, if there is uncertainty in the output of the tagger, it can be a lattice with multiple tags for each position.

The grammar G is first compiled into a phrase transducer P,[6] which takes an input sequence I and outputs the same sequence, but with pairs of start and end symbols—[S] and [E], respectively—inserted to indicate possible NPs (see figure 1). At runtime, RewriteFST computes an output lattice $L = I \circ P$ using FST composition;[7] since it is non-deterministic, L includes all overlapping and nested spans, rather than just the longest match. Finally, FilterFST traverses L to find all edges with a [S] symbol. From each one, it performs a depth-first search to find all paths to an edge with an [E] symbol, accumulating all [S]- and [E]-delimited spans.[8]

In table 1, we provide a comparison of FilterFST and the three matching strategies described in §2.3.

---

[5]We used the ARK POS tagger for tweets (Gimpel et al., 2011; Owoputi et al., 2013) and used Stanford CoreNLP for all other corpora (Toutanova et al., 2003; Manning et al., 2014).

[6]We used `foma` (Hulden, 2009; Beesley and Karttunen, 2003) to compile G into P. `foma` was designed for building morphological analyzers; it allows a developer to write a grammar in terms of readable production rules with intermediate categories. The rules are then compiled into a single, compact FST.

[7]We implemented the FST composition using *OpenNLP* (Allauzen et al., 2007) and *pyfst* (http://pyfst.github.io/).

[8]There are alternatives to this FST approach, such as a backtracking algorithm applied directly to the original grammar's FSA to retrieve all spans starting at each position in the input.

4 Experimental Results

In this section, we provide experimental results comparing NPFST to the baselines described in §2 in terms of yield, recall, efficiency, and interpretability. As desired, NPFST has a low yield and high recall, and efficiently extracts highly interpretable phrases.

4.1 Yield and Recall

Yield refers to the number of phrases extracted by a method, while recall refers to a method's ability to recover the most relevant or important phrases, as determined by a human. Because relevance and importance are domain-specific concepts that are not easy to define, we compared the methods using three named-entity recognition (NER) data sets: mentions of ten types of entities on Twitter from the WNUT 2015 shared task (Baldwin et al., 2015); mentions of proteins in biomedical articles from the BioNLP shared task 2011 (Kim et al., 2011); and a synthetic data set of named entities in New York Times articles (Sandhaus, 2008), identified using Stanford NER (Manning et al., 2014). Named entities are undoubtedly relevant and important phrases in all three of these different domains.[9] For each data set, we defined a method's yield to be the total number of spans that it extracted and a method's recall to be the percentage of the (labeled) named entity spans that were present in its list of extracted spans.[10]

---

[9]Although we use NER data sets to compare the methods' yield and recall, social scientists are obviously interested in analyzing other phrases, such as "heath care reform," which have a less psycholinguistically concrete status (Brysbaert et al., 2014). We focus on these kinds of phrases in §4.3 and §5.

[10]We assumed that all methods extracted all unigram spans.

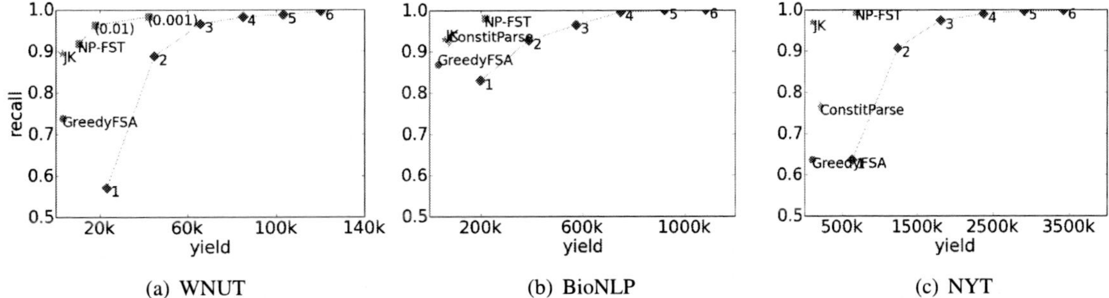

(a) WNUT   (b) BioNLP   (c) NYT

Figure 2: Recall versus yield for AllNGrams(K) with $K = 1, \ldots, 6$, ConstitParse, JK, (SimpleNP, $K = \infty$, GreedyFSA), and NPFST. A good method should have a low yield, but high recall—i.e., the best methods are in the top-left corner of each plot. For visual clarity, the y-axis starts at 0.5. We omit yield and recall values for AllNGrams(K) with $K > 6$ because recall approaches an asymptote. For the WNUT data set, we omit yield and recall values for ConstitParse because there is no reliable constituent parser for tweets. As described in §4.1, we also show yield and recall values for NPFST run on input lattices (denoted by 0.01 and 0.001).

Figure 2 depicts recall versus yield[11] for NPFST and the following baseline methods: AllNGrams(K) with different values of K, ConstitParse,[12] JK, and (SimpleNP, $K = \infty$, GreedyFSA). Because the yield and recall values for (SimpleNP, $K = 3$, FilterFSA) are the same as those of JK, we omit these values from figure 2. We also omit yield and recall values for (FullNP, $K = \infty$, FilterEnum) and (FullNP, $K = \infty$, FilterFSA) because they are identical to those of NPFST. Finally, we omit yield and recall values for (FullNP, $K = \infty$, GreedyFSA) because our implementation of GreedyFSA (using standard Python libraries) is too slow to use with FullNP.

A good method should have a low yield, but high recall—i.e., the best methods are in the top-left corner of each plot. The pattern-based methods all achieved high recall, with a considerably lower yield than AllNGrams(K). ConstitParse achieved a lower yield than NPFST, but also achieved lower recall. JK performed worse than NPFST, in part because it can only extract 2- and 3-grams, and, for example, the BioNLP data set contains mentions of proteins that are as long as eleven tokens (e.g., "Ca2+/calmodulin-dependent protein kinase (CaMK) type IV/Gr"). Finally, (SimpleNP, $K = \infty$, GreedyFSA) performed much worse than JK because it cannot extract overlapping or nested spans.

---

[11]The WNUT data set is already tokenized; however, we accidentally re-tokenized it in our experiments. Figure 2 therefore only depicts yield and recall for the 1,278 (out of 1,795) tweets for which our re-tokenization matched the original tokenization.

[12]We used the Stanford CoreNLP shift–reduce parser.

Method	Time
AllNGrams(∞)	44.4 ms
ConstitParse	825.3 ms
JK	45.3 ms
(SimpleNP, $K = 3$, FilterFSA)	46.43 ms
(SimpleNP, $K = \infty$, GreedyFSA)	39.34 ms
NPFST	82.2 ms

Table 2: Timing results for AllNGrams(∞), ConstitParse, JK, (SimpleNP, $K = 3$, FilterFSA), (SimpleNP, $K = \infty$, GreedyFSA), and NPFST on ten articles from the BioNLP data set; AllNGrams(∞) is equivalent to AllNGrams(56) in this context. The pattern-based methods' times include POS tagging (37.1 ms), while ConstitParse's time includes parsing (748 ms).

For the WNUT data set, NPFST's recall was relatively low (91.8%). To test whether some of its false negatives were due to POS-tagging errors, we used NPFST's ability to operate on an input lattice with multiple tags for each position. Specifically, we constructed an input lattice I using the tags for each position whose posterior probability was at least t. We experimented with $t = 0.01$ and $t = 0.001$. These values increased recall to 96.2% and 98.3%, respectively, in exchange for only a slightly higher yield (lower than that of AllNGrams(2)). We suspect that we did not see a greater increase in yield, even for $t = 0.001$, because of posterior calibration (Nguyen and O'Connor, 2015; Kuleshov and Liang, 2015).

117

4.2 Efficiency

We used ten articles from the BioNLP data set to compare the methods' preprocessing and run-time costs. Table 2 contains timing results[13] for AllNGrams(∞), ConstitParse, JK, (SimpleNP, $K = 3$, FilterFSA), and (SimpleNP, $K = \infty$, GreedyFSA), and NPFST. We omit results for (FullNP, $K = \infty$, FilterEnum), (FullNP, $K = \infty$, FilterFSA), and (FullNP, $K = \infty$, GreedyFSA) because they are too slow to compete with the other methods.

POS tagging is about twenty times faster than parsing, which is helpful for social scientists who may not have fast servers. NPFST is slightly slower than the simpler pattern-based methods; however, 80% of its time is spent constructing the input I and traversing the output lattice L, both of which are implemented in Python and could be made faster.

4.3 Interpretability

When analyzing text corpora, social scientists often examine ranked lists of terms, where each term is ranked according to some score. We argue that multiword phrases are more interpretable than unigrams when stripped from their surrounding context and presented as a list. In §4.3.1 we explain how to merge related terms, and in §4.3.2, we provide ranked lists that demonstrate that NPFST extracts more interpretable phrases than other methods.

4.3.1 Merging Related Terms

As described in §3.2, NPFST extracts overlapping and nested spans. For example, when run on a data set of congressional bills about crime, NPFST extracted "omnibus crime control and safe streets act," as well as the nested phrases "crime control" and "safe streets act." Although this behavior is generally desirable, it can also lead to repetition in ranked lists. We therefore outline an high-level algorithm for merging the highest-ranked terms in a ranked list.

The input to our algorithm is a list of terms L. The algorithm iterates through the list, starting with the highest-ranked term, aggregating similar terms according to some user-defined criterion (e.g., whether the terms share a substring) until it has generated C distinct term clusters. The algorithm then selects a single term to represent each cluster. Finally, the al-

gorithm orders the clusters' representative terms to form a ranked list of length C. By starting with the highest-ranked term and terminating after C clusters have been formed, this algorithm avoids the inefficiency of examining all possible pairs of terms.

4.3.2 Ranked Lists

To assess the interpretability of the phrases extracted by NPFST, we used three data sets: tweets about climate change, written by (manually identified) climate deniers;[14] transcripts from criminal trials at the Old Bailey in London during the 18th century;[15] and New York Times articles from September, 1993. For each data set, we extracted phrases using ConstitParse, JK, and NPFST and produced a list of terms for each method, ranked by count. We excluded domain-specific stopwords and any phrases that contained them.[16] Finally, we merged related terms using our term-merging algorithm, aggregating terms only if one term was a substring of another, to produce ranked lists of five representative terms. Table 4.3 contains these lists, demonstrating that NPFST produces highly interpretable phrases.

5 Case Study: Finding Partisan Terms in U.S. Congressional Legislation

Many political scientists have studied the relationship between language usage and party affiliation (Laver et al., 2003; Monroe et al., 2008; Slapin and Proksch, 2008; Quinn et al., 2010; Grimmer and Stewart, 2013). We present a case study, in which we use NPFST to explore partisan differences in U.S. congressional legislation about law and crime. In §5.1, we describe our data set, and in §5.2, we explain our methodology and present our results.

5.1 The Congressional Bills Corpus

We used a new data set of 97,221 U.S. congressional bills, introduced in the House and Senate between

---

[13]We used Python's *timeit* module.

[14]https://www.crowdflower.com/data/sentiment-analysis-global-warmingclimate-change-2/

[15]http://www.oldbaileyonline.org/

[16]For example, for the tweets, we excluded phrases that contained "climate" and "warming." For the Old Bailey transcripts, we excluded phrases that contained "st." or "mr." (e.g., "st. john" or "mr. white"). We also used a regular expression to exclude apparent abbreviated names (e.g., "b. smith") and used a stopword list to exclude dates like "5 of february." For the New York Times articles, we excluded phrases that contained "said."

Data Set	Method	Ranked List
Twitter	unigrams	snow, #tcot, al, dc, gore
	JK	al gore's, snake oil science, snow in dc, mine safety
	NPFST	al gore's, snake oil science, 15 months, snow in dc, *bunch of snake oil science
Old Bailey	unigrams	jacques, goodridge, rust, prisoner, sawtell
	ConsitParse	the prisoner, the warden, the draught, the fleet, the house
	JK	middlesex jury, public house, warrant of attorney, baron perryn, justice grose
	NPFST	middlesex jury, public house, warrant of attorney, baron perryn, *middlesex jury before lord loughborough
NYT	unigrams	will, united, one, government, new
	ConstitParse	he united states, the government, the agreement, the president, the white house
	JK	united states, united nations, white house, health care, prime minister
	NPFST	united states, united nations, white house, health care, *secretary of state warren christopher

Table 3: Ranked lists of representative terms for unigrams, ConstitParse, JK, and NPFST. For NPSFT, we include the highest-ranked phrase of length four or more (on its own line, denoted by *) in order to highlight the kinds of longer phrases that JK is unable to extract. For the Twitter data set, we omit results for ConstitParse because there is no reliable constituent parser for tweets.

1993 and 2014. We created this data set by scraping the Library of Congress website.[17] We used Stanford CoreNLP to tokenize and POS tag the bills. We removed numbers and punctuation, and discarded all terms that occurred in fewer than five bills. We also augmented each bill with its author, its final outcome (e.g., did it survive committee deliberations, did it pass a floor vote in the Senate) from the Congressional Bills Project (Adler and Wilkerson, 2014), and its major topic area (Purpura and Hillard, 2006).

For our case study, we focused on a subset of 488 bills, introduced between 2013 and 2014, that are primarily about law and crime. We chose this subset because we anticipated that it would clearly highlight partisan policy differences. For example, the bills include legislation about immigration enforcement and about incarceration of low-level offenders—two areas where Democrats and Republicans tend to have very different policy preferences.

5.2 Partisan Terms

We used NPFST to extract phrases from the bills, and then created ranked lists of terms for each party using the informative Dirichlet[18] feature selection

method of Monroe et al. (2008). This method computes a z-score for each term that reflects how strongly that term is associated with Democrats over Republicans—a positive z-score indicates that Democrats are more likely to use the term, while a negative z-score indicates that Republications are more likely to use the term. We merged the highest-ranked terms for each party, aggregating terms only if one term was a substring of another and if the terms were very likely to co-occur in a single bill,[19] to form ranked lists of representative terms. Finally, for comparison, we also used the same approach to create ranked lists of unigrams, one for each party.

Figure 3 depicts z-score versus term count, while table 4 lists the twenty highest-ranked terms. The unigram lists suggest that Democratic lawmakers focus more on legislation related to mental health, juvenile offenders, and possibly domestic violence, while Republican lawmakers focus more on illegal immigration. However, many of the highest-ranked unigrams are highly ambiguous when stripped from their surrounding context. For example, we do not know whether "domestic" refers to "domestic violence," "domestic terrorism," or "domestic programs" without manually reviewing the origi-

---

[17]http://congress.gov/

[18]In order to lower the z-scores of uninformative, high-frequency terms, we set the Dirichlet hyperparameters to be proportional to the term counts from our full data set of bills.

[19]We used the correlation between the terms' tf-idf vectors determine how likely the terms were to co-occur in a single bill.

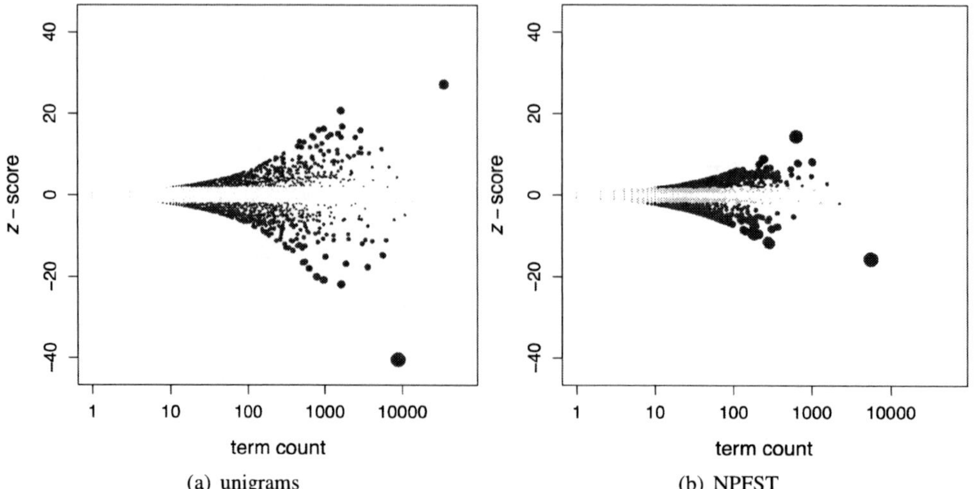

(a) unigrams   (b) NPFST

Figure 3: z-score versus term count. Each dot represents a single term and is sized according to that term's z-score. Terms that are more likely to be used by Democrats are shown in blue; terms that are more likely to be used by Republicans are shown in dark red.

nal bills (e.g., using a keyword-in-context interface (O'Connor, 2014)). Moreover, many of the highest-ranked Republican unigrams, such as "communication," are not unique to law and crime.

In contrast, the phrase-based lists are less ambiguous and much more interpretable. They include names of bills (which are often long) and important concepts, such as "mental health," "victims of domestic violence," "interstate or foreign commerce," and "explosive materials." These lists suggest that Democratic lawmakers have a very strong focus on programs to prevent child abuse and domestic violence, as well as issues related to mental health and gang violence. Republican lawmakers appear to focus on immigration and incarceration. This focus on immigration is not surprising given the media coverage between 2013 and 2014; however, there was much less media coverage of a Democratic focus on crime-related legislation during that time period.

These results suggest that social scientists will be less likely to draw incorrect conclusions from ranked lists of terms if they include multiword phrases. Because phrases are less ambiguous than unigrams, social scientists can more quickly discover meaningful term-based associations for further exploration, without undertaking a lengthy process to validate their interpretation of the terms.

6   Conclusions and Future Work

Social scientists typically use a unigram BOW representation when analyzing text corpora, even though unigram analyses do not preserve meaningful multiword phrases. To address this limitation, we presented a new phrase-based method, NPFST, for enriching a unigram BOW. NPFST is suitable for many different kinds of English text; it does not require any specialized configuration or annotations.

We compared NPFST to several other methods for extracting phrases, focusing on yield, recall, efficiency, and interpretability. As desired, NPFST has a low yield and high recall, and efficiently extracts highly interpretable phrases. Finally, to demonstrate the usefulness of NPFST for social scientists, we used NPFST to explore partisan differences in U.S. congressional legislation about law and crime. We found that the phrases extracted by NPFST were less ambiguous and more interpretable than unigrams.

In the future, we plan to use NPFST in combination with other text analysis methods, such as topic modeling; we have already obtained encouraging preliminary results. We have also experimented with modifying the FullNP grammar to select broader classes of phrases, such as subject–verb and verb–object constructions (though we anticipate that more structured syntactic parsing approaches will eventually be useful for these kinds of constructions).

120

Method	Party	Ranked List
unigrams	Democrat	and, deleted, health, mental, domestic, inserting, grant, programs, prevention, violence, program, striking, education, forensic, standards, juvenile, grants, partner, science, research
	Republican	any, offense, property, imprisoned, whoever, person, more, alien, knowingly, officer, not, united, intent, commerce, communication, forfeiture, immigration, official, interstate, subchapter
NPFST	Democrat	mental health, juvenile justice and delinquency prevention act, victims of domestic violence, child support enforcement act of u.s.c., fiscal year, child abuse prevention and treatment act, omnibus crime control and safe streets act of u.s.c., date of enactment of this act, violence prevention, director of the national institute, former spouse, section of the foreign intelligence surveillance act of u.s.c., justice system, substance abuse criminal street gang, such youth, forensic science, authorization of appropriations, grant program
	Republican	special maritime and territorial jurisdiction of the united states, interstate or foreign commerce, federal prison, section of the immigration and nationality act, electronic communication service provider, motor vehicles, such persons, serious bodily injury, controlled substances act, department or agency, one year, political subdivision of a state, civil action, section of the immigration and nationality act u.s.c., offense under this section, five years, bureau of prisons, foreign government, explosive materials, other person

Table 4: Ranked lists of unigrams and representative phrases of length two or more for Democrats and Republicans.

Our open-source implementation of NPFST is available at http://slanglab.cs.umass.edu/phrases/.

Acknowledgments

We thank the anonymous reviewers for their comments (especially the suggestion of FSA backtracking) on earlier versions of this work. We also thank Ken Benoit, Brian Dillon, Chris Dyer, Michael Heilman, and Bryan Routledge for helpful discussions. MD was supported by NSF Grant DGE-1144860.

Appendix: FullNP Grammar

The following foma grammar defines the rewrite phrase transducer P:

```
# POS tag categories. "Coarse" refer to the Petrov Univeral tag set.
# We directly use PTB tags, but for Twitter, we assume they've been
# preprocessed to coarse tags.
# CD is intentionally under both Adj and Noun.
define Adj1      [JJ | JJR | JJS | CD | CoarseADJ];
define Det1      [DT | CoarseDET];
define Prep1     [IN | TO | CoarseADP];
define Adv1      [RB | RBR | RBS | CoarseADV];
# Note that Twitter and coarse tags subsume some of this under VERB.
define VerbMod1 [Adv1 | RP | MD | CoarsePRT];
# PTB FW goes to CoarseX, but we're excluding CoarseX since for Gimpel et al.'s
# Twitter tags, that's usually non-constituent-participating things like URLs.
define Noun      [NN | NNS | NNP | NNPS | FW | CD | CoarseNOUN | CoarseNUM];
define Verb      [VB | VBD | VBG | VBN | VBP | VBZ | CoarseVERB];
define AnyPOS    [O  |  Adj1|Det1|Prep1|Adv1|VerbMod1|Noun|Verb |
    CoarseDOT|CoarseADJ|CoarseADP|CoarseADV|CoarseCONJ|CoarseDET|
    CoarseNOUN|CoarseNUM|CoarsePRON|CoarsePRT|CoarseVERB|CoarseX
]
define Lparen    ["-LRB-" | "-LSB-" | "-LCB-"];  # Twitter doesnt have this.
define Rparen    ["-RRB-" | "-RSB-" | "-RCB-"];
# Ideally, auxiliary verbs would be VerbMod, but PTB gives them VB* tags.


# single-word coordinations
define Adj       Adj1 [CC Adj1]*;
define Det       Det1 [CC Det1]*;
define Adv       Adv1 [CC Adv1]*;
define Prep      Prep1 [CC Prep1]*;
define VerbMod   VerbMod1 [CC VerbMod1]*;


# NP (and thus BaseNP) have to be able to stand on their own.  They are not
# allowed to start with a determiner, since it's usually extraneous for our
# purposes. But when we want an NP right of something, we need to allow
# optional determiners since they're in between.
define BaseNP    [Adj|Noun]* Noun;
define PP        Prep+ [Det|Adj]* BaseNP;
define ParenP    Lparen AnyPOS^{1,50} Rparen;
define NP1       BaseNP [PP | ParenP]*;
define NP        NP1 [CC [Det|Adj]* NP1]*;

regex NP -> START ... END;
write att compiled_fsts/NP.attfoma
```

References

[Abney1997] Steven Abney. 1997. Part-of-speech tagging and partial parsing. In *Corpus-based methods in language and speech processing*, pages 118–136. Springer.

[Adler and Wilkerson2014] E. Scott Adler and John Wilkerson. 2014. Congressional Bills Project: (1980-2004).

[Allauzen et al.2007] Cyril Allauzen, Michael Riley, Johan Schalkwyk, Wojciech Skut, and Mehryar Mohri. 2007. OpenFST: A general and efficient weighted finite-state transducer library. In *Implementation and Application of Automata*, pages 11–23. Springer.

[Baldwin et al.2015] Timothy Baldwin, Marie-Catherine de Marneffe, Bo Han, Young-Bum Kim, Alan Ritter, and Wei Xu. 2015. Shared tasks of the 2015 workshop on noisy user-generated text: Twitter lexical normalization and named entity recognition. In *Proceedings of the Workshop on Noisy User-generated Text*, pages 126–135, Beijing, China, July. Association for Computational Linguistics.

[Bamman and Smith2014] David Bamman and Noah A. Smith. 2014. Unsupervised discovery of biographical structure from text. *Transactions of the Association for Computational Linguistics*, 2:363–376.

[Beesley and Karttunen2003] Kenneth R. Beesley and Lauri Karttunen. 2003. *Finite-state morphology: Xerox tools and techniques*. CSLI, Stanford.

[Benoit and Nulty2015] Kenneth Benoit and Paul Nulty. 2015. More than unigrams can say: Detecting meaningful multi-word expressions in political text. *MPSA Working Paper*, pages 1–19.

[Brysbaert et al.2014] Marc Brysbaert, Amy Beth Warriner, and Victor Kuperman. 2014. Concreteness ratings for 40 thousand generally known English word lemmas. *Behavior Research Methods*, 46(3):904–911.

[Chuang et al.2012] Jason Chuang, Christopher D. Manning, and Jeffrey Heer. 2012. "Without the clutter of unimportant words": Descriptive keyphrases for text visualization. *ACM Transactions on Computer-Human Interaction (TOCHI)*, 19(3):19.

[Dunning1993] Ted Dunning. 1993. Accurate methods for the statistics of surprise and coincidence. *Computational Linguistics*, 19:61–74.

[Frantzi et al.2000] Katerina Frantzi, Sophia Ananiadou, and Hideki Mima. 2000. Automatic recognition of multi-word terms: The c-value/nc-value method. *International Journal on Digital Libraries*, 3(2):115–130.

[Gimpel et al.2011] Kevin Gimpel, Nathan Schneider, Brendan O'Connor, Dipanjan Das, Daniel Mills, Jacob Eisenstein, Michael Heilman, Dani Yogatama, Jeffrey Flanigan, and Noah A. Smith. 2011. Part-of-speech tagging for Twitter: Annotation, features, and experiments. In *Proceedings of the 49th Annual Meeting of the Association for Computational Linguistics: Human Language Technologies: short papers-Volume 2*, pages 42–47. Association for Computational Linguistics.

[Grimmer and Stewart2013] Justin Grimmer and Brandon M. Stewart. 2013. Text as data: The promise and pitfalls of automatic content analysis methods for political texts. *Political Analysis*, 21(3):267–297.

[Grimmer2010] Justin Grimmer. 2010. A Bayesian hierarchical topic model for political texts: Measuring expressed agendas in Senate press releases. *Political Analysis*, 18(1):1–35.

[Hannah and Wallach2014] Lauren Hannah and Hanna Wallach. 2014. Topic summarization: From word lists to phrases. In *Proceedings of the NIPS Workshop on "Modern Machine Learning and Natural Language Processing"*.

[Hulden2009] Mans Hulden. 2009. Foma: A finite-state compiler and library. In *Proceedings of the 12th Conference of the European Chapter of the Association for Computational Linguistics: Demonstrations Session*, pages 29–32. Association for Computational Linguistics.

[Justeson and Katz1995] John S. Justeson and Slava M. Katz. 1995. Technical terminology: Some linguistic properties and an algorithm for identification in text. *Natural Language Engineering*, 1(01):9–27.

[Kim et al.2010] Su Nam Kim, Timothy Baldwin, and Min-Yen Kan. 2010. Evaluating n-gram based evaluation metrics for automatic keyphrase extraction. In *Proceedings of the 23rd international conference on computational linguistics*, pages 572–580. Association for Computational Linguistics.

[Kim et al.2011] Jin-Dong Kim, Sampo Pyysalo, Tomoko Ohta, Robert Bossy, Ngan Nguyen, and Jun'ichi Tsujii. 2011. Overview of BioNLP shared task 2011. In *Proceedings of the BioNLP Shared Task 2011 Workshop*, pages 1–6. Association for Computational Linguistics.

[Kuleshov and Liang2015] Volodymyr Kuleshov and Percy S. Liang. 2015. Calibrated structured prediction. In *Advances in Neural Information Processing Systems*, pages 3456–3464.

[Laver et al.2003] Michael Laver, Kenneth Benoit, and John Garry. 2003. Extracting policy positions from political texts using words as data. *The American Political Science Review*, 97(2):311–331.

[Manning and Schütze1999] Christopher D. Manning and Hinrich Schütze. 1999. *Foundations of Statistical Natural Language Processing*. MIT Press.

[Manning et al.2014] Christopher D. Manning, Mihai Surdeanu, John Bauer, Jenny Finkel, Steven J.

Bethard, and David McClosky. 2014. The Stanford CoreNLP natural language processing toolkit. In *Association for Computational Linguistics (ACL) System Demonstrations*, pages 55–60.

[Marcus et al.1993] Mitchell P. Marcus, Mary Ann Marcinkiewicz, and Beatrice Santorini. 1993. Building a large annotated corpus of English: The Penn Treebank. *Computational Linguistics*, 19(2):313–330.

[Monroe et al.2008] Burt L. Monroe, Michael P. Colaresi, and Kevin M. Quinn. 2008. Fightin' words: Lexical feature selection and evaluation for identifying the content of political conflict. *Political Analysis*, 16:372–403.

[Nguyen and O'Connor2015] Khanh Nguyen and Brendan O'Connor. 2015. Posterior calibration and exploratory analysis for natural language processing models. In *Proceedings of the 2015 Conference on Empirical Methods in Natural Language Processing*, pages 1587–1598. Association for Computational Linguistics.

[O'Connor2014] B O'Connor. 2014. MITEXTEX-PLORER : Linked brushing and mutual information for exploratory text data analysis. In *ACL 2014 Workshop on Interactive Language Learning, Visualization, and Interfaces*.

[Owoputi et al.2013] Olutobi Owoputi, Brendan O'Connor, Chris Dyer, Kevin Gimpel, Nathan Schneider, and Noah A. Smith. 2013. Improved part-of-speech tagging for online conversational text with word clusters. In *Proceedings of NAACL*.

[Petrov et al.2011] Slav Petrov, Dipanjan Das, and Ryan McDonald. 2011. A universal part-of-speech tagset. *arXiv preprint arXiv:1104.2086*.

[Purpura and Hillard2006] Stephen Purpura and Dustin Hillard. 2006. Automated classification of congressional legislation. *Proceedings of The 2006 International Conference on Digital Government Research*, pages 219–225.

[Quinn et al.2010] Kevin M. Quinn, Burt L. Monroe, Michael Colaresi, Michael H. Crespin, and Dragomir R. Radev. 2010. How to analyze political attention with minimal assumptions and costs. *American Journal of Political Science*, 54(1):209–228.

[Roche and Schabes1997] Emmanuel Roche and Yves Schabes. 1997. *Finite-State Language Processing*. MIT Press.

[Sandhaus2008] Evan Sandhaus. 2008. The New York Times Annotated Corpus. *Linguistic Data Consortium*, LDC2008T19.

[Slapin and Proksch2008] Jonathan B Slapin and Sven-Oliver Proksch. 2008. A scaling model for estimating time-serial positions from texts. *American Journal of Political Science*, 52(3):705–722.

[Toutanova et al.2003] K. Toutanova, Dan Klein, Christopher D. Manning, and Yoram Singer. 2003. Feature-rich part-of-speech tagging with a cyclic dependency network. In *Proceedings of the 2003 Conference of the North American Chapter of the Association for Computational Linguistics on Human Language Technology-Volume 1*, pages 173–180.

[Vadas and Curran2011] David Vadas and James R. Curran. 2011. Parsing noun phrases in the Penn Treebank. *Computational Linguistics*, 37(4):753–809.

[Yogatama et al.2015] Dani Yogatama, Lingpeng Kong, and Noah A. Smith. 2015. Bayesian optimization of text representations. In *Proceedings of the 2015 Conference on Empirical Methods in Natural Language Processing*, pages 2100–2105. Association for Computational Linguistics.

News Sentiment and Cross-Country Fluctuations[*]

Samuel P. Fraiberger
Northeastern Network Science Institute
177 Huntington Avenue, Boston, MA 02114
Harvard Institute for Quantitative Social Sciences
1737 Cambridge St, Cambridge, MA 02138
`s.fraiberger@neu.edu`

Abstract

What is the information content of news-based measures of sentiment? How are they related to aggregate economic fluctuations? I construct a sentiment index by measuring the net amount of positive expressions in the corpus of Economic news articles produced by Reuters over the period 1987 - 2013 and across 12 countries. The index successfully tracks fluctuations in Gross Domestic Product (GDP) at the country level, is a leading indicator of GDP growth and contains information to help forecast GDP growth which is not captured by professional forecasts. This suggests that forecasters do not appropriately incorporate available information in predicting future states of the economy.

1   Introduction

To date, there is limited cross-country evidence for the role that sentiment might play in explaining aggregate economic fluctuations. In this paper, I show how measures of aggregate beliefs extracted from news articles are related to GDP growth. I build upon a recent and fast-growing literature which relates information extracted from text to economic and financial variables ((Tetlock, 2007), (Baker et al., 2016), (Garcia, 2013)). The approach commonly used in this literature measures sentiment using pre-existing dictionaries. [1]

---

[*]The author gratefully acknowledges financial support from the IMF Research Department.

[1]An alternative approach employed in (Choi and Varian, 2012) uses Google search results to forecast near-term values of economic indicators.

I build my sentiment index by measuring the net amount of positive expressions in the collection of Economic news articles from Reuters covering 12 countries over the period 1987 - 2013. The index successfully tracks GDP growth over time and across countries. Is sentiment a leading indicator of GDP growth? I estimate an autoregressive model GDP growth to which I add news-based sentiment measures. Coefficients on news-based sentiment measures are jointly significant at the country level for 10 out of 12 countries in my sample. Sentiment variables reduce in-sample forecast errors of GDP growth by 9.1% on average across countries compared to an autogressive process. This indicates that news sentiment is a leading indicator of GDP growth.

Do news-based sentiment measures simply aggregate other well-established leading indicators? I test whether news-based sentiment measures contain information which is not reflected in professional forecasters' expectations. I run predictive regressions of annual GDP growth on consensus forecasts data at different forecasting horizons. I then add to the regressions my news sentiment index measured prior to the release of the consensus forecasts. Including sentiment reduces in-sample forecast errors by 19% on average across countries. News-based sentiment measures contain information which is not included in forecasters' expectations. Reductions in forecast errors are larger for longer forecasting horizons, which reflect the fact the long-term forecast are inherently hard. Reductions in forecast errors are also larger during bad times, which indicates that forecasters might be underreacting to bad news.

Proceedings of 2016 EMNLP Workshop on Natural Language Processing and Computational Social Science, pages 125–131,
Austin, TX, November 5, 2016. ©2016 Association for Computational Linguistics

	# Articles	Avg. # Words	Start Date	End Date
Argentina	19007	338	6/1987	9/2013
Australia	31792	456	12/1998	7/2013
Brazil	32952	315	6/1987	9/2013
India	64306	384	6/1987	9/2013
Indonesia	22791	356	6/1987	9/2013
Japan	69607	408	12/1998	3/2012
New Zealand	20238	498	12/1998	8/2013
South Africa	30319	342	6/1987	9/2013
South Korea	32203	348	5/1987	9/2013
Sweden	10106	318	12/1998	11/2012
Switzerland	21499	351	12/1998	5/2013
United Kingdom	86182	422	12/2000	1/2013

Table 1: News Corpus Summary Statistics.

2　News-based Sentiment

2.1　Data Description

My dataset contains news articles extracted from Factiva.com, an online database which provides access to news archives from around the world. One can retrieve articles by querying a set of tags such as the source, the main topics and the locations associated with an article. A proprietary algorithm attributes topics and location tags to articles and is constant across the database.

Table (1) presents summary statistics of the news articles in my corpus. I focus on articles produced by Reuters News, which is the most comprehensive stream of news over time and across countries. I have collected all the news articles containing the topics tag "Economic news" and covering a set of 12 countries: Argentina, Australia, Brazil, India, Indonesia, Japan, New Zealand, Sweden, Switzerland, South Africa, South Korea, and the United Kingdom. The time window is December 1998 to September 2013 for developed countries (Australia, Japan, New Zealand, Sweden, Switzerland, and the United Kingdom), and June 1987 to September 2013 for developing countries (Argentina, Brazil, India, Indonesia, South Africa and South Korea). For each article, I have automatically extracted the timestamp, the title, the main text, the topics and the locations tags.

Positive	IDF	Negative	IDF
strong	1.95	limited	1.10
support	2.08	debt	1.61
help	2.08	cut	1.79
recovery	2.30	crisis	1.95
good	2.48	late	2.30
gains	2.56	deficit	2.30
boost	2.56	risk	2.30
easing	2.64	concerns	2.56
agreement	2.64	recession	2.64
highest	2.64	unemployment	2.64
better	2.77	weak	2.64
positive	2.77	decline	2.64
confidence	2.83	slowdown	2.83
steady	2.83	problems	2.83
agreed	2.83	risks	2.89
balance	2.83	concern	2.94
helped	2.83	slow	3.00
open	2.89	losses	3.04
strength	3.09	fears	3.04
stronger	3.09	negative	3.04
provide	3.14	fail	3.04

Table 2: The 20 Most Frequent Negative and Positive Words.

2.2　Text Processing

I combine dictionaries of positive and negative words compiled by (Loughran and McDonald, 2011) for financial texts and by (Young and Soroka, 2012) for political and economic texts. I search for inflections of each word in these dictionaries which are present in my corpus. Given a root tonal word (e.g. "lose"), I retrieve all the inflected words in the news corpus ("losing", "looser", "lost", "loss", etc ...) and add them to the dictionaries. I check the relevance of the most frequent words and eliminate the ones which are irrelevant. My dictionary of positive words contains 3,527 items and the one with negative words contains 7,109 items.

Table 2 shows that the most frequent positive and negative words indeed reflect the sentiment typically associated with economic and financial outcomes.

Here is an example of an article in which the main location tag is Argentina (in bold) and one of the topic tags is "Economic news" (in bold):[2]

---

[2]The words included in my dictionaries are underlined.

Title: Argentina's Peronists defend Menem's labor reforms.

Timestamp: 1996-09-02

Text: BUENOS AIRES, Sept 2 (Reuters) - The Argentine government Monday tried to counter criticisms of President Carlos Menem's proposals for more flexible labor laws, arguing that not just workers would contribute to new unemployment insurance. Menem angered trade unions, already in disagreement over his fiscal austerity programmes, by announcing a labor reform package Friday including suspending collective wage deals and replacing redundancy payouts with unemployment insurance.

Topics: Labor/Personnel Issues, Corporate/Industrial News, Economic/Monetary Policy, **Economic News**, Political/General News, Labor Issues, Domestic Politics

Locations: **Argentina**, Latin America, South America

The dictionary-based approach is straightforward and transparent, yet some words are not properly classified. To improve accuracy, I normalize 373 negative forms such as "no longer", "neither", "not having", etc ... to "not" as proposed in (Young and Soroka, 2012). I then build a second pair of lists of positive and negative expressions which appear preceded by a "not". A positive (negative) word preceded by a "not" is classified as negative (positive). Finally, I normalize 783 ambiguous expressions to correctly account for their tone. For instance, the expression "lose support" would be classified as neutral, so I normalize it to be counted as negative.

2.3 Sentiment Index

Using this classification of tonal expressions, a simple measure sentiment is the difference between the fraction of positive expressions and the fraction of negative expressions in each article. This measure is unlikely to capture all the nuances of a text, but it is likely to give a good indication of how news tone varies across country and over time.

Let t_{ij} be the number of occurrences of word i in article j. Let n_{ij} (p_{ij}) be the number of occurrences of negative (positive) word i in document j. Corre-

spondingly, let $\bar{p}_{ij}$ ($\bar{n}_{ij}$) the number of occurrences of negative (positive) word i in document j preceded by a "not".

The positivity of article j is given by:

$$\pi_j = \frac{\sum_i p_{ij} + \sum_i \bar{p}_{ij} - \sum_i \bar{n}_{ij}}{\sum_i t_{ij}}. \tag{1}$$

In the numerator, the first term corresponds to the weighted sum of all the positive words. The second term corresponds to the weighted sum of negative words preceded by a "not". The last term corresponds to the weighted sum of positive words preceded by a "not".

Similarly, the negativity of article j is given by:

$$\nu_j = \frac{\sum_i n_{ij} + \sum_i \bar{n}_{ij} - \sum_i \bar{p}_{ij}}{\sum_i t_{ij}}. \tag{2}$$

The net positivity of article j is given by:

$$s_j = \pi_j - \nu_j. \tag{3}$$

3 Sentiment and GDP Growth

Figure (1) shows that my sentiment index successfully tracks fluctuations in GDP growth at the country level. The first natural question is whether or not sentiment is a leading indicator of GDP growth.

3.1 Granger Causality Tests

To show this, I estimate the autoregressive distributed lag model described by equation (4):

$$y_{t,c} = \alpha + \sum_{i=1}^{p} \beta_{i,c} y_{t-i,c} + \sum_{i=1}^{q} \gamma_{i,c} \pi_{t-i,c} + \sum_{i=1}^{q} \zeta_{i,c} \nu_{t-i,c} + \epsilon_{t,c}, \tag{4}$$

where $y_{t,c}$ is the log GDP growth between t and $t+3$ months in country c and $\epsilon_{t,c}$ is the error term. I first estimate an autoregressive process of GDP growth at a quarterly frequency and at the country level by choosing the number of lags p which minimizes the AIC criterion. I then add monthly lags of positive

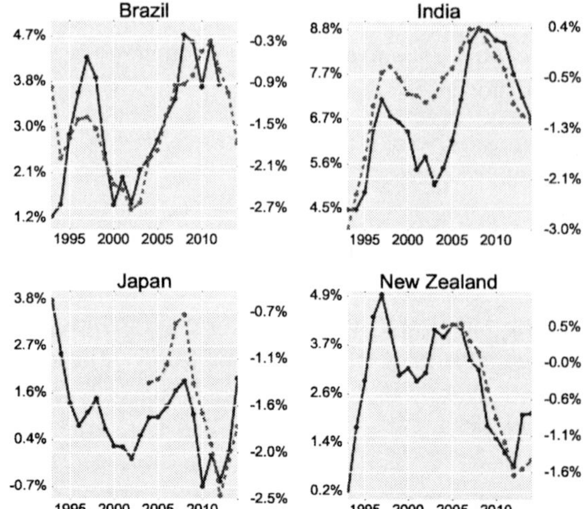

Figure 1: News Sentiment and GDP growth per Country. *Time series of my benchmark sentiment index (dotted line) and GDP growth (full line) at a yearly frequency. Sentiment measures are computed at the article level and averaged at a yearly frequency. I then apply a 3-year moving average to smooth the series. News articles come from Factiva.com, GDP growth comes from the International Financial Statistics Database (IFS).*

and negative sentiment (averaged at a monthly frequency), again choosing the number of lag values q using the AIC criterion.

Table (3) shows that lags of negative sentiment are a leading indicator of GDP growth at the country level for 9 out of the 12 countries in my sample. Lags of positive sentiment are a leading indicator of GDP growth for half of the country in my sample. This evidence is consistent with previous literature using news-based measures of sentiment which finds that most of the textual information is contained in negative words ((Loughran and McDonald, 2011)). In the case of India however, while I cannot reject the hypothesis that lags of negative sentiment are jointly equal to zero, I can reject the hypothesis that lags of positive sentiment are jointly equal to zero. This suggests that positive sentiment measures might also be worth considering as a leading indicator of GDP growth.

Figure (2) shows that on average across countries, forecast errors of next quarter GDP growth diminish by 9.1% when news-based sentiment measures are included in the ADL(p,q) model described by equa-

	$F\,[\pi]$	$p\,[\pi]$	$F\,[\nu]$	$p\,[\nu]$	$F\,[\pi,\nu]$	$p\,[\pi,\nu]$	N
Argentina	8.76**	1.7E-06	4.67**	9.8E-04	4.87**	2.6E-05	86
Australia	2.34	1.1E-01	3.65**	3.2E-02	1.84	1.3E-01	64
Brazil	1.81	1.3E-01	4.87**	1.0E-03	3.04**	4.4E-03	66
India	2.55**	3.1E-02	1.01	4.3E-01	1.94*	5.1E-02	63
Indonesia	0.82	4.5E-01	5.94**	5.1E-03	3.03**	2.7E-02	57
Japan	8.25**	5.9E-03	7.61**	8.0E-03	5.27**	8.2E-03	61
New Zealand	3.69**	3.1E-02	3.33**	4.3E-02	2.13*	8.9E-02	64
South Africa	1.25	2.6E-01	1.46	1.5E-01	1.36	1.6E-01	101
South Korea	4.82**	5.9E-06	5.34**	1.4E-06	4.13**	1.4E-06	98
Sweden	5.76**	6.4E-04	3.61**	1.1E-02	3.60**	2.1E-03	63
Switzerland	2.00	1.6E-01	2.74	1.0E-01	1.50	2.3E-01	64
United Kingdom	0.14	7.1E-01	4.07**	4.9E-02	2.14	1.3E-01	55

Table 3: Granger Causality Tests. *Significance tests of the coefficient estimates of the autoregressive distributed lag model described by equation (4) at a quarterly frequency and at the country level. The number of lags p and q are chosen using the AIC criterion. I test for the joint significance of lags of positive sentiment π (column 1 and 2), lags of negative sentiment ν (column 3 and 4), and the union of lags of positive and negative sentiment (π, ν) (column 5 and 6). For each test of joint significance, I report F-statistics and p-values. ** and * indicate that coefficients are jointly significantly different from zero at the 0.05 and 0.10 levels or better, respectively. News articles come from Factiva.com, GDP growth comes from the International Financial Statistics Database (IFS).*

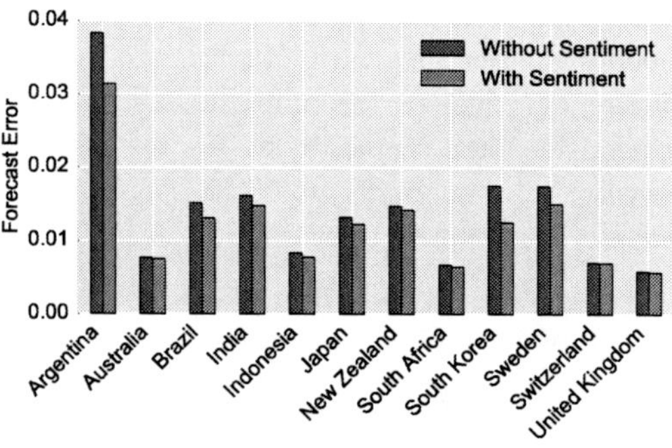

Figure 2: Reductions in GDP Growth Forecast Errors Using Sentiment. *Forecast errors (measured by the regressions' Root Mean Square Error) of predictive regressions of GDP growth estimated with an AR(p) process (in blue) and when news-based measures of sentiment are also included in the regression (in green). News articles come from Factiva.com, GDP growth comes from the International Financial Statistics Database (IFS).*

tion (4) compared to an AR(p) process.[3]

3.2 News Sentiment and Consensus Forecast

Several aggregate time series (e.g. weekly initial jobless claims, monthly payroll employment, etc...) are well known for containing information to help measure current economic conditions ((Aruoba et al., 2009)). Does my sentiment index simply combine information already contained in these well-known leading indicators? Obtaining data on leading indicators of GDP growth across countries is challenging, but these leading indicators should presumably be included in professional forecasters' information set. Since 1989, Consensus Economics Inc. provides a monthly survey of professional forecasters who are asked to forecast annual GDP growth across countries. For each realization of yearly GDP growth, the dataset contains GDP growth forecasts made by public and private economic institutions for each horizon h=1,...,24 months. (Fildes and Stekler, 2002) show that survey-based consensus forecasts are most of the time more accurate than those generated by time series models. The other advantage of forecasts produced by Consensus Economics is its common format for a large cross section of emerging market countries. If professional forecasters use all available information in producing their forecasts, the information contained in my news-based sentiment measures should not reduce the forecast errors of predictive regressions of GDP growth using consensus forecasts.

Predictive regressions of GDP growth using consensus forecasts and news-based sentiment measures are described by equation (5):

$$y_{t,c} = \alpha + \beta y_{t-h,c} + \gamma \sum_{i=1}^{q} \pi_{t-h-i,c} + \zeta \sum_{i=1}^{q} \nu_{t-h-i,c} + \epsilon_{t,c}, \tag{5}$$

where $y_{t,c}$ is the log GDP growth between t and $t + 12$ months in country c and $\epsilon_{t,c}$ is the error term. First, I estimate predictive regressions of GDP growth on consensus forecasts at the country level

for each horizon h = 1, ... , 24. Because sample sizes are small, estimating coefficients for each lagged measure of sentiment would lead to large standard errors. I instead include moving averages of my positive and negative sentiment measures (averaged at a monthly frequency); the moving average horizon q is chosen by minimizing regressions' forecast errors.[4]

On average across countries and horizons, forecast errors diminish by 19% when news-based sentiment measures are included in predictive regressions of GDP growth on consensus forecasts. The top right panel of figure (3) shows that, on average across horizons, forecast errors diminish for each country in my sample. The top left panel shows that this reduction is larger for longer horizon: the average reduction in forecast error goes from 12% for horizons up to 12 months, to 25% for horizons longer than 12 months. This evidence supports a model of information frictions where forecasters slowly incorporate textual information in forming their forecasts.

It is well established that forecast errors tend to be larger during bad times. Does the reduction in forecast errors resulting from the inclusion of sentiment measures differentially improve forecasts of good and bad times? I fit an H-P filter to quarterly GDP growth times series at the country level ((Hodrick and Prescott, 1997)). Good (bad) times are defined to be the periods when the realized annual GDP growth is above (below) the trend produced by the H-P filter. I use the estimates of the model defined by equation (5) and I separately compute the forecast errors measured during good and bad times. The middle column of figure (3) presents forecast errors of good times and the right column presents forecast errors of bad times.

Forecast errors of good times diminish by 13% on average as a result of the inclusion sentiment measures in equation (5). The improvement in forecast error goes up to 21% during bad times. The middle left and bottom left panel of figure (3) shows that the same result holds if I restrict the sample to short (long) forecasting horizons: during good times, forecast errors diminish by 10% (15%) on av-

---

[3]All the regressions' forecast errors are measured in sample by computing the regressions' root mean square errors (RMSE).

[4]To be clear, sentiment variables are lagged to only include information released prior to the forecasts.

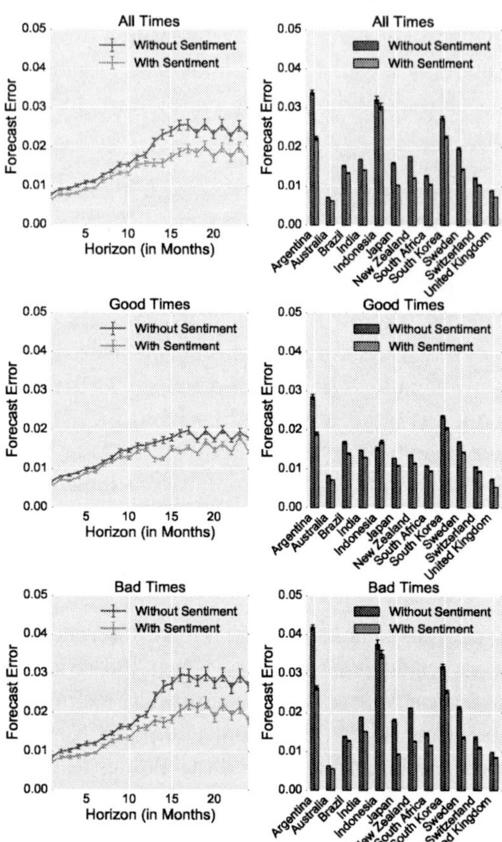

Figure 3: Reduction in GDP Growth Forecast Errors. *Changes in forecast errors (measured in RMSE) across countries and horizons when news-based sentiment measures are included in predictive regressions of GDP growth on consensus forecasts for GDP growth (see equation (5)). In the left column, forecast errors are averaged across countries. In the right column they are averaged across horizons. The left panel shows forecast errors during both good and bad times; the middle panel shows forecast errors during good times; the right panel shows forecast errors during bad times. Good and bad times are determined with respect to an HP filter estimated on quarterly GDP growth data. A period is considered to be a good (bad) time if annual GDP growth is above (below) the trend estimated by the HP filter. Errors bars represent standard errors. News articles come from Factiva.com, GDP growth comes from the International Financial Statistics Database (IFS), consensus forecasts come from Consensus Economics, Inc.*

erage; during bad times they diminish by 16% (28%) on average.

If forecasters where simply slowly incorporating information but correctly assigning weights when updating their forecasts, I should not observe a difference in changes in predictive accuracy between good and bad times. The fact that reductions in forecast error are larger in bad times than in good times suggests that forecasters tend to underreact to negative information.

4 Conclusion and Future Work

This paper describes the information content of news-based measures of sentiment and their relationship to fluctuations in GDP growth. Sentiment measures tracks fluctuations in GDP and we show that they are a leading indicator of GDP growth at the country level for 10 out of 12 countries in our sample. Sentiment measures contain information which is not accounted for by professional forecasters. News-based sentiment measures lead to a 19% average reduction in forecast error of GDP growth relative to consensus forecasts. Reductions in forecast errors are larger for longer forecasting horizons which suggests that forecasters slowly incorporate textual information into their forecasts. Reductions in forecast errors are also larger during bad times which indicates that forecasters tend to underreact to bad news.

From a policy perspective, news-based measures of sentiment provide a direct, real-time, automated and inexpensive measures of aggregate sentiment about current and future economic conditions, especially for countries for which official statistics might be sparse, inaccurate or noisy. As a result, it could help policy makers react in a more efficient manner to changes in economic conditions.

References

[Aruoba et al.2009] S. Boragan Aruoba, Francis X. Diebold, and Chiara Scotti. 2009. Real-time measurement of business conditions. *Journal of Business and Economic Statistics*, 27:417– 427.

[Baker et al.2016] Scott Baker, Nicolas Bloom, and S.J. Davis. 2016. Measuring economic policy uncertainty. *Quarterly Journal of Economics, Forthcoming*.

[Choi and Varian2012] Hyunyoung Choi and Hal Varian. 2012. Predicting the present with google trends. *The Economic Records*, 88:2–9.

[Fildes and Stekler2002] Robert Fildes and Herman Stekler. 2002. The state of macroeconomic forecasting. *Journal of Macroeconomics*, 24(4):435–468.

[Garcia2013] Diego Garcia. 2013. Sentiment during recession. *Journal of Finance*, 68(3):1267–1300.

[Hodrick and Prescott1997] Robert Hodrick and Edward C. Prescott. 1997. Postwar u.s. business cycles: An empirical investigation. *Journal of Money, Credit, and Banking*, 29(1):1–16.

[Jurafsky and Martin2009] Daniel Jurafsky and James H. Martin. 2009. *Speech and Language Processing*. Prentice Hall, Upper Saddle River, NJ.

[Loughran and McDonald2011] Tim Loughran and Bill McDonald. 2011. When is a liability not a liability? textual analysis, dictionaries, and 10-ks. *Journal of Finance*, 66(1):35–65.

[Nordhaus1987] William Nordhaus. 1987. Forecasting efficiency: Concepts and applications. *Review of Economics and Statistics*, 69(4).

[Tetlock2007] Paul C. Tetlock. 2007. Giving content to investor sentiment: The role of media in the stock market. *The Journal of Finance*, 62(3):1139–1168.

[Young and Soroka2012] Lori Young and Stuart Soroka. 2012. Affective news: The automated coding of sentiment in political texts. *Political Communication*, 29:205–231.

The Clinical Panel:
Leveraging Psychological Expertise During NLP Research

Glen Coppersmith
Qntfy
glen@qntfy.com

Kristy Hollingshead
IHMC
kseitz@ihmc.us

H. Andrew Schwartz
Stony Brook University
has@cs.stonybrook.edu

Molly E. Ireland
Texas Tech University
molly.ireland@ttu.edu

Rebecca Resnik
Rebecca Resnik & Assoc., LLC
drrebeccaresnik@gmail.com

Kate Loveys
Qntfy
kate@qntfy.com

April Foreman
Veterans Affairs
acf@docforeman.com

Loring Ingraham
George Washington University
ingraham@gwu.edu

Abstract

Computational social science is, at its core, a blending of disciplines—the best of human experience, judgement, and anecdotal case studies fused with novel computational methods to extract subtle patterns from immense data. Jointly leveraging such diverse approaches effectively is decidedly nontrivial, but with tremendous potential benefits. We provide frank assessments from our work bridging the computational linguistics and psychology communities during a range of short and long-term engagements, in the hope that these assessments might provide a foundation upon which those embarking on novel computational social science projects might structure their interactions.

1 Introduction

Cross-discipline collaboration is critical to computational social science (CSS), amplified by the complexity of the behaviors measured and the data used to draw conclusions. Academic tradition divides courses, researchers, and departments into quantitative ($\mathbb{Q}$s) and humanities ($\mathbb{H}$s), with collaboration more common within $\mathbb{Q}$ disciplines (e.g., engineering and computer science are required for many pursuits in robotics) than across the $\mathbb{Q}$-$\mathbb{H}$ divide (e.g., computational poetry). Ideally, long term collaborations across the $\mathbb{Q}$-$\mathbb{H}$ divide will serve CSS best, but establishing such relationships is challenging and the success of any pairing is hard to predict. How does one find the most technologically-forward $\mathbb{H}$s? Which are the most patient-centered $\mathbb{Q}$s?

Any cross-discipline collaboration requires bridging a gap with some level of familiarization and adaptation, as well as establishment of common ground, common semantics, and common language (Snow, 1959). With intra-$\mathbb{Q}$ endeavors like robotics, many of these commonalities exist (e.g., everyone involved in the endeavor has likely taken calculus and basic programming classes). CSS, however, draws techniques and deep understanding from both $\mathbb{Q}$ and $\mathbb{H}$ disciplines, which makes establishing such commonalities an even larger task. This paper outlines the various ways in which the Computational Linguistics and Clinical Psychology (CLPsych) community has bridged the semantic chasm between the required $\mathbb{Q}$ and $\mathbb{H}$ partners, in the hopes that some of the successful techniques and lessons learned can be adapted for other CSS collaborations. We highlight the actions taken by researchers from both sides to cross the $\mathbb{Q}$ and $\mathbb{H}$ divide. Briefly, we believe in the Gestalt of these approaches—they mutually reinforce and serve to establish a community and maintain commonality, even as research progresses. Concretely, we focus on three categories of approaches: integrated conferences (Section 2), a channel for continual exchange (Section 3), and intensive research workshops (Section 4).

Forging a new successful collaboration is tricky, with expectations on both sides often proving to be a mismatch to reality. For example, due to a lack of understanding of how language analyses are accomplished, $\mathbb{H}$ may expect *feats of magic* from $\mathbb{Q}$s, or for $\mathbb{Q}$s to provide an unrealistic amount of tedious data grunt work. On the other side, $\mathbb{Q}$s may expect

Proceedings of 2016 EMNLP Workshop on Natural Language Processing and Computational Social Science, pages 132–137,
Austin, TX, November 5, 2016. ©2016 Association for Computational Linguistics

diagnostic criteria to be concrete or may not fully appreciate the need to control for sample biases. From an $\mathbb{H}$ perspective, social and cultural barriers may prevent engagement with $\mathbb{Q}$s: $\mathbb{H}$ researchers may be more sensitive to prejudices about research methods in the so-called soft sciences, and misunderstandings may emerge from stereotypes about expressive $\mathbb{H}$s and cold $\mathbb{Q}$s (as well as their underlying kernels of truth). $\mathbb{Q}$s may design tools and methods without proper consideration for making them accessible to $\mathbb{H}$ colleagues, or without a patient-centered design for the patients that $\mathbb{H}$s work with. At a minimum, there is a general ignorance to some of the findings in the other field, and in the extreme, there is complete dismissal of others' concerns or research.

In any $\mathbb{Q}$-$\mathbb{H}$ collaboration, the tendency to lapse into using specific semantically-laden terminology may lead to confusion without recognizing that the other side needs more explanation. For examples of this[1], "self-medicate" is a clinical $\mathbb{H}$ euphemism for destructive behavior involving alcohol or drugs. Similarly, the "suicide zone" is a series of related cognitive phenomena sometimes apparent before a suicide attempt. These terms carry a well-understood and experienced semantic context for the practicing clinicians, but the $\mathbb{Q}$ collaborators lack this nuance. Similarly, $\mathbb{Q}$ researchers are familiar with certain methods in presenting results and graphs, so DET-curves and notched box plots are well-understood to $\mathbb{Q}$s, but require explanation and analysis to be informative to many $\mathbb{H}$s. This effect is amplified when working intensely with a dataset, letting the researchers become intimately (and in cases overly) familiar with it, and the assumptions and limitation of it. This highlights a need to take a step back when presenting graphs or other visual results to collaborators on the other side of the $\mathbb{Q}$-$\mathbb{H}$ divide. Creating clear data and result visualizations was a vital lesson learned to interface successfully between $\mathbb{H}$ and $\mathbb{Q}$ collaborators.

Many of the other lessons learned from our collaborations over the years took us back to basics:

1. Ask whether the analysis really answers the question for which it was motivated.

2. Step through each component of a figure (e.g., explain the axes).

3. Present potential conclusions that might be drawn from these results.

4. Allow for questions and discussion at each step.

In addition to familiarity with the data, familiarity with the statistics and data displays can also impede collaborators' understanding of the results. Clinical $\mathbb{H}$s have typically been exposed to statistics courses within their discipline, which likely cover variance, ANOVAs, MANOVAs, t-tests, χ^2, and standard error of measurement. However, exposure of many machine learning approaches to measurement and analysis is not included, although those with more recent training in computational social science may have more familiarity with these stereotypical $\mathbb{Q}$ approaches. Quite aside from techniques, typical ways to report results differ significantly: F-measure, precision/recall, or true positives/true negatives are common for $\mathbb{Q}$s whereas $\mathbb{H}$s are more familiar with sensitivity/specificity. The strength of a $\mathbb{Q}$-$\mathbb{H}$ collaboration comes largely from learning from one another, of learning to take advantage of an $\mathbb{H}$'s strength in hypothesis testing and a $\mathbb{Q}$'s abilities in advanced predictive modeling, computation, and algorithms.

In CLPsych, each side of these nascent collaborations approached a research problem differently—the $\mathbb{Q}$s often favored bottom-up, data-driven analysis rather than the more traditional and top-down approach generally taken by $\mathbb{H}$s first forming then formally testing a series of hypotheses based on prior knowledge. Though these different approaches have many commonalities and may achieve the same goal, initial discussions in some of the collaborations were needed to overcome the hurdle of different starting assumptions. This co-education across the $\mathbb{Q}$-$\mathbb{H}$ divide was, and continues to be, continual process.

2 Psychologists as Discussants

The CLPsych workshops, co-located at computational linguistic conferences since 2014, have been instrumental in bringing together the computational linguistics and clinical psychology communities (Resnik et al., 2014; Mitchell et al., 2015; Hollingshead and Ungar, 2016). These workshops took care

---

[1]Sometimes referred to as code words (http://rationalwiki.org/wiki/Code_word) or groupspeak (Nguyen et al., 2015).

to have the NLP and Psych constituencies integrated at every sensible step: program committee, reviews, dialog, and co-presentation.

The call for papers made explicit that the papers are to be informative to and understood by both the computer science and the psychology constituencies. Papers that did not meet this standard were harshly reviewed and consistently rejected. All papers were reviewed by both computational linguistics and psychology researchers, and authors were given a chance to edit their submissions in response to the peer-review comments prior to the submission of the camera-ready papers. Concretely, this allowed the authors to incorporate the reviewing psychologists' views, even prior to publication and presentation at the workshop.

Once at the workshop, each presentation was followed by a discussant from the other constituency (i.e., each $\mathbb{Q}$ presentation was followed by an $\mathbb{H}$ discussant and vice versa). This discussant had the paper well ahead of time and was given the chance to prepare a presentation to complement or respond to the paper. Without exception, this enriched the presented material with fresh insight from a novel perspective. The discussants served to expose the researchers and audience alike to the way such work is interpreted by the other constituency. Critically, though, the discussants took care to restate some of the assumptions and findings as how they would expect their constituency to phrase and interpret it – which provided a potent method for establishing and reinforcing common vocabulary and semantics. Together, these effects led to strong semantic foundations and ongoing dialogs between constituencies, ultimately giving rise to increased communication between the workshop participants at the workshop itself and throughout the year.

3   Online Communities & Continual Engagement

Early in this process, CLPsych was fortunate that a group of researchers and clinicians from the suicide prevention community ($\mathbb{H}$s) came upon some popular press coverage of recent research and reached out to the $\mathbb{Q}$ researchers involved (Coppersmith et al., 2014a; Coppersmith et al., 2014b). *#SPSM* (Sui-

cide Prevention and Social Media[2]) is a social media community that focuses on innovation in suicide prevention. They have a weekly broadcast from a topic relevant to suicide prevention, and invited some of the CLPsych work to be presented. Since the first meeting in February 2014, a number of the NLP members ($\mathbb{Q}$s) from CLPsych have been guests on their show, where they have been able to discuss with a primarily $\mathbb{H}$ panel and audience the myriad ways in which research in this space may inform suicide prevention and mental healthcare more generally. *#SPSM* was keen to bring NLP and data science researchers into their community and provided a platform for continual dialog.

Through this platform, the $\mathbb{Q}$-$\mathbb{H}$ dialog was able to extend outside the context of workshops and move to a less-formal conversational style, such that NLP members of the CLPsych community received deeper exposure to clinicians who might eventually benefit from their research. This dialog begat familiarity and lowered the barrier for interaction— common semantics and language were established, which allowed for efficient communication of ideas, preliminary results, and next steps for the $\mathbb{Q}$ researchers who became part of this community.

Beyond the direct effects on research, the *#SPSM* community has also trained the $\mathbb{Q}$ researchers of some of the unwritten rules, cultural norms, and social codes of the mental health community. While mental health might be an extreme case in their sensitivity to language usage, given the discrimination many in the community face, all fields have some equivalent linguistic, political, or historical touchpoints. For example, the colloquial phrase "commit suicide" carries with it a strong negative connotation for the result of a neurological condition, as the term "commit" has a generally negative connotation associated with criminal behavior. Anyone unaware that the suicide prevention community tends to use "die by suicide" in place of "commit suicide" will inadvertently be perceived as crass, discriminating, and out-of-touch with the community that might benefit from their research (Singer and Erreger, 2015).

The *#SPSM* community helped the $\mathbb{Q}$ researchers to understand the important context of their work and the realities of the mental healthcare system. Access

---

[2]http://spsmchat.com or *#SPSM* on social media channels.

to the community also helped to impress upon ℚ researchers the potential impact of the work they are doing, encouraging the work to continue and reshaping it for greater impact and utility. New partnerships have been borne out of online discussions. In turn, the ℚ researchers helped the *#SPSM*'ers to understand the realm of the possible in data science. Informed discussion of data, access, and policy has become a recurring *#SPSM* theme.

From this ℚ-ℍ partnership, the ℍs came to understand what was needed to do successful ℚ research—labeled data—and became advocates for that. The ℍs were able to clearly articulate the barriers to releasing some of the most sensitive data, and collectively the ℚs and ℍs created a method to gather the data necessary to support research (at the data donation site `OurDataHelps.org`) and work with the mental healthcare and lived experience communities to spread the word and collect donations.

4   The Clinical Panel

The CLPsych community was given a chance to work together in a concerted manner at the 2016 Frederick Jelinek memorial workshop, hosted by the Center for Language and Speech Processing at Johns Hopkins University (Hollingshead et al., 2016). Novel datasets were made available for the workshop to advance the analysis of mental health through social media:

1. The Social Mediome project at the University of Pennsylvania provided electronic medical records and paired Facebook data from users who opted in to the study (Padrez et al., 2015);

2. Qntfy provided anonymized data from users who discussed mental health diagnoses or suicide attempts publicly on Twitter (Coppersmith et al., 2015; Coppersmith et al., 2016); and

3. `OurDataHelps.org` provided anonymized Twitter data for users who attempted suicide.

A team of researchers, primarily ℚs and primarily from NLP and data science, came to Johns Hopkins University for 6 weeks to explore temporal patterns of social media language relevant for mental health. In order to make sure the analyses were on the right path and to get some of the benefits of the CLPsych discussants in real time, a *clinical panel* was formed.

This panel was comprised of practicing clinicians, people with lived experience with mental health issues, epidemiologists, and psychology researchers. This was, from the start, an organic non-hierarchical cross-disciplinary experience, as we set out to establish precedent for a mutually respectful and collaborative environment.

During a weekly one hour video conference, the fulltime workshop researchers presented findings from the week's analysis, and were able to raise questions from the data. The ℍs on the panel continuously translated the visual to the clinical. The clinical panel was quick to offer corroboration, counterfactuals and alternate explanations to the presented results, as well as suggesting follow-on analyses. In some cases, these follow-on analyses led to productive lines of research with clear clinical applications. At the same time, it was difficult to maintain a balance between the ℚ-proposed lines of research on changes in language over time and meeting some of the ℍ shorter-term questions on changes in behavior over time, unrelated to language.

Most importantly, this weekly conference provided the panel a real-time and interactive medium to share their clinical experiences with the NLP researchers performing the analyses. For example, clinicians recounted various phenomena that would show up as increased variability over time. This allowed the NLP researchers to quickly adapt and incorporate measures of variability in all analyses going forward. In another example, one of the key findings from the workshop was inspired by an ℍ suggestion that we try to illuminate the "suicide zone"—a period of time before a suicide attempt where one's behavior is markedly different. Critically, the timeliness of this feedback allowed the adjustment to take place early in the workshop, when there was still sufficient time to adjust the immediate research trajectory. The benefit of this might be most stark when examined in contrast to the (perhaps) yearly feedback one might expect from published papers or conference presentations.

Collectively, both ℚs and ℍs involved in these clinical panels had great respect for each other's expertise, knowledge, and willingness to step outside of their discipline. While this healthy respect made for excellent ongoing interaction, it had a tendency to hamper voicing of criticism early on. With some

Benefits/ Successes	*Video-conference clinical panels*: timely interactive feedback from clinicians on novel data findings.
	Clinicians as discussants: immediate interpretation and feedback to presentations, which builds rapport, common semantics, and common vocabulary.
	Clinicians on program committee: fosters findings that are interesting and accessible to all disciplines.
	Continual engagement: ongoing dialog outside of conferences, which serves to refine common semantic picture.
	Problem framing: initial discussions of experimental setups led to framing data-driven, exploratory analysis as hypothesis-driven tests.
Pitfalls/ Challenges	*Publishing in mainstream NLP conferences*: difficult to balance sophistication of method (highly regarded for NLP publications) with general interpretability (necessary for social scientific impact).
	Long-term goals: expectation of new results at regular collaborative check-ins can motivate a team toward short-sighted tasks.
	Fundamental assumptions: understanding, explicitly stating, and challenging fundamental assumptions can create emotionally charged exchanges.

Table 1: Summarized successes and pitfalls of various collaborative interactions between NLP researchers and psychology experts.

frequency, a contrary view to a publicly-expressed viewpoint was harbored by one of the participants, but only shared privately after the panel rather than voicing it publicly and risking damage to these new relationships. While this has merit to building relationships, it does make rapid scientific progress difficult. We feel that finding ways to foster constructive challenging of assumptions would have made the panel even more effective within the limited duration workshop.

To summarize, the clinical panel provided great benefits in their ability to drive the research in more clinically impactful directions than would come from Qs alone. They also were invaluable in keeping the research aligned with the ultimate goal of helping people and provided a regular source of motivation. This approach is not without a significant startup cost to establish common language and semantics, the occasional danger of shortsighted research tasks before the next weekly meeting, and both sides' reluctance to criticize unfamiliar ideas.

5   Conclusion

As we explore the role that computational linguistics and NLP has in psychology, it is important to engage with clinical psychologists and psychology researchers for their insight and complementary knowledge. Our Q-$\mathbb{H}$ collaborations taught us (1) the power of these collaborations comes from diverse experience, which also means diverse needs, (2) establishing common language and semantics is a continual process, and (3) regular engagement keeps one motivated and focused on the important questions. These partnerships are the result of many forms of continual contact and, most importantly, a mutual respect and desire to see progress.

Acknowledgments

This work is the collection of the entire CLPsych community's efforts, and for that we are most grateful. Philip Resnik's intellectual influence are evident in this work and community, and bear special mention, as does that of Margaret Mitchell and Lyle Ungar. Some of the work reported here was carried out during the 2016 Jelinek Memorial Summer Workshop on Speech and Language Technologies, which was supported by Johns Hopkins University via DARPA LORELEI Contract No. HR0011-15-2-0027, and gifts from Microsoft, Amazon, Google, and Facebook.

References

Glen Coppersmith, Mark Dredze, and Craig Harman. 2014a. Quantifying mental health signals in Twitter. In *Proceedings of the ACL Workshop on Computational Linguistics and Clinical Psychology.*

Glen Coppersmith, Craig Harman, and Mark Dredze. 2014b. Measuring post traumatic stress disorder in Twitter. In *Proceedings of the 8th International AAAI Conference on Weblogs and Social Media (ICWSM).*

Glen Coppersmith, Mark Dredze, Craig Harman, and Kristy Hollingshead. 2015. From ADHD to SAD: Analyzing the language of mental health on Twitter through self-reported diagnoses. In *Proceedings of the Workshop on Computational Linguistics and Clinical Psychology: From Linguistic Signal to Clinical Reality*, Denver, Colorado, USA, June. North American Chapter of the Association for Computational Linguistics.

Glen Coppersmith, Kim Ngo, Ryan Leary, and Anthony Wood. 2016. Exploratory analysis of social media prior to a suicide attempt. In *Proceedings of the Workshop on Computational Linguistics and Clinical Psychology: From Linguistic Signal to Clinical Reality*, San Diego, California, USA, June. North American Chapter of the Association for Computational Linguistics.

Kristy Hollingshead and Lyle Ungar, editors. 2016. *Proceedings of the Workshop on Computational Linguistics and Clinical Psychology: From Linguistic Signal to Clinical Reality*. North American Association for Computational Linguistics, San Diego, California, USA, June.

Kristy Hollingshead, H Andrew Schwartz, and Glen Coppersmith. 2016. Detecting risk and protective factors of mental health using social media linked with electronic health records. In *3rd annual Frederick Jelenik Memorial Summer Workshop / 22nd annual Applied Language Technology Workshop at the Center for Language and Speech Processing at Johns Hopkins University.*

Margaret Mitchell, Glen Coppersmith, and Kristy Hollingshead, editors. 2015. *Proceedings of the Workshop on Computational Linguistics and Clinical Psychology: From Linguistic Signal to Clinical Reality*. North American Association for Computational Linguistics, Denver, Colorado, USA, June.

Viet-An Nguyen, Jordan Boyd-Graber, Philip Resnik, and Kristina Miler. 2015. Tea party in the house: A hierarchical ideal point topic model and its application to Republican legislators in the 112th congress. In *Proceedings of ACL.*

Kevin A Padrez, Lyle Ungar, Hansen Andrew Schwartz, Robert J Smith, Shawndra Hill, Tadas Antanavicius, Dana M Brown, Patrick Crutchley, David A Asch, and Raina M Merchant. 2015. Linking social media and medical record data: a study of adults presenting to an academic, urban emergency department. *BMJ quality & safety*, pages bmjqs–2015.

Philip Resnik, Rebecca Resnik, and Margaret Mitchell, editors. 2014. *Proceedings of the Workshop on Computational Linguistics and Clinical Psychology: From Linguistic Signal to Clinical Reality*. Association for Computational Linguistics, Baltimore, Maryland, USA, June.

Jonathan Singer and Sean Erreger. 2015. Let's talk about suicide: #LanguageMatters. http://www.socialworker.com/feature-articles/practice/lets-talk-about-suicide-languagematters/.

Charles Percy Snow. 1959. *The two cultures and the scientific revolution*. University Press.

Are You a Racist or Am I Seeing Things?
Annotator Influence on Hate Speech Detection on Twitter

Zeerak Waseem
University of Copenhagen
Copenhagen, Denmark
`csp265@alumni.ku.dk`

Abstract

Hate speech in the form of racism and sexism is commonplace on the internet (Waseem and Hovy, 2016). For this reason, there has been both an academic and an industry interest in detection of hate speech. The volume of data to be reviewed for creating data sets encourages a use of crowd sourcing for the annotation efforts.

In this paper, we provide an examination of the influence of annotator knowledge of hate speech on classification models by comparing classification results obtained from training on expert and amateur annotations. We provide an evaluation on our own data set and run our models on the data set released by Waseem and Hovy (2016).

We find that amateur annotators are more likely than expert annotators to label items as hate speech, and that systems trained on expert annotations outperform systems trained on amateur annotations.

1 Introduction

Large amounts of hate speech on exists on platforms that allow for user generated documents, which creates a need to detect and filter it (Nobata et al., 2016), and to create data sets that contain hate speech and are annotated for the occurrence of hate speech. The need for corpus creation must be weighted against the psychological tax of being exposed to large amounts of abusive language (Chen, 2012).

A number of studies on profanity and hate speech detection, have crowdsourced their annotations due to the resources required to annotate large data sets and the possibility of distributing the load onto the crowd (Warner and Hirschberg, 2012; Nobata et al., 2016). Ross et al. (2016) investigate annotator reliability for hate speech annotation, concluding that *"hate speech is a fuzzy construct that requires significantly better definitions and guidelines in order to be annotated reliably"*.

Hate speech is hard to detect for humans (Sue et al., 2007), which warrants a thorough understanding of the benefits and pitfalls of crowdsourced annotation. This need is reinforced by previous studies, which utilize crowdsourcing of hate speech without knowledge on the quality of crowdsourced annotations for hate speech labeling.

In addition, it is important to understand how different manners of obtaining labeling can influence the classification models and how it is possible to obtain good annotations, while ensuring that annotators are not likely to experience adverse effects of annotating hate speech.

Our contribution We provide annotations of $6,909$ tweets for hate speech by annotators from CrowdFlower and annotators that have a theoretical and applied knowledge of hate speech, henceforth *amateur* and *expert* annotators[1]. Our data set extends the Waseem and Hovy (2016) data set by $4,033$ tweets. We also illustrate, how amateur and expert annotations influence classification efforts. Finally, we show the effects of allowing majority voting on classification and agreement between the amateur and expert annotators.

---

[1]Data set available at http://github.com/zeerakw/hatespeech

Proceedings of 2016 EMNLP Workshop on Natural Language Processing and Computational Social Science, pages 138–142,
Austin, TX, November 5, 2016. ©2016 Association for Computational Linguistics

2   Data

Our data set is obtained by sampling tweets from the 130k tweets extracted by Waseem and Hovy (2016). The order of the tweets is selected by our database connection, thus allowing for an overlap with the data set released by Waseem and Hovy (2016). We find that there is an overlap of $2,876$ tweets (see Table 1) between the two data sets.

	Racism	Sexism	Neither
Count	1	95	2780

Table 1: Overlap between our data set and Waseem and Hovy (2016), denoted by their labels

Given the distribution of the labels in Waseem and Hovy (2016) and our annotated data set (see Table 2), it is to be expected the largest overlap occurs with tweets annotated as negative for hate speech. Observing Table 2, we see that the label distribution in our data set generally differs from the distribution in Waseem and Hovy (2016). In fact, we see that the amateur majority voted labels is the only distribution that tends towards a label distribution similar to Waseem and Hovy (2016), while the labels the amateurs fully agreed upon and the expert annotations have similar distributions.

	Racism	Sexism	Neither	Both
Expert	1.41%	13.08%	84.19%	0.70%
Amateur Majority	5.80%	19.00%	71.94%	1.50%
Amateur Full	0.69%	14.02%	85.15%	0.11%
Waseem and Hovy (2016)	11.6%	22.6%	68.3%	–

Table 2: Label distributions of the three annotation groups and Waseem and Hovy (2016).

Our annotation effort deviates from Waseem and Hovy (2016). In addition to "racism", "sexism", and "neither", we add the label "both" for tweets that contain both racism and sexism. We add this label, as the intersection of multiple oppressions can differ from the forms of oppression it consists of (Crenshaw, 1989), and as such becomes a unique form of oppression. Thus, we introduce a labeling scheme that follows an intersectional approach (Crenshaw, 1989). We do not require annotators to follow links. Instead, we ask them to annotate tweets only containing links as "Neither".

Expert Annotations   We recruit feminist and anti-racism activists to annotate the data set. We present the annotators with the tests from Waseem and Hovy (2016). If a tweet fails any of the tests, the annotators are instructed to label it as the relevant form of hate speech. Expert annotators are given the choice of skipping tweets, if they are not confident in which label to assign, and a "Noise" label in case the annotators are presented with non-English tweets. Due to privacy concerns, all expert annotators are treated as a single entity.

Amateur Annotations   Amateur annotators are recruited on CrowdFlower without any selection, to mitigate selection biases. They are presented with $6,909$ tweets that have been annotated by the expert annotators. The amateur annotators are not provided with the option to skip tweets, as they are not presented tweets the experts had skipped or labeled as "Noise".

Annotator agreement   Considering annotator agreement, we find that the inter-annotator agreement among the amateur annotators is $\kappa = 0.57$ ($\sigma = 0.08$).

	Majority Vote	Full Agreement
Expert	0.34	0.70

Table 3: Kappa scores comparing majority voted label and full agreement with expert annotations.

The low agreement in Table 2 provides further evidence to the claim by Ross et al. (2016) that annotation of hate speech is a hard task. Table 2 suggests that if only cases of full agreement are considered, it is possible to obtain good annotations using crowdsourcing.

Overlap   Considering the overlap with the Waseem and Hovy (2016), we see that the agreement is extremely low (mean pairwise $\kappa = 0.14$ between all annotator groups and Waseem and Hovy (2016)). Interestingly, we see that the vast majority of disagreements between our annotators and Waseem and Hovy (2016), are disagreements where our annotators do not find hate speech but Waseem and Hovy (2016) do.

3   Evaluation

We evaluate the influence of our features on the classification task using 5-fold cross validation to assess

	Feature	Amateur			Expert		
		F1	Recall	Precision	F1	Recall	Precision
Close	*Character n-gram*	86.41	88.53%	87.21%	91.24	92.49%	92.73%
	Token n-gram	86.37	88.60%	87.68%	91.55	92.92%	91.50%
	Token unigram	86.46	88.68%	87.74%	91.15	92.41%	92.37%
	Skip-grams	86.27	88.53%	87.62%	91.53	92.92%	91.59%
	Length	83.16	86.31%	86.14%	86.43	89.17%	88.07%
Middling	**Binary Gender**	76.64	82.47%	83.11%	77.77	84.76%	71.85%
	Gender Probability	86.37	88.60%	87.68%	81.30	86.35%	85.63%
	Brown Clusters	84.50	87.27%	86.59%	87.74	90.03%	90.10%
	POS (Spacy)	76.66	80.17%	75.38%	80.49	84.54%	79.08%
	POS (Ark)	73.86	79.06%	72.41%	80.07	85.05%	81.08%
Distant	AHST	71.71	80.17%	82.05%	55.40	68.28%	46.62%

Table 4: Scores for each individual feature on amateur (majority voting) and expert annotations.

the influence of the features listed in Table 4 for each annotator group.

Model Selection We perform a grid search over all possible feature combinations to find the best performing features. We find that the features with the highest performance are not necessarily the features with the best performance. For instance, token unigrams obtains the highest F1-score, precision, and the second highest recall on the amateur annotations, yet this feature fails to classify the minority classes.

Features We use a range of features focusing on both the textual information given in the tweets as well as extra-linguistic information including POS tags obtained using Gimpel et al. (2011) and Spacy[2].

In Table 4[3], we see that the most significant features trained on majority voted amateur annotations emphasize extra-linguistic features while the most significant features trained on expert annotations emphasize the content of the tweets.

Brown Clusters and Length We highlight the use of Brown Clusters (Brown et al., 1992) and length features (as inspired by Nobata et al. (2016)), as these are the only two features that classify the minority classes for both amateur and expert annotators. We use an in-house mapping of brown clusters, replacing unigrams with cluster identifiers.

We follow Nobata et al. (2016), in their use of the length of comments in tokens, and the average length of the words in a tweet.

Author Historical Salient Terms Given the promising results obtained for sarcasm detection (Bamman and Smith, 2015), we calculate the Author Historical Salient Terms (AHST). We obtain up to 3200 tweets for each user in our data set, calculate the TF-IDF scores, and identify the top 100 terms. We then add a binary feature signifying the occurrence of each of these 100 terms.

Interestingly, this feature performs worse than any other feature. Particularly when trained on expert annotations, suggesting that hate speech may be more situational or that users engaging in hate speech, do not only, or even primarily engage in hate speech.

Gender Following the indication that gender can positively influence classification scores (Waseem and Hovy, 2016), we compute the gender of the users in our data set. To counteract the low coverage in Waseem and Hovy (2016), we use a lexicon trained on Twitter (Sap et al., 2014) to calculate the probability of gender. Using these probabilities we assign binary gender. Both the probability of a gender for a user and the binary gender are used as individual features. We find that using gender information only contributes to the classification score for amateur annotators.

Minority Class Misclassification We find that some features trained on expert and amateur annotations result in misclassification on the minority classes, including identifying no instances of the mi-

---

[2]www.spacy.io
[3]Italics signify the best performing feature on expert annotations, bold signify the best performing features on amateur annotations (majority voting). These best performing features are then used for the respective "best" feature sets.

Feature Set	Amateur			Expert		
	F1	Recall	Precision	F1	Recall	Precision
Close	86.39	88.60%	87.59%	91.24	92.49%	92.67%
Middling	84.07	86.76%	85.43%	87.81	90.10%	88.53%
Distant	71.71	80.17%	82.05%	77.77	84.76%	71.85%
All	86.39	88.60%	87.59%	90.77	92.20%	92.23%
Best	83.88	86.68%	85.54%	91.19	92.49%	92.50%
Baseline	70.84	79.80%	63.69%	77.77	84.76%	71.85%

Table 5: Scores obtained for each of the feature sets.

nority classes (see Table 4). These misclassifications of the minority classes are largely due to the small number of instances in those classes. In spite of this, we do not believe that only boosting the size of the minority classes is a good approach, as we should seek to mimic reality in our data sets for hate speech detection.

Results Running our system on the Waseem and Hovy (2016) data set, we find that our best performing system does not substantially outperform on the binary classification task Waseem and Hovy (2016) ($F1_{ours}$: 70.05, $F1_{WH}$: 69.94). We find that our system performs significantly worse than Waseem and Hovy (2016) on the multi-class classification ask ($F1_{ours}$: 53.43, $F1_{WH}$: 73.89).

Interestingly, the main cause of error is false positives. This holds true using both amateur and expert annotations. We mitigate personal bias in our annotations, as multiple people have participated in the annotation process. Waseem and Hovy (2016) may suffer from personal bias, as the only the authors annotated, and only the annotations positive for hate speech were reviewed by one other person.

It is our contention that hate speech corpora should reflect real life, in that hate speech is a rare occurrence comparatively. Given that some of our features obtain high F1-scores, in spite of not classifying for the minority classes, we suggest that the unweighted F1-score may not be an appropriate metric to evaluate classification on hate speech corpora.

4 Related Work

Most related work in the field of abusive language detection has focused on detecting profanity using list-based methods to identify offensive words (Sood et al., 2012; Chen et al., 2012). These methods traditionally suffer from a poor recall and do not address hate speech. While Sood et al. (2012) incorporate edit distances to find variants of slurs, they are not able to find terms that do not occur in these lists. Nobata et al. (2016) address this, by using comprehensive lists of slurs obtained from Hatebase[4].

Waseem and Hovy (2016) and Ross et al. (2016) focus on building corpora which they annotate for containing hate speech. Our work closely resembles Waseem and Hovy (2016), as they also run classification experiments on a hate speech data set. Waseem and Hovy (2016) obtain an F1-score of 73.91 on their data set, using character n-grams and gender information.

Nobata et al. (2016) employ a wide array of features for abusive language detection, including but not limited to POS tags, the number of blacklisted words in a document, n-gram features including token and character n-grams and length features. The primary challenge this paper presents, is the need for good annotation guidelines, if one wishes to detect specific subsets of abusive language.

5 Conclusion

We find that using expert annotations can produce models that perform comparably to previous classification efforts. Our best model is on par with previous work on the Waseem and Hovy (2016) data set for the binary classification task but under-performs for the multi-class classification task.

We suggest that a weighted F1-score be applied in evaluation of classification efforts on hate speech corpora, such that misclassification on minority classes is penalized.

Our annotation and classification results expand on the claim of Ross et al. (2016) that hate speech is hard to annotate without intimate knowledge of hate speech. Furthermore, we find that considering only cases of full agreement among amateur annota-

---

[4]www.hatebase.org

tors can produce relatively good annotations as compared to expert annotators. This can allow for a significant decrease in the annotations burden of expert annotators by asking them to primarily consider the cases in which amateur annotators have disagreed.

Future Work We will seek to further investigate the socio-linguistic features such as gender and location. Furthermore, we will expand to more forms of hate speech. Finally, we will review the negative class in Waseem and Hovy (2016).

References

David Bamman and Noah Smith. 2015. Contextualized sarcasm detection on twitter.

Peter F. Brown, Peter V. deSouza, Robert L. Mercer, Vincent J. Della Pietra, and Jenifer C. Lai. 1992. Class-based n-gram models of natural language. *Comput. Linguist.*, 18(4):467–479, December.

Ying Chen, Yilu Zhou, Sencun Zhu, and Heng Xu. 2012. Detecting offensive language in social media to protect adolescent online safety. In *Privacy, Security, Risk and Trust (PASSAT), 2012 International Conference on and 2012 International Conference on Social Computing (SocialCom)*, pages 71–80. IEEE, September.

Adrian Chen. 2012. Inside facebook's outsourced anti-porn and gore brigade, where 'camel toes' are more offensive than 'crushed heads'. `http://gawker.com/5885714/` `inside-facebooks-outsourced-anti-\` `\porn-and-gore-brigade-where-camel-\` `\toes-are-more-offensive-than-crushed-\` `\heads`. Last accessed on July 4th, 2016.

Kimberle Crenshaw. 1989. Demarginalizing the intersection of race and sex: A black feminist critique of antidiscrimination doctrine, feminist eory and antiracist politics. *University of Chicago Legal Forum*, 1989(1).

Kevin Gimpel, Nathan Schneider, Brendan O'Connor, Dipanjan Das, Daniel Mills, Jacob Eisenstein, Michael Heilman, Dani Yogatama, Jeffrey Flanigan, and Noah A. Smith. 2011. Part-of-speech tagging for twitter: Annotation, features, and experiments. In *Proceedings of the 49th Annual Meeting of the Association for Computational Linguistics: Human Language Technologies: Short Papers - Volume 2*, HLT '11, pages 42–47, Stroudsburg, PA, USA. Association for Computational Linguistics.

Chikashi Nobata, Joel Tetreault, Achint Thomas, Yashar Mehdad, and Yi Chang. 2016. Abusive language detection in online user content. In *Proceedings of the 25th International Conference on World Wide Web*, WWW '16, pages 145–153, Republic and Canton of Geneva, Switzerland. International World Wide Web Conferences Steering Committee.

Björn Ross, Michael Rist, Guillermo Carbonell, Benjamin Cabrera, Nils Kurowsky, and Michael Wojatzki. 2016. Measuring the reliability of hate speech annotations: The case of the european refugee crisis. Bochum, Germany, September.

Maarten Sap, Gregory Park, Johannes Eichstaedt, Margaret Kern, David Stillwell, Michal Kosinski, Lyle Ungar, and Hansen Andrew Schwartz. 2014. Developing age and gender predictive lexica over social media. In *Proceedings of the 2014 Conference on Empirical Methods in Natural Language Processing (EMNLP)*, pages 1146–1151, Doha, Qatar, October. Association for Computational Linguistics.

Sara Owsley Sood, Judd Antin, and Elizabeth F. Churchill. 2012. Using crowdsourcing to improve profanity detection. In *AAAI Spring Symposium: Wisdom of the Crowd*, volume SS-12-06 of *AAAI Technical Report*. AAAI.

Derald Wing Sue, Christina M Capodilupo, Gina C Torino, Jennifer M Bucceri, Aisha Holder, Kevin L Nadal, and Marta Esquilin. 2007. Racial microaggressions in everyday life: implications for clinical practice. *American Psychologist*, 62(4).

William Warner and Julia Hirschberg. 2012. Detecting hate speech on the world wide web. In *Proceedings of the Second Workshop on Language in Social Media*, LSM '12, pages 19–26, Stroudsburg, PA, USA. Association for Computational Linguistics.

Zeerak Waseem and Dirk Hovy. 2016. Hateful symbols or hateful people? predictive features for hate speech detection on twitter. In *Proceedings of the NAACL Student Research Workshop*, San Diego, California, June. Association for Computational Linguistics.

Disentangling Topic Models:
A Cross-cultural Analysis of Personal Values through Words

Steven R. Wilson and **Rada Mihalcea**
University of Michigan
steverw@umich.edu, mihalcea@umich.edu

Ryan L. Boyd and **James W. Pennebaker**
University of Texas at Austin
ryanboyd@utexas.edu, pennebaker@mail.utexas.edu

Abstract

We present a methodology based on topic modeling that can be used to identify and quantify sociolinguistic differences between groups of people, and describe a regression method that can disentangle the influences of different attributes of the people in the group (e.g., culture, gender, age). As an example, we explore the concept of personal values, and present a cross-cultural analysis of value-behavior relationships spanning writers from the United States and India.

1 Introduction

Topic modeling describes a family of approaches that capture groups of related words in a corpus. In these frameworks, a *topic* can be thought of as a group of words found to be related to a higher level concept. Generally, a topic is represented as a set of numbers that describe the degree to which various words belong, which often takes the form of a probability distribution over words. Several topic modeling approaches have been proposed in the past, including Latent Dirichlet Allocation (Blei et al., 2003), Correlated Topic Models (Blei and Lafferty, 2006), Hierarchical Dirichlet Processes (Teh et al., 2012), and the Meaning Extraction Method (MEM) (Chung and Pennebaker, 2008), among others. Topic modeling has been a useful way to handle myriad tasks, including dimensionality reduction (Lacoste-Julien et al., 2009), data exploration (Blei, 2012), creation of features that are used for downstream tasks such as document classification (Zhu et al., 2009), twitter hashtag recommendation (Godin et al., 2009), and authorship attribution (Steyvers et al., 2004).

In this paper, we use topic modeling to explore sociolinguistic differences between various groups of authors by identifying groups of words that are indicative of a target process. We introduce a number of strategies that exemplify how topic modeling can be employed to make meaningful comparisons between groups of people. Moreover, we show how regression analysis may be leveraged to disentangle various factors influencing the usage of a particular topic. This facilitates the investigation of how particular traits are related to psychological processes.

We provide an example application in which we investigate how this methodology can be used to understand personal values, their relationships to behaviors, and the differences in their expression by writers from two cultures. To carry out these analyses, we examine essays from a multicultural social survey and posts written by bloggers in different countries. Our results show that culture plays an important role in the exploration of value-behavior relationships

Our contributions include: 1) a new sociolinguistic geared methodology that combines topic modeling with linear regression to explore differences between groups, while specifically accounting for the potential influence of different attributes of people in the group; 2) a cross-cultural study of values and behaviors that uses this methodology to identify differences in personal values between United States (US) and India, as well as culture-specific value-behavior links; and 3) a social survey data set containing free response text as well as a corpus of blog posts writ-

Proceedings of 2016 EMNLP Workshop on Natural Language Processing and Computational Social Science, pages 143–152,
Austin, TX, November 5, 2016. ©2016 Association for Computational Linguistics

ten by authors from two countries.

2 Methodology

2.1 Topic Modeling with the Meaning Extraction Method

While several topic modeling methods are available, we use the MEM as it has been shown to be particularly useful for revealing dimensions of authors' thoughts while composing a document (Kramer and Chung, 2011; Lowe et al., 2013). The MEM was first used as a content analysis approach for understanding dimensions along which people think about themselves as inferred from self descriptive writing samples. Given a corpus in which the authors are known to be writing in a way that is reflective of a certain psychological construct (e.g., self concept), the MEM can be used to target that construct and automatically extract groups of words that are related to it. Note that the MEM is a general framework for identifying topics in a corpus, and is one of many approaches that could be taken toward this goal. While our methodology allows for flexibility in decision making during the process, we opt for the original MEM setting proposed in (Chung and Pennebaker, 2008) and leave the investigation of the effectiveness alternative configurations for future work.

The standard MEM begins with a particular series of preprocessing steps, which we perform using the Meaning Extraction Helper (Boyd, 2015). This tool tokenizes and lemmatizes the words in each document, then filters out function words as well as rare words (those used in less than 5% of documents). Each of the documents is then converted into a binary vector indicating the presence of a given word with a value of 1 and the absence of a word with a 0. This approach is taken in order to focus on whether or not documents contain particular words without taking into account word frequency.

Based on the notion that word co-occurrences can lead to psychologically meaningful word groupings, we then perform principal components analysis on the correlation matrix of these document vectors, and apply the varimax rotation (Kaiser, 1958),[1] which, in terms of the language analysis domain, is

---

[1]We use the implementation of the varimax rotation from the stats package of CRAN (cran.r-project.org).

formulated as the orthogonal rotation that satisfies:

$$max \sum_t^T \left(\sum_w^V {f_{wt}}^4 - \frac{\left(\sum_w^V {f_{wt}}^2 \right)}{|V|} \right)$$

where T represents the set of topics ($|T| = k$, the number of topics specified as a parameter to the model), V is the vocabulary of all the words in the data set, and f_{tw} is the factor loading of word (variable) w for topic (factor) t. The goal of this rotation is to increase structural simplicity and interpretability while maintaining factorial invariance.

For many topic modeling approaches, the raw membership relation m_{RAW} for a word w in a topic, or "theme", t, may be defined directly as: $m_{RAW}(t, w) = f_{wt}$ where f_{wt} is the factor loading of w for t (or posterior probability of w belonging to t, depending on the paradigm being used). However, the MEM traditionally takes a thresholding approach to words' membership to a topic: any word with a factor loading of at least .20 for a particular component is retained as part of the theme, (words with loadings of less than -.20 reflect concepts at the opposite end of a bipolar construct). Functionally, then, we define the threshold membership relation m_{THRESH} for a word w to a new theme t:

$$m_{THRESH}(t, w) = \begin{cases} 1 & \text{if } f_{wt} > \tau, \\ -1 & \text{if } f_{wt} < -\tau, \\ 0 & otherwise. \end{cases}$$

We follow (Chung and Pennebaker, 2008) and choose a threshold of $\tau = .2$.

2.2 Topic Regression Analysis

To measure the degree to which a particular topic is used more (or less) by one group than another, we fit and subsequently analyze a series of regression models. For each document d and theme t, we assign a usage score by the function:

$$s(t, d) = \frac{\sum_w^d m(t, w)}{|d|},$$

assuming that a document is an iterable sequence of words and m is the chosen membership relation. When using m_{THRESH}, this score is essentially a normalized count of words in a document that belong to a particular theme minus the total number of words that were found to be in opposition to that theme (those words for which $m(t, w) = -1$).

We then regress the normalized score:

$$s_{NORM}(t, i, D) = \frac{|D| \cdot s(t, d_i)}{\sum_{d \in D} s(t, d)}$$

against variables encoding attributes of interest pertaining to each document d_i, such as the author's membership to a certain group, in order to determine the influence of these attributes on $s_{NORM}(t, i, D)$. Here, D represents all documents in the corpus and d_i is the ith document in D.

After fitting the regression models, we can interpret the coefficient attached to each attribute as the expected change in the usage of a particular theme as a result of a unit increase in the attribute, holding all other modeled attributes constant. For example, if we have a variable measuring the gender of the document's author, encoded as 0 for male and 1 for female, we can explore the degree to which gender has an expected relationship with the usage of a theme while controlling for other possible confounding factors that are included in the regression model. With this formulation, a binary variable with a predicted coefficient of, e.g., .15 would indicate an expected 15% increase in the usage of a theme between the group encoded as 1 (female, in our example) over the group encoded as 0 (male). Furthermore, we check for interactions between the attributes through a two-level factorial design regression analysis.

2.3   Relationships Between Sets of Themes

It may also be desirable to quantify the relationships between two different sets of themes. If the same set of authors have written texts that are known to relate to multiple categories of interest, perhaps psychological constructs (e.g., an essay about personality and another about mental health), the MEM can be run for each category of writing in order to generate several sets of themes.

At this point, this is equivalent to treating each writing type as a distinct meaning extraction task where the texts from a corpus C_1 generates T_1 and another corpus C_2 generates T_2, where C_1 and C_2 are collections of documents belonging to distinct categories (e.g., stances on a political issue and views of morality). We are then able to take a look at the relationships *within* or *between* the constructs as expressed in texts of C_1 and C_2. We use the previously defined s function to assign a score to each writing sample $d \in C_i$ for each topic $t \in T_i$ so that all documents are represented as vectors of topic scores, with each element corresponding to one of the k topics. Transposing the matrix made up of these vectors gives vectors for each topic with a length equal to the number of documents in the corpus. We then use these topic vectors to compute the Pearson correlation coefficient between any pair of themes. In order to ensure that correlations are not inflated by the presence of the same word in both themes, we first remove words that appear in any theme in T_1 from all themes in T_2 (or vice versa). When using an m function that gives a continuous nonzero score to (nearly) every word for every topic, it would be advisable to use a threshold in this case, rather than absence/presence. That is, remove any words from any theme $t_i \in T_1$ with $|m(t_i, w)| > \phi$ from every topic $t_j \in T_2$ for which it is also the case that $|m(t_j, w)| > \phi$, for some small value ϕ.

These quantified topical relationships are then used as a way to look at differences between two groups of people in a new way (e.g., differences between Republicans and Democrats). To illustrate, assume that we have two groups of writers, G_1 and G_2, and writers from each group have created two documents each, one belonging to C_1 and the other to C_2, on which we have applied the MEM to generate sets of themes T_1 and T_2 and computed $s(t, d)$ scores. Then, for the group G_1, we can use the aforementioned approach to compute the relationship between every theme in T_1 and every theme in T_2 and compare these relationships to those found for another group of people, G_2. Also, we are able to compute the relationships between themes that are found when combining texts from both writer groups into a single corpus (written by $G_1 \cup G_2$) and examine how these differ from the relationships found when only considering one of the groups.

Since many correlations will be computed during this process, and each is considered an individual statistical test, correction for multiple hypothesis testing is in order. This is addressed using a series of 10K Monte Carlo simulations of the generation of the resulting correlation matrix in order to compute statistical significance, following the multivariate permutation tests proposed by Yoder et al. (2004). Each iteration of this approach involves randomly shuffling the topic usage scores for every topic, then recomputing the correlations to determine how often a given correlation coefficient would be found if the usage scores of themes by a user were randomly chosen. Observed coefficient values larger than the coefficient at the $1-\alpha/2$ percentile or smaller than the coefficient at the $\alpha/2$ percentile of all simulated coefficients are labeled as significant.

3 Example Application: Personal Values

As an example application of this methodology, we take a look at the psychological construct of *values* and how they are expressed differently by people from India and people from the US. In psychological research, the term *value* is typically defined as a network of ideas that a person views to be desirable and important (Rokeach, 1973). Psychologists, historians, and other social scientists have long argued that people's basic values predict their behaviors (Ball-Rokeach et al., 1984; Rokeach, 1968); it is generally believed that the values which people hold tend to be reliable indicators of how they will actually think and act in value-relevant situations (Rohan, 2000). Further, human values are thought to generalize across broad swaths of time and culture (Schwartz, 1992) and are deeply embedded in the language that people use on a day-to-day basis (Chung and Pennebaker, 2014).

While values are commonly measured using tools such as the Schwartz Values Survey (SVS), a well established questionnaire that asks respondents to rate value items on a Likert-type scale (Schwartz, 1992), it has recently been shown that the MEM is another useful way to measure specific values, and can be applied to open-ended writing samples (Boyd et al., 2015). We show how the MEM can be used to target the concept of values to create useful themes that summarize the main topics people discuss when reflecting on their personal values in two different cultural groups. While doing this, we seek to avoid overlooking culture, which is a considerable determiner of an individual's psychology (Heine and Ruby, 2010). Importantly, research studies that fo-

cus exclusively on very specific people groups may reach false conclusions about the nature of observed effects (Henrich et al., 2010; Peng et al., 1997).

Since values are theorized to relate to a person's real-world behaviors, we also use the MEM to learn about people's recent activities and which values these activities link to most strongly within different cultural groups. Furthermore, we show how the themes that we discover can be used to study cultural value and behavior differences in a new social media data set.

4 Data Collection

4.1 Open-Ended Survey Data

We set out to collect data that captures the types of things people from the different cultural groups generally talk about when asked about their values and behaviors. To do this, we collect a corpus of writings from US and Indian participants containing responses to open-ended essay questions. The choice to use participants from both the US and India was grounded in three practical concerns. First, both countries have a high degree of participation in online crowdsourcing services. Second, English is a commonly-spoken language in both countries, making direct comparisons of unigram use relatively straight-forward for the current purposes. Lastly, considerable research has shown that these two cultures are psychologically unique in many ways (Misra and Gergen, 1993), making them an apt test case for the current approach.

We construct two sections of a social survey that is designed using Qualtrics survey software and distributed via Mechanical Turk (MTurk). Participants are asked to respond to the following prompt:

> *For the next 6 minutes (or more), write about your central and most important values that guide your life. Really stand back and explore your deepest thoughts and feelings about your basic values. [...]*

Additionally, since values are theorized to be related to real-world behaviors, we would like to collect some information about what people had been doing recently. Therefore, participants are also asked to write about their activities from the past week. The order of the two essay questions (values and behaviors) is randomized.

In order to guarantee an adequate amount of text for each user, we only retain surveys in which respondents write at least 40 words in each of the writing tasks. Additionally, each essay is manually checked for coherence, plagiarism, and relevance to the prompt. Within the survey itself, multiple "check" questions were randomly placed as a means of filtering out participants who were not paying close attention to the instructions; no surveys are used in the current analyses from participants who failed these check questions. After this filtering process, we choose the maximum number of surveys that would still allow for an equal balance of data from each country. Since there were more valid surveys from the US than from India, a random subsample is drawn from the larger set of surveys to create a sample that is equivalent in size to the smaller set. These procedures result in 551 completed surveys from each country, or 1102 surveys in total, each with both a value and behavior writing component.

In the set of surveys from India, 35% of respondents reported being female and 53% reported that they were between 26 and 34 years old. 96% reported having completed at least some college education. For the respondents from the US, 63% reported being female and 38% were between the ages of 35 and 54 (more than any other age range). 88% reported having had some college education.

4.2 Blog Data

To further explore the potential of this approach, we would like to apply our sets of themes to a naturalistic data source that is unencumbered by researcher intervention. While survey data is easily accessible and fast to collect, it may not necessarily reflect psychological processes as they occur in the real world. Thus, for another source of data, we turn to a highly-trafficked social media website, Google Blogger.[2]

We create a new corpus consisting of posts scraped from Google Blogger. First, profiles of users specifying that their country is India or the US are recorded until we have amassed 2,000 profiles each. Then, for each public blog associated with each profile (a user may author more than one blog), we collect up to 1,000 posts. Since a disproportionate number of these posts were written in more re-

cent months, we balance the data across time by randomly selecting 1,000 posts for each country for each month between January 2010 and September 2015. This way, there should not be a bias toward a particular year or month when the bloggers may have been more active in one of the countries. Each post is stripped of all HTML tags, and the titles of the posts are included as part of the document.

5 Results

5.1 Targeted Topic Extraction

First, we apply the MEM to the set of values essays, C_{VALUES}, from all respondents of the social survey. The set of extracted value-relevant themes, T_{VALUES}, is displayed in Table 1. The number of themes, k, is chosen for topical interpretability (e.g., in this case, $k = 15$). As with other topic modeling methods, slight variations in theme retention are possible while still reaching the same general conclusions. The theme names were manually assigned and are only for reference purposes; each theme is itself a collection of words with scores of either +1 or -1. For each theme, sample words that had a positive score are given. Note that each word may appear in more than one theme. The themes are listed in descending order by proportion of explained variance in the text data.

Table 2 shows the behavior themes (T_{BEHAV}). Most of these themes are rich in behavioral content. However, a few themes capture words used

Theme	Example Words
Respect others	people, respect, care, human, treat
Religion	god, heart, belief, religion, right
Family	family, parent, child, husband, mother
Hard Work	hard, work, better, honest, best
Time & Money	money, work, time, day, year
Problem solving	consider, decision, situation, problem
Relationships	family, friend, relationship, love
Optimism	enjoy, happy, positive, future, grow
Honesty	honest, truth, lie, trust, true
Rule following	moral, rule, principle, follow
Societal	society, person, feel, thought, quality
Personal Growth	personal, grow, best, decision, mind
Achievement	heart, achieve, complete, goal
Principles	important, guide, principle, central
Experiences	look, see, experience, choose, feel

Table 1: Themes extracted by the MEM from the values essays, along with example words.

---

[2]http://www.blogger.com

in more of a structural role when composing a text descriptive of one's past events (for example, Days and Daily routine). The theme labeled MTurk is a byproduct of the data collection method used, as it is expected that many of those surveyed would mention spending some time on the site within the past week.

5.2 Topic Regression Analysis

As we explore the differences in theme usage between cultures, we attempt to control for the influences of other factors by adding gender (x_G) and age (x_A) variables to the regression model in addition to country (x_C):

$$y_i = \beta_0 + \beta_1 x_{Ci} + \beta_2 x_{Gi} + \beta_3 x_{Ai} + \epsilon_i$$

where $y_i = s_{NORM}(t, i, D)$ for theme t and the document in D with index i. We set the country indicative variable, x_C, equal to 0 if the author of a document is from the US, and 1 if the author is from India. $x_G = 0$ indicates male, $x_G = 1$ indicates female. x_A is binned into (roughly) 10 year intervals so that a unit increase corresponds to an age difference of about a decade with higher numbers corresponding to older ages. No significant interactions

Theme	Example Words
Days	monday, tuesday, friday, sunday, today
Everyday activ.	shower, coffee, lunch, eat, sleep
Chores	clean, laundry, dish, cook, house
Morning	wake, tea, morning, office, breakfast
Consumption	tv, news, eat, read, computer
Time	week, hour, month, day, minute
Child care	daughter, son, ready, school, church
MTurk	computer, mturk, survey, money
Grooming	tooth, dress, hair, brush, shower
Video games	play, game, video, online, talk
Home leisure	television, snack, show, music, listen
Commuting	move, house, drive, work, stay
Family	sister, brother, birthday, phone, visit
Road trip	drive, meet, plan, car, trip
Daily routine	daily, regular, routine, activity, time
Completion	end, complete, finish, leave, weekend
Friends	friend, visit, movie, together, fun
Hobbies	garden, read, exercise, write, cooking
School	attend, class, work, project, friend
Going out	shop, restaurant, food, family, member
Taking a break	break, fast, chat, work, routine

Table 2: Themes extracted by the MEM from the behavior essays, along with example words.

between country, gender, and age were detected at $\alpha = .05$ using level-2 interactions. The predicted regression coefficients are shown in Figure 1.

Even when using the same set of topics, we see cultural differences coming into play. Culture coefficients for the value themes show that Hard work and Respect for others were predominately talked about by Americans. Indian authors tended to invoke greater rates of the Problem Solving, Rule Following, Principles, and Optimism themes. The theme containing words relating to the value of one's Family had a significant coefficient indicating that it is generally used by females more than males.

5.3 Value-behavior Relationships

Next, we look at how usage of words from the value themes relates to usage of words from the behavior themes. Table 3 shows the correlations between topics in T_{VALUES} and T_{BEHAV}. These correlations were computed three times: once each for texts written by only people from India, texts written by only by people from the US, and for the entire set of texts. Overall, all but three of the behavior themes have observable links to the values measured in at least one of the cultural groups.

Looking more closely at the results, we see that only one of the value-behavior relationships is shared by these two cultures: the value of Family is positively related to the behavior Child care. This result is also identified when looking at the combination of texts from both cultures. One potential explanation for this is that, as we have shown, the use of words from the Family theme is more related to a person's gender than her/his culture, so removing texts from one culture will not affect the presence of this relationship. On the other hand, when considering only the text from American survey respondents, we notice that the value of Hard work is related to Chores. However, if we ignored these writing samples and only analyzed the texts from Indian authors, we saw that this same theme of Hard work is related to Consumption and Home leisure. The combined set of texts captures all three relationships. This may hint at the solution of simply combining the texts in the first place, but further investigation showed that some of the relationships only emerged when examining texts from a single country. For example, we would not learn that American authors who

	Respect others	Religion	Family	Hard work	Time & money	Problem solving	Relationships	Optimism	Honesty	Rule following	Societal	Personal growth	Achievement	Principles	Experiences
Days															
Everyday activities													●		
Chores				●◆	◇	◇									
Morning				◇		◆		◆		◆				◆	
Consumption				■◆									●		
Time	○														
Child Care			●■◆				●◆								
MTurk				◆				◇							
Grooming													●		
Video games				◆											
Home leisure				■◆											
Commuting						◇		□◇						◇	
Family	●													◇	
Road trip				●											
Daily routine	◇			◇		◆	●◆	◆		◆					
Completion															
Friends											●				
Hobbies	●												●		
School		◇				◆		◆						◆	
Going out								■							
Taking a break															

Table 3: Coverage of behavior MEM themes (rows) by value MEM themes (columns) for two different cultures. All results significant at $\alpha = .05$ (two-tailed).

USA only: ● : $r > 0$, ○ : $r < 0$, **India only:** ■ : $r > 0$, □ : $r < 0$, **Combined:** ◆ : $r > 0$, ◇ : $r < 0$

wrote about Achievement in their values essay were more likely to have talked about Personal Grooming when listing their recent activities, or that Indian authors who used words from the value theme of Honesty probably wrote more words from the Going Out theme.

5.4 Applying Themes to Social Media Data

For the blog data, C_{BLOGS}, we perform topic modeling procedures that are parallel to those described earlier, with one exception: due to an extreme diversity in the content of blog posts, the threshold at which rare words were removed was set to 1% in order to capture a greater breadth of information. We found that a large number of themes (nearly 60) was required in order to maximize interpretability and keep unrelated topics from mixing. Spatial limitations preclude the presentation of all themes in the current paper, therefore, we present those themes that were later found to be most related to personal values in Table 4.[3]

Since value-relevant themes, T_{VALUES}, were established using the MEM on the value survey essays, value-specific language can be captured in the blog data without the need for a separate MEM procedure to be conducted. Themes in Table 4, then, reflect a broader, more naturalistic set of concepts being discussed by bloggers in the real world (T_{BLOGS}) that can then be linked with their value-relevant language as measured by computing $s(d, t)$ for $d \in C_{BLOGS}$ and $t \in S_{VALUES}$. As was done in the value-behavior comparison using only the survey data, all words that appeared in any value theme were removed from all of the blog themes so that relationships were not confounded by predictor/criterion theme pairs containing overlapping sets of words. We present the themes found when looking at blog posts from each culture individually as well as the

---

[3]A complete list of themes and unigram loadings are available from the first author by request.

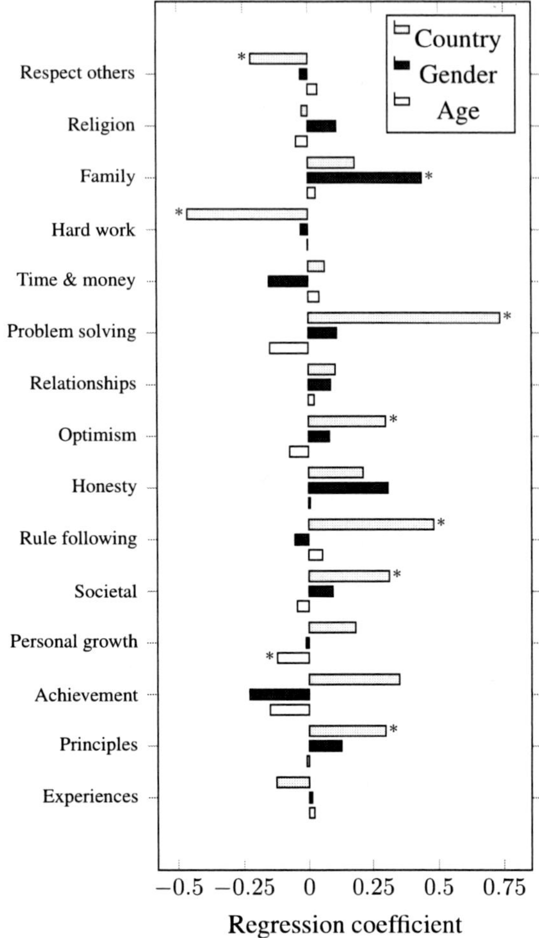

Figure 1: Coefficients for the Country, Gender, and Age variables in regression model. For Country, Gender, and Age, negative values indicate a US, male, or younger bias toward the theme, respectively, and positive values indicate an Indian, female, or older bias toward the theme, respectively. * indicates $p < .001$.

full combined corpus in Table 5.

In this dataset, we saw a similar trend as in Table 3: the particular cultural composition of the corpus changes the observed relationships. However, the association between the Religion 1 blog theme and the Religion, Honesty, and Experiences value themes was present in both US and India when considered in isolation, as well as in the combined corpus. The Tech industry theme was negatively correlated with a large number of value themes, which alludes to the idea that the words in this theme are actually an indicator of less value-related language in general. Many of the relationships found in one of the cultures were also found using the combined corpus, but only in the US data did we see a significant increase in respectful language for blogs talking about the environment; only in India did we find a negative relationship between the value theme of Personal growth and posts about the Stock market.

6   Conclusions

We have presented a methodology that can be used to employ topic models to the understanding of sociolinguistic differences between groups of people, and to disentangle the effects of various attributes on a person's usage of a given topic. We showed how this approach can be carried out using the MEM topic modeling method, but leave the framework general and open to the use of other topic modeling approaches.

As an example application, we have shown how topic models can be used to explore cultural differences in personal values both qualitatively and quantitatively. We utilized a open-ended survey as well

Theme	Example Words
Religion 1	jesus, glory, saint, angel, pray
Outdoorsman	farm, hunt, wild, duty, branch
Government	government, department, organization
Religion 2	singh, religion, praise, habit, wise
Profiles	french, russian, male, female, australia
Personal life	cry, job, sleep, emotion, smile
Financial	sector, money, trade, profit, consumer
School	school, university, grade, teacher
Stock market	trade, market, close, investor, fund
Tech industry	software, google, microsoft, ceo
Sports	league, play, win, team, score
Cooking	recipe, delicious, prepare, mix, kitchen
US Politics	washington, obama, debt, law, america
Job openings	requirement, candidate, opening, talent
Crime	murder, police, crime, incident
Film industry	direct, film, movie, actor, musical
India & China	india, china, representative, minister
Space exploration	mars, mission, space, flight, scientist
Environment	weather, earth, bird, storm, ocean
Indian city living	delhi, financial, tax, capital, chennai
Beauty	gold, pattern, hair, mirror, flower
Happy fashion	clothes, funny, awesome, grand

Table 4: Sample themes extracted by the MEM from the blog data, along with example words.

	Respect others	Religion	Family	Hard work	Time & money	Problem solving	Relationships	Optimism	Honesty	Rule following	Societal	Personal growth	Achievement	Principles	Experiences
Religion 1		●■◆	◆	◇					●■◆				◆	◆	○□◇
Outdoorsman				●◆							●◆	●◆			
Government	◇				◇		□◇	□◇			□◇				
Religion 2									■◆						
Profiles		□◇					■◆								
Personal life				●◆	■◆		◆			◇	●◆	●◆			
Financial	□◇				◇		○□◇		□◇		◇			□◇	
the School					■◆										
Stock market			◇				○	■◆	□◇		◇	□			
Tech industry	○◇	◇	○□◇		○◇	□◇	○□◇	○□◇	□◇		○□◇			○□◇	○
Sports		◇		■◆	■			◇			○◇				
Cooking	○				○										
US politics				◇				◇			□◇				◇
Job openings		□◇						□							■◆
Crime					○◇		○◇								
Film industry	□◇				○	□◇			◇	□				○◇	○
India + China								◇	□◇		◇				
Space exploration		□◇	□◇		◇					□	◇				
Indian city living	◇	□◇	□			□					◇			□	◇
Environment	●														
Beauty								◇							
Happy fashion									●	■	○◇				

Table 5: Coverage of blog MEM themes (rows) by value MEM themes (columns) for two different cultures. Correlations significant at $\alpha = .05$ (two-tailed) are presented.

USA only: ● : $r > 0$, ○ : $r < 0$, **India only**: ■ : $r > 0$, □ : $r < 0$, **Combined**: ◆ : $r > 0$, ◇ : $r < 0$

as a new collection of blog data.[4] The topics extracted from these texts by the MEM provide a high level descriptive summary of thousands of writing samples, and examining regression models gives insight into how some topics are used differently in US and India. We found that the underlying culture of the group of writers of the text has a significant effect on the conclusions that are drawn, particularly when looking at value-behavior links. In the future, we hope to explore how well culture-specific themes are able to summarize texts from the cultures from which they are derived in comparison with themes that were generated using texts from many cultures. While we focused on differences between Indian and American people, the proposed approach could also be used to understand differences in topic usage between members of any groups, such as liberals vs. conservatives, computer scientists vs. psychologists, or at-risk individuals vs. the general population.

Acknowledgments

This material is based in part upon work supported by the National Science Foundation (#1344257), the John Templeton Foundation (#48503), the Michigan Institute for Data Science, and the National Institute of Health (#5R01GM112697-02). Any opinions, findings, and conclusions or recommendations expressed in this material are those of the authors and do not necessarily reflect the views of the National Science Foundation, the John Templeton Foundation, the Michigan Institute for Data Science, or the National Institute of Health. Finally, we would like to thank Konstantinos Pappas for providing the code used to collect the blog data.

---

[4] The survey data as well as the code used to download the blogs along with the list of profile URLs are available from the first author upon request.

References

Sandra Ball-Rokeach, Milton Rokeach, and Joel W. Grube. 1984. *The Great American Values Test: Influencing Behavior and Belief Through Television*. Free Press, New York, New York, USA.

David Blei and John Lafferty. 2006. Correlated topic models. *Advances in neural information processing systems*, 18:147.

David M Blei, Andrew Y Ng, and Michael I Jordan. 2003. Latent Dirichlet Allocation. *Journal of Machine Learning Research*, 3(4-5):993–1022.

David M Blei. 2012. Probabilistic topic models. *Communications of the ACM*, 55(4):77–84.

Ryan L Boyd, Steven R Wilson, James W Pennebaker, Michal Kosinski, David J Stillwell, and Rada Mihalcea. 2015. Values in words: Using language to evaluate and understand personal values. In *Ninth International AAAI Conference on Web and Social Media*.

Ryan L. Boyd. 2015. MEH: Meaning Extraction Helper (Version 1.4.05) [Software] Available from http://meh.ryanb.cc.

Cindy K. Chung and James W. Pennebaker. 2008. Revealing dimensions of thinking in open-ended self-descriptions: An automated meaning extraction method for natural language. *Journal of Research in Personality*, 42:96–132.

Cindy K Chung and James W Pennebaker. 2014. Finding values in words: Using natural language to detect regional variations in personal concerns. In *Geographical psychology: Exploring the interaction of environment and behavior*, pages 195–216.

Fréderic Godin, Viktor Slavkovikj, Wesley De Neve, Benjamin Schrauwen, and Rik Van de Walle. 2013. Using topic models for twitter hashtag recommendation. In *Proceedings of the 22nd international conference on World Wide Web companion*, pages 593–596. International World Wide Web Conferences Steering Committee.

Steven J Heine and Matthew B Ruby. 2010. Cultural psychology. *Wiley Interdisciplinary Reviews: Cognitive Science*, 1(2):254–266.

Joseph Henrich, Steven J Heine, and Ara Norenzayan. 2010. The weirdest people in the world? *Behavioral and brain sciences*, 33(2-3):61–83.

Henry F Kaiser. 1958. The varimax criterion for analytic rotation in factor analysis. *Psychometrika*, 23(3):187–200.

Adam DI Kramer and Cindy K Chung. 2011. Dimensions of self-expression in facebook status updates. In *Fifth International AAAI Conference on Weblogs and Social Media*.

Simon Lacoste-Julien, Fei Sha, and Michael I Jordan. 2009. Disclda: Discriminative learning for dimensionality reduction and classification. In *Advances in neural information processing systems*, pages 897–904.

Robert D Lowe, Derek Heim, Cindy K Chung, John C Duffy, John B Davies, and James W Pennebaker. 2013. In verbis, vinum? relating themes in an open-ended writing task to alcohol behaviors. *Appetite*, 68:8–13.

Girishwar Misra and Kenneth J. Gergen. 1993. On the place of culture in psychological science. *International Journal of Psychology*, 28(2):225.

Kaiping Peng, Richard E Nisbett, and Nancy YC Wong. 1997. Validity problems comparing values across cultures and possible solutions. *Psychological methods*, 2(4):329.

Meg J. Rohan. 2000. A Rose by Any Name? The Values Construct. *Personality and Social Psychology Review*, 4(3):255–277.

Milton Rokeach. 1968. *Beliefs, Attitudes, and Values.*, volume 34. Jossey-Bass, San Francisco.

Milton Rokeach. 1973. *The nature of human values*, volume 438. Free press New York.

Shalom H. Schwartz. 1992. Universals in the Content and Structure of Values: Theoretical Advances and Empirical Tests in 20 Countries. *Advances in Experimental Social Psychology*, 25:1–65.

Mark Steyvers, Padhraic Smyth, Michal Rosen-Zvi, and Thomas Griffiths. 2004. Probabilistic author-topic models for information discovery. In *Proceedings of the tenth ACM SIGKDD international conference on Knowledge discovery and data mining*, pages 306–315. ACM.

Yee Whye Teh, Michael I Jordan, Matthew J Beal, and David M Blei. 2012. Hierarchical dirichlet processes. *Journal of the american statistical association*.

Paul J Yoder, Jennifer Urbano Blackford, Niels G Waller, and Geunyoung Kim. 2004. Enhancing power while controlling family-wise error: an illustration of the issues using electrocortical studies. *Journal of Clinical and Experimental Neuropsychology*, 26(3):320–331.

Wayne Xin Zhao, Jing Jiang, Jianshu Weng, Jing He, Ee-Peng Lim, Hongfei Yan, and Xiaoming Li. 2011. Comparing twitter and traditional media using topic models. In *Advances in Information Retrieval*, pages 338–349. Springer.

Jun Zhu, Amr Ahmed, and Eric P Xing. 2009. Medlda: maximum margin supervised topic models for regression and classification. In *Proceedings of the 26th annual international conference on machine learning*, pages 1257–1264. ACM.

Author Index

Association for Computational Linguistics
209 N. Eighth Street
Stroudsburg, Pennsylvania 18360

ISBN 978-1-5108-3148-3